Adaptive Finance

About the Authors

Frank J. Fabozzi is a professor of practice at the Carey Business School at Johns Hopkins University, Baltimore. He is the editor of *The Journal of Portfolio Management* and coeditor of the *The Journal of Financial Data Science.* Fabozzi has served on the board of directors of the BlackRock Fixed Income Funds, the BlackRock Equity-Liquidity Funds, the BlackRock BCIA Funds, and the Guardian Mutual Funds and Guardian Annuity Funds. He has taught at the Massachusetts Institute of Technology (MIT), Yale University, Princeton University, the EDHEC Business School (Nice, France), New York University, Rutgers University, and Carnegie Mellon University. The recipient of the CFA Institute's 2007 C. Stewart Sheppard Award and the 2015 James R. Vertin Award, he was inducted into the Fixed Income Society's Hall of Fame in 2002. He holds a doctorate in economics from the Graduate Center of the City University of New York and an honorary doctorate of Humane Letters from Nova Southeastern University, Davie, Florida.

Sergio Focardi is a professor at the University of Genoa—DIME, Italy, where he teaches risk management and financial engineering. He is also the founder of the consulting firm Economics and Complexity. Focardi has taught complexity economics at Franklin University, Lugano, Switzerland. Previously he was a professor of finance at the Pôle Universitaire Léonard de Vinci, Paris–La Defense, France, and a researcher at the De Vinci Research Center after spending three years as a visiting professor of finance at the State University of New York at Stony Brook, Long Island, and lecturing at Princeton University. He holds a degree in electronic engineering from the University of Genoa, Italy, and a PhD in mathematical finance from the University of Karlsruhe, Germany. He cofounded the Interdisciplinary Research Center in Economics & Finance at the University of Genoa. He is the author or coauthor of twenty books and more than one hundred peer-reviewed papers.

Adaptive Finance

Embracing Uncertainty and Complexity

Frank J. Fabozzi and Sergio Focardi

The MIT Press
Cambridge, Massachusetts
London, England

The MIT Press
Massachusetts Institute of Technology
77 Massachusetts Avenue
Cambridge, MA 02139
mitpress.mit.edu

The MIT Press would like to thank the anonymous peer reviewers who provided comments on drafts of this book. The generous work of academic experts is essential for establishing the authority and quality of our publications. We acknowledge with gratitude the contributions of these otherwise uncredited readers.

This book was set in Stone Serif and Stone Sans by Westchester Publishing Services. Printed and bound in the United States of America.

Library of Congress Cataloging-in-Publication Data

Names: Fabozzi, Frank J. author | Focardi, Sergio M. author
Title: Adaptive finance : embracing uncertainty and complexity / Frank J. Fabozzi and Sergio Focardi.
Description: Cambridge, Massachusetts : The MIT Press, [2026] | Includes bibliographical references.
Identifiers: LCCN 2025017065 (print) | LCCN 2025017066 (ebook) | ISBN 9780262051415 paperback | ISBN 9780262051422 pdf | ISBN 9780262051439 epub
Subjects: LCSH: Finance
Classification: LCC HG173 .F248 2026 (print) | LCC HG173 (ebook) | DDC 332—dc23/eng/20250919
LC record available at https://lccn.loc.gov/2025017065
LC ebook record available at https://lccn.loc.gov/2025017066

10 9 8 7 6 5 4 3 2 1

EU Authorised Representative: Easy Access System Europe, Mustamäe tee 50, 10621 Tallinn, Estonia | Email: gpsr.requests@easproject.com

Dedicated to the memory of Carolyn Jonas

Contents

Preface

In this book, we present a forward-thinking exploration of the evolving world of finance that addresses the most pressing challenges and emerging trends facing financial markets today. Our objective is to illuminate how traditional economic and financial models, which long have dominated the field, are being reassessed and in some cases superseded in light of recent developments in behavioral science, mathematics, and technology. In today's environment of rising complexity, rapid technological change, and persistent global uncertainty, financial professionals and academics face risks and market dynamics that traditional theories no longer fully explain. This book seeks to provide the intellectual foundation needed to confront these challenges.

The chapters cover a wide range of topics, from behavioral finance and causal models to quantum finance and innovations in financial systems, thus offering a comprehensive view of the critical forces shaping the future of finance. The chapters are ordered to guide the reader in a logical progression from more established frameworks, such as behavioral finance, to cutting-edge fields such as quantum finance and complexity science. This discursive flow mirrors the journey that finance as a discipline is undergoing, from refining classical theories to incorporating novel methodologies.

Each chapter is designed to stand alone as a complete work. As a result, readers may notice some overlap in coverage, mainly where chapters address interconnected themes, such as market risk, behavioral finance, or the evolving role of quantitative models. This intentional overlap ensures that each chapter can be read independently without requiring the reader to follow a specific sequence. This makes the book accessible for comprehensive reading and selective exploration of topics.

Throughout this book, we refer to "economics and finance" because the two are inseparable in understanding market behavior and decision-making under uncertainty. Economics provides the foundational frameworks for understanding incentives, market structures, and systemic interactions. Finance builds on these foundations to address capital allocation, portfolio construction, risk management, and valuation.

At times, we use "economics" when discussing general principles or behavioral drivers that extend beyond financial markets and "finance" when the discussion is oriented explicitly toward investment decisions, market dynamics, or asset pricing. Where the term "economics and finance" appears, it reflects the integrated approach of *Adaptive Finance*: leveraging the insights of both disciplines to address the complexity of modern markets.

In each chapter, we discuss innovative frameworks that challenge traditional assumptions governing economic and financial thought, offering readers a critique of existing models and practical alternatives. By weaving together established knowledge with cutting-edge insights, we hope to provide a comprehensive yet forward-looking perspective on how finance must adapt to an ever-evolving global landscape.

The deliberate progression from foundational financial theories to speculative new ideas mirrors the journey of finance as a discipline, guiding the reader from well-established principles toward the frontiers of economic and financial thought. We hope the book invites readers to rethink finance in times of significant change and uncertainty.

1 Introduction: Breaking Boundaries in Modern Finance

The world of finance is in the midst of an unprecedented transformation driven by an intricate web of technological advances, evolving economic and financial theories, and a growing awareness of environmental risks. This transformation marks a turning point in understanding, navigating, and predicting financial markets. At its core, finance is shifting from the familiar terrain of rational models and dynamic equilibria to a new paradigm in which complexity, uncertainty, and innovation play central roles in shaping outcomes. Today's financial professionals must confront a landscape characterized by increasing interconnectedness, global volatility, and the limits of traditional methods in addressing these multifaceted challenges. This book explores the forces driving that transformation and offers a roadmap for adapting to the new realities of modern finance.

The foundational models in finance, relied on for decades, are based on assumptions that no longer fully align with the realities of modern markets. Concepts such as the efficient market hypothesis and the rational expectations theory, which have dominated financial thinking, assume that market agents act rationally and that markets operate efficiently, processing all available information to arrive at optimal outcomes. However, these assumptions often fail in practice, as evidenced by the 2007–2008 Global Financial Crisis (GFC), market bubbles, and periodic market crashes of recent years. Markets, far from efficient, exhibit volatility, unpredictability, and periods of irrational exuberance or panic. The limitations of these classical models in modern finance have driven the need for new approaches that embrace the inherent complexity of financial systems and better account for human behavior and external risks.

This shift in thinking reflects a broader realization that financial markets are complex, adaptive systems—ecosystems in which many factors interact dynamically, often in unpredictable and nonlinear ways. The increasing role of data science (i.e., artificial intelligence, machine learning, and big data) and technology (i.e., quantum computing) adds layers of complexity by creating new market dynamics that are both faster and more opaque. These advances, while offering powerful tools for decision-making, also introduce new risks, such as algorithmic trading–induced market crashes or systemic vulnerabilities in an interconnected financial ecosystem.

In this book, we address this critical juncture in the evolution of finance. Each chapter focuses on a crucial aspect of modern financial thought and practice, from behavioral finance and quantum mechanics to causal modeling. Together, these chapters paint a comprehensive picture of the emerging trends reshaping how we understand financial markets, offering theoretical insights and practical strategies for navigating the complexities of the modern financial environment. The overarching theme of the book is the need to embrace innovation and complexity not as challenges to be managed but as essential components of a more resilient, adaptive financial system.

One of the defining features of today's financial landscape is the speed at which change occurs. The rise of digital currencies, blockchain, and decentralized finance is disrupting traditional banking models, while advances in data science are revolutionizing how financial data are analyzed and acted upon. At the same time, the increasing frequency and severity of global crises—whether driven by domestic or geopolitical tensions, technological disruptions, or climate-related disasters—are forcing financial institutions to rethink their risk management strategies. These rapid changes underscore the limitations of traditional financial models, which often assume stable markets and predictable outcomes. In this new era, the ability to adapt to uncertainty, anticipate emerging risks, and leverage innovation is not just an advantage, it is a necessity.

We also recognize that today's challenges cannot be fully understood or addressed through a single lens. The complexities of modern financial systems require a multidisciplinary approach that draws on insights from economics, psychology, physics, and environmental science. Behavioral finance, for example, has shown that investors' decision-making processes are often influenced by cognitive biases and emotional responses, challenging the notion of rational market participants. On the other hand, complexity science provides tools for understanding the interconnected, nonlinear dynamics that characterize financial markets. At the same time, quantum finance introduces new probabilistic frameworks for managing uncertainty in ways that classical models cannot.

In addition to the technical and theoretical advances reshaping finance, there is a growing recognition of the importance of ethical and social responsibility. The GFC, driven partly by unchecked financial innovation and a lack of regulatory oversight, highlighted the dangers of prioritizing short-term profits over long-term stability. Today, with the global push toward sustainability and the integration of environmental, social, and governance (ESG) principles, the financial industry is beginning to take a more holistic approach, balancing profitability with the need to address broader social and environmental challenges. This shift toward responsible investing is not just a moral imperative, it is increasingly seen as a prudent strategy for managing long-term risks and ensuring the resilience of financial systems in an era of heightened global uncertainty.

Ultimately, this book is about the future of finance and the tools, models, and frameworks that will shape that future. Each chapter delves into a critical area of financial innovation and complexity, offering insights that are as relevant to practitioners in the field as they are to academics and policymakers. Whether exploring the integration of behavioral insights into quantitative models, the application of quantum probability to market dynamics, or the role of data-driven decision-making in navigating technological disruption, this book provides a comprehensive guide to understanding and managing the complexities of modern finance.

This book's objective is to provoke thought, inspire innovation, and encourage a flexible, adaptive approach to finance, embracing complexity and uncertainty to build a resilient system for the twenty-first century.

FOUNDATIONS OF A NEW FINANCIAL PARADIGM

In the following chapters, we explore the theoretical foundations and practical implications of this new financial paradigm, offering readers a deep dive into the critical forces shaping the future of finance. Each chapter provides a unique perspective on the changing financial landscape, from the behavioral anomalies that challenge traditional market assumptions to the quantum frameworks that offer new ways of modeling uncertainty. Together they form a comprehensive narrative that explains where we are and offers insights into where we are headed.

Behavioral Finance

Chapter 2, "Behavioral Finance and Its Integration into Quantitative Models," addresses how behavioral finance has fundamentally shifted our understanding of financial markets. Unlike traditional finance, which assumes that investors are rational actors who always seek to maximize their utility, behavioral finance incorporates psychological insights to explain why investors' behavior frequently deviates from a rational paradigm. This chapter traces the development of behavioral finance, beginning with the foundational work of such scholars as Daniel Kahneman and Amos Tversky, who introduced the concepts of prospect theory and loss aversion, which reveal how investors weigh potential gains and losses asymmetrically.

In addition to exploring these cognitive biases, the chapter examines how behavioral finance integrates with quantitative models. Traditional models such as the capital asset pricing model (CAPM) and the Black-Scholes option pricing model assume rational behavior, but behavioral finance offers an alternative: models that account for psychological factors. The chapter discusses the behavioral CAPM and prospect theory–based models, which help provide a more nuanced understanding of risk, return, and investor behavior. These models seek to explain market anomalies such as the equity premium puzzle, where the actual stock returns are far higher than what traditional models predict based on risk.

Another key theme is the application of behavioral finance in portfolio management. As the financial industry becomes more data-driven, behavioral insights are being incorporated into algorithmic trading, robo-adviser offerings, and smart beta strategies. These applications reflect a shift toward using data and behavioral insights to anticipate and respond to market inefficiencies attributable to human behavior. The chapter also discusses the role of behavioral finance in risk management, where understanding investor psychology is crucial to predicting market movements during periods of stress.

The chapter concludes with real-world case studies, such as the dot-com bubble and the GFC, highlighting the critical role of cognitive biases such as overconfidence and herding behavior in these events. The case studies illustrate the practical relevance of behavioral finance in understanding and predicting market behavior, particularly in periods of extreme volatility.

As the financial landscape becomes more complex, behavioral finance will likely continue to play an increasingly important role in academic research and practical investment management.

Causal Models

In chapter 3, "Toward a Comprehensive Economic Framework: The Role of Causal Models," the focus shifts from behavioral biases to the deeper causal mechanisms that drive financial outcomes. Traditional economic and financial models often rely on correlations to predict market behavior, but correlation does not imply causation. This chapter highlights the importance of causal modeling, which attempts to identify and quantify the underlying causes of market movements, thereby offering a more reliable foundation for decision-making.

Causal models are particularly valuable when policy interventions or regulatory changes produce ripple effects throughout the financial system. Causal models can be used to simulate the impact of these policy interventions and predict their outcomes. By modeling counterfactual scenarios—what would happen if a particular policy were implemented—causal models provide a more detailed understanding of how changes in one area can influence the broader economy.

The chapter also explores the integration of causal models with machine learning (ML) and artificial intelligence (AI). With the rise of big data, financial institutions are increasingly turning to AI-driven causal models to help them make sense of vast amounts of information and identify key drivers of market behavior. These models are descriptive and prescriptive, allowing institutions to take more proactive approaches to risk management and investment strategies. The integration of causal models with AI is helping firms move from merely reacting to market changes to anticipating them.

A key challenge discussed in the chapter is identifying true causal relationships in highly complex and interconnected markets. Financial systems are influenced by many factors, many of which interact in nonlinear ways, making it hard to disentangle cause from effect. The chapter critiques current methods, arguing that while causal models are a significant advance, they must be used carefully to avoid oversimplification. The chapter concludes by looking at future directions in causal modeling, including how advances in econometrics and AI could help address these challenges.

Complexity in Financial Modeling

Chapter 4, "The Integration of Complexity Science into Financial Modeling," introduces the idea that financial markets behave more like complex adaptive systems than traditional models suggest. In traditional financial theory, markets are assumed to trend toward equilibrium, where supply meets demand and prices reflect all available information. However, complexity science challenges this assumption, presenting markets as dynamic systems in which numerous interacting agents give rise to unpredictable and emerging behaviors.

A major concept in complexity science is that of feedback loops—both positive and negative—that amplify or dampen market movements. For instance, during a market crash, a negative feedback loop might occur as falling asset prices lead to panic selling, further driving prices down. Conversely, positive feedback loops can stabilize markets when, for example, falling prices attract new buyers, who help correct the initial downturn. These feedback mechanisms are central to understanding market volatility and systemic risk, and the chapter discusses how traditional models have failed to capture these dynamics.

Agent-based models (ABMs) are one of the most promising tools in complexity science for understanding financial markets. ABMs simulate the behavior of individual agents—such as investors, firms, or regulators—and how their interactions create broader market patterns. These models allow researchers to explore how changes in agent behavior can lead to market bubbles, crashes, or periods of stability. The chapter provides examples of how ABMs have been used to model such phenomena as high-frequency trading, where the interactions of algorithmic traders can lead to flash crashes.

Network theory is another key component of complexity science discussed in this chapter. Financial markets are highly interconnected, and the failure of one institution or market segment can have cascading effects on the entire system. Network theory helps researchers analyze these interdependencies and assess systemic risk. For example, the GFC illustrated how interconnectedness through mortgage-backed securities and other financial instruments allowed the collapse of a few institutions to trigger a global economic meltdown. The chapter explores how network theory can be applied to identify vulnerabilities in financial systems and to develop strategies for building more resilient markets.

Mathematical Modeling

Chapter 5, "The Role of Mathematical Modeling and New Economic Thinking in Modern Finance," traces the evolution of mathematical finance from its origins to its current state, focusing on how new economic thinking is reshaping the field. Mathematical models have long been a cornerstone of finance, providing tools to quantify risk, price financial instruments, and optimize portfolios. However, the limitations of these models have become increasingly apparent, particularly during financial crises.

The chapter begins by discussing foundational models such as the CAPM and the Black-Scholes model, which have dominated financial theory for decades. These models rely on assumptions such as market efficiency and normal distribution of returns—assumptions that often break down in real-world markets, particularly during periods of extreme volatility. The GFC exposed these limitations, prompting a reevaluation of the role of mathematical models in finance.

One of the major critiques of traditional mathematical models is their inability to account for fat tails—the extreme events that occur more frequently than predicted by normal distribution. This chapter describes advanced techniques such as the use of extreme value theory and generalized autoregressive conditional heteroskedasticity (GARCH) models, which provide a more realistic representation of market volatility. These statistical techniques permit better risk management, particularly in scenarios where traditional models underestimate the likelihood of extreme losses.

In addition to critiquing traditional models, the chapter discusses how new economic thinking is reshaping financial theory. Behavioral economics, complexity science, and interdisciplinary approaches influence how we model financial markets. The chapter highlights the importance of integrating these new insights with mathematical rigor, offering a more holistic approach to understanding risk and uncertainty in modern finance. The chapter concludes by examining the future of mathematical modeling, suggesting that a pluralistic approach incorporating behavioral and complexity-based models will be essential for navigating the challenges of today's financial markets.

Emerging Risks

Chapter 6, "Emerging Risks and the Future of Quantitative Finance," focuses on the new risks that have emerged in the financial industry as a result of technological advances, climate change, and geopolitical shifts. Traditional risk management models, which focus on market, credit, and liquidity risks, are increasingly inadequate for addressing the complexity of these emerging risks. This chapter explores the nature of these risks and how they reshape the financial landscape.

One of the most pressing risks discussed in the chapter is cyber risk. As the financial industry becomes more digitized, the potential for cyberattacks—such as data breaches, ransomware, and hacking—has grown exponentially. Cyber risk poses a unique challenge because it is not easily quantifiable using traditional risk metrics. The chapter explores how financial institutions use ML and advanced analytics to assess and manage cyber risk and the role of scenario analysis in preparing for potential cyber incidents.

Climate risk is another emerging threat that is reshaping financial markets. As the effects of climate change become more pronounced, financial institutions are increasingly integrating environmental risks into their investment strategies. The chapter discusses how physical climate risks, such as hurricanes and floods, and transition risks, such as regulatory changes aimed at reducing carbon emissions, influence asset prices and investment decisions. Investing that incorporates ESG factors is highlighted as a key strategy for managing these risks.

Geopolitical risks, such as trade wars, sanctions, and political instability, are also discussed in detail. The chapter draws on the U.S.-China trade war and other examples to illustrate how geopolitical tensions can disrupt global supply chains, affect currency markets, and create volatility in commodity prices. These risks are complicated to model because they are often driven by political decisions, which are difficult to predict.

The chapter concludes by exploring the future of risk management in the context of these emerging threats. It argues that the financial industry must move beyond traditional risk models and adopt more flexible, dynamic approaches to account for global markets' growing complexity and interconnectedness. This step includes greater use of ML, scenario analysis, and stress testing to anticipate and mitigate the impact of emerging risks.

Quantum Finance

Quantum finance, a revolutionary new way of understanding uncertainty in financial markets, is the subject of chapter 7, "Entangling Markets: The Role of Quantum Probability in Financial Systems." Traditional finance models are based on classical probability, which assumes that the behavior of financial markets can be understood by representing markets as idealized objects. However, these classical models are proving increasingly inadequate as markets become more volatile and unpredictable. Quantum finance offers an alternative by applying the principles of quantum mechanics, such as superposition and entanglement, to financial systems.

Quantum probability differs from classical probability in that it allows multiple potential outcomes to exist simultaneously until an observation collapses them into a single result. This approach has profound implications for financial modeling, particularly in understanding market volatility and self-reflexivity. The chapter explains how concepts such as superposition can be used to model financial instruments such as options, where the price can exist simultaneously in multiple states of valuation until an investor acts.

Entanglement is another key concept in quantum finance. In quantum mechanics, entanglement refers to the correlation of particles such that the state of one particle instantly affects the state of another, even if they are far apart. This concept can be applied to financial markets to model the interconnectedness of different asset classes or markets. For example, a shock in one market can quickly spread to others, creating a ripple effect that classical models struggle to capture.

The chapter also explores the practical applications of quantum finance, particularly in option pricing and portfolio management. By applying quantum stochastic processes, financial institutions can develop more flexible models for assessing modern markets' inherent uncertainty and reflexivity. The chapter concludes by discussing the potential of quantum finance to revolutionize the field by offering a more robust framework for managing risk and uncertainty in an increasingly complex financial environment.

Rethinking Economics

Chapter 8, "Rethinking Economics and Finance Through Complexity and Empirical Approaches," critiques mainstream economic models that rely on overly simplistic rational behavior and market equilibrium assumptions. These models, while applicable in certain contexts, are increasingly inadequate for understanding the complexity of modern financial markets, which are characterized by uncertainty, volatility, and nonlinear dynamics.

The chapter's central theme is the role of uncertainty in financial markets. Traditional models often assume that market participants have access to all relevant information and can make rational decisions based on that information. However, markets are driven by uncertainty in terms of information availability and market participants' behavior. The chapter introduces Knightian uncertainty, which arises in situations where the probability of outcomes cannot be known in advance. This type of uncertainty is particularly relevant in financial markets, where unexpected events, such as the collapse of Lehman Brothers or the COVID-19 pandemic, can trigger widespread market disruption.

The chapter also critiques the reliance on equilibrium models, which assume that markets naturally tend toward a state of balance in which supply equals demand. In contrast, complexity science suggests that markets are constantly evolving and often are far from equilibrium. This perspective is supported by empirical evidence showing that markets are frequently characterized by periods of extreme volatility, bubbles, and crashes. The chapter explores how complexity-based models, which focus on the interactions between agents and the emergence of new market dynamics, provide a more realistic understanding of financial markets.

In addition to critiquing traditional models, the chapter highlights alternative economic and financial modeling approaches. These include ABMs, which simulate the behavior of individual market participants to explore how their interactions give rise to broader market patterns. The chapter also discusses the importance of empirical validation, proposing that models should be tested against real-world data rather than relying solely on theoretical assumptions.

Financial Innovation

Chapter 9, "Navigating Financial Innovation: From Data-Driven Decisions to Technological Disruption," explores the transformative impact of technological innovation on financial markets. Over the past few decades, advances in data analytics, AI, and blockchain technology have reshaped the financial landscape, creating new opportunities and risks. This chapter examines how financial institutions leverage these innovations to gain a competitive edge and addresses the ethical and regulatory challenges that come with them.

One of the chapter's key themes is the role of data-driven decision-making in finance. With the rise of big data, financial institutions now have access to vast information that can inform investment strategies, optimize risk management, and improve customer experiences. The chapter discusses how ML algorithms analyze these data, identify patterns, and predict market behavior. These algorithms are particularly valuable in such areas as algorithmic trading, where they can be used to execute trades at high speeds based on real-time data.

Blockchain technology is another primary focus of the chapter. Blockchain has the potential to revolutionize financial markets by providing a decentralized, secure, and transparent way of recording transactions. The chapter explores the impact of blockchain in areas such as digital currencies, smart contracts, and decentralized finance. It addresses the regulatory challenges associated with blockchain, particularly the problem of ensuring that these technologies are used ethically and responsibly.

The chapter also discusses the ethical implications of financial innovation. While AI and blockchain offer significant benefits, they pose concerns over privacy, bias, and inequality. For example, AI algorithms can sometimes reinforce biases in financial decision-making, leading to unfair outcomes. Financial institutions must adopt strong ethical frameworks and regulatory oversight to ensure innovation serves the broader public interest.

The chapter concludes by exploring the future of financial innovation, suggesting that the most successful institutions will be those that balance the benefits of technological disruption with the need for ethical responsibility and risk management.

EMBRACING INNOVATION, COMPLEXITY, AND ADAPTATION IN FINANCE

Financial markets are complex, adaptive systems shaped by behavioral, technological, and environmental forces. These interconnected dynamics require models that are both flexible and resilient, capable of accounting for feedback loops, emerging behaviors, and unforeseen disruptions. Addressing this complexity calls for a pluralistic, interdisciplinary approach that integrates insights from behavioral finance, complexity science, and environmental sustainability while moving beyond the limits of traditional equilibrium-based models.

Each chapter in this book offers a distinct perspective on the future of finance, from the role of cognitive biases in decision-making to the causal relationships that drive market outcomes and the implications of climate change for financial stability. Together, these perspectives emphasize the need to rethink the fundamental assumptions that have long guided financial theory and to embrace adaptive models suited to today's complex environment.

Effectively managing today's interconnected and fast-evolving risks requires a holistic approach that extends beyond traditional market, credit, and liquidity models. Financial institutions must integrate advanced tools, such as scenario analysis, stress testing, and machine learning, into risk management frameworks to anticipate and mitigate the impact of emerging threats, from cyber events to climate-related disruptions and geopolitical shocks.

One of the key takeaways from this book is the role of technological innovation in shaping the future of finance. From the use of AI in algorithmic trading to the potential of blockchain to revolutionize financial transactions, technology is transforming how financial markets operate. However, innovation also brings new risks, including the potential for market manipulation, systemic vulnerabilities, and ethical concerns related to privacy and bias. As we explore in the final chapters, balancing the benefits of technological disruption with the need for robust regulatory frameworks and transparency will be critical to ensuring that financial innovation contributes to long-term stability rather than short-term volatility.

Climate change represents another critical frontier in the evolution of finance. As global efforts to mitigate the impacts of climate change accelerate, financial institutions will play an increasingly central role in driving the transition to a sustainable, low-carbon economy. Integrating ESG criteria into investment strategies is one of the most promising developments in recent years, offering a framework for aligning financial goals with broader social and environmental objectives. However, as the chapter on climate risk illustrates, integrating these considerations into financial decision-making will require the development of new models and tools capable of capturing both the physical and transition risks associated with climate change.

Traditional models, while applicable in the past, are increasingly inadequate for understanding the forces shaping modern markets. Throughout the book, we argue for a more adaptive and interdisciplinary approach that combines the rigor of quantitative analysis with insights into behavioral science, complexity theory, and environmental economics. By adopting such an approach, we can build a financial system that is not only more resilient in the face of shocks and disruptions but also more aligned with the broader challenges and opportunities of the twenty-first century.

In addition to the theoretical advances discussed in this book, there are also important practical implications for financial professionals. As the world becomes more data-driven, the ability to harness and analyze vast amounts of information will be a critical competitive advantage. ML and AI are already revolutionizing how financial institutions make decisions, but these technologies also raise important ethical and regulatory questions. Financial professionals will need to navigate these challenges while staying ahead of the curve regarding technological innovation. Moreover, the increasing importance of sustainability in finance means that professionals must develop new skills and expertise in ESG investing, climate risk modeling, and sustainable finance.

Ultimately, this book is not just a collection of chapters on individual topics in finance but a cohesive narrative that invites readers to rethink the discipline's future. It challenges the status quo, encouraging financial professionals, academics, and policymakers to adopt a more holistic, interdisciplinary approach to modern markets' challenges. The world of finance is more complex, interconnected, and uncertain than ever before, but it is also full of opportunities for those willing to innovate and adapt.

The insights presented in this book provide a roadmap for navigating this evolution, offering both a critique of existing models and a vision for the future. By embracing the complexity of modern markets and integrating new tools and perspectives into our understanding of finance, we can build a more resilient, adaptive financial system—one that can thrive in an increasingly uncertain and dynamic world.

2 Behavioral Finance and Its Integration into Quantitative Models

EMBRACING BEHAVIORAL FINANCE IN FINANCIAL SYSTEMS

Behavioral finance has fundamentally altered our understanding of financial markets by challenging the traditional assumption that investors are wholly rational actors. Instead, it reveals that psychological factors and cognitive biases play a significant role in financial decision-making, often leading to outcomes that deviate from those predicted by classical financial theories. By integrating insights from psychology into economic models, behavioral finance provides a more nuanced view of investor behavior and market dynamics.

Financial crises and the growing awareness of human behavioral variances have profoundly influenced the evolution of financial theory. Traditionally, financial models were grounded in the efficient market hypothesis and the assumption that investors are rational actors, always seeking to maximize utility based on available information. However, the limitations of these models became evident, particularly during major financial disruptions, such as the 2007–2008 Global Financial Crisis (GFC). This crisis highlighted how irrational behavior, fueled by cognitive biases, can deviate drastically from classical economic models, leading to catastrophic market failures.

The GFC marked a pivotal moment for behavioral finance. It showcased the failures of traditional financial models to account for psychological influences on investor behavior, including expressions of bias such as loss aversion, overconfidence, and herding. These behaviors exacerbated the market collapse as investors scrambled to avoid losses, further amplifying the downward spiral.

In response, behavioral economists' work gained prominence. Their research provided a framework for understanding why markets deviate from rational expectations, offering insights into the psychological factors driving market bubbles, crashes, and anomalies. By incorporating prospect theory and concepts such as mental accounting, behavioral finance addresses the limitations of traditional models, offering a more accurate representation of market dynamics.

As behavioral finance has evolved, it has significantly influenced financial modeling and investment management practices. Traditional models such as the capital asset pricing model (CAPM) and the Black-Scholes option pricing model (Black & Scholes, 1973), which assume investor rationality, have been expanded to integrate psychological factors. New frameworks, such as the behavioral CAPM and prospect theory–based models, offer a more comprehensive understanding of risk, return, and market behavior by accounting for the cognitive biases that have an impact on financial decisions. As the field continues to evolve, its influence will likely grow in both academic research and practical investment management.

This chapter explores behavioral finance's significant contributions to modern financial theory and its integration into investment management practices. We begin by reviewing behavioral finance's historical and theoretical foundations. We then examine various cognitive biases, such as loss aversion, overconfidence, anchoring, and herding, and their influence on financial decision-making. These biases often lead to market anomalies that are poorly explained by traditional finance models. The chapter also delves into integrating behavioral finance into quantitative models, highlighting advances such as the behavioral CAPM and prospect theory–based frameworks. These models have proved essential in providing more accurate assessments of risk and return by accounting for psychological influences. Finally, we explore the practical applications of behavioral finance in investment management, including in smart beta strategies, robo-adviser protocols, and risk management.

HISTORICAL AND THEORETICAL FOUNDATIONS OF BEHAVIORAL FINANCE

At the core of behavioral finance is the work of Kahneman and Tversky (1979), whose seminal development of prospect theory reshaped economic thinking. Their research demonstrated that individuals make decisions based not on absolute outcomes but relative to a reference point and that losses weigh more heavily on them than equivalent gains, a bias known as *loss aversion*. Prospect theory was revolutionary because it challenged the rational choice models that dominated economics. Kahneman and Tversky's work laid the groundwork for behavioral economics, providing a framework to understand why investors often make seemingly irrational decisions.

Thaler expanded on these ideas with his contributions to behavioral economics. In Thaler (1985), he introduced the concept of *mental accounting*, whereby individuals divide their money into separate accounts based on subjective criteria.[1] Mental accounting affects how people spend, invest, and perceive gains and losses. In Thaler and Sunstein (2008), the concept of *nudging* was introduced: the authors explained how small interventions can guide people toward making better decisions without restricting their freedom of choice. The concept has been widely influential in both policymaking and financial decision-making. Kahneman, Knetsch, and Thaler (1991) described how people overvalue things they own, making them more sensitive to losses than to gains (i.e., loss aversion), which the authors refer to as the *endowment effect*. Therefore, people prefer things to remain the same, which Kahneman and coworkers call the *status quo bias*.[2]

Behavioral Life-Cycle Hypothesis

Shefrin and Thaler (1988) introduced the behavioral life-cycle hypothesis and explained how psychological factors such as self-control and mental accounting influence individuals' financial decisions. This theory builds on the traditional life-cycle hypothesis,[3] which assumes that individuals plan their consumption and saving behavior rationally over their lifetime, aiming to smooth consumption across different phases of life. The behavioral life-cycle hypothesis challenges this notion by incorporating psychological factors, such as self-control, mental accounting, and framing, that influence individuals' decisions about saving, spending, and investing.

The behavioral life-cycle hypothesis is critical for asset management because it provides insights into why individuals often fail to make optimal financial decisions, particularly regarding saving for retirement and managing long-term investments. According to Shefrin and Thaler, individuals are prone to biases and emotional influences, such as mental accounting, self-control problems, and framing. With respect to mental accounting, investors mentally assign their wealth to different accounts (current needs, savings, future-oriented retirement funds) and make decisions in isolation rather than considering their total financial situation. As for self-control problems, investors struggle to save consistently and tend to overspend. Financially, framing effects occur when the way choices are presented affects decision-making, such as how risk or rewards are framed in the context of investment options.

In asset management, the behavioral life-cycle hypothesis helps professionals understand why clients may struggle with saving enough for long-term goals such as retirement, may prefer certain types of investments over others owing to short-term needs, or may make suboptimal decisions influenced by emotional factors. By recognizing these behavioral biases, asset managers can design better investment strategies that consider the psychological realities of investor behavior, encouraging better saving and investment habits through tailored advice and financial products.

Behavioral Portfolio Theory

Statman and Shefrin (2000) developed behavioral portfolio theory (BPT) as an alternative to the widely accepted modern portfolio theory (MPT), fundamentally challenging its assumptions about investor behavior. While MPT, developed by Markowitz (1952), assumes rational investors who diversify to optimize risk and return, BPT posits that investors create portfolios shaped by multiple, often conflicting goals influenced by emotional and financial objectives. This is evident from various researchers' analysis following the GFC, which underscored how investor psychology plays a central role in shaping market behavior (Fabozzi, Focardi, & Jonas, 2014; Fabozzi, Focardi, & Ma, 2005).

In BPT, Statman and Shefrin (2000) posit that investors do not always aim to maximize utility. Instead, they pursue multiple, often conflicting objectives driven by emotional and financial goals. This means that investors are not purely rational actors as MPT assumes. Instead, they are influenced by fear, greed, and emotional satisfaction, which shape their portfolio choices. As a result, portfolios are constructed to satisfy both the desire for financial security and the lure of potentially high returns, even when such a balance may not be optimal in traditional risk-return terms.

One of the critical insights of BPT is that investors build their portfolios in a manner that more closely resembles a pyramid of assets rather than the holistic, fully diversified portfolio suggested by MPT. In the pyramid structure, safer, lower-risk investments form the base, providing security and peace of mind. These could include such assets as bonds, savings deposits, or other low-risk vehicles. At the peak of the pyramid are riskier, potentially higher-reward assets, such as stocks or speculative investments, which are included to satisfy the investor's aspirational goals of achieving higher returns. This contrasts with the idea in MPT that all investments should fit into a single diversified portfolio that minimizes risk for a given level of expected return.

The construction of a portfolio in the layered manner suggested by MPT highlights the dual objectives investors often have: establishing a "downside protection" layer to safeguard against significant losses and an "upside potential" layer to chase gains. Investors manage these layers according to both rational assessments of risk and emotional factors, such as fear of loss (leading to a heavier weight on the base layer) and greed (leading to greater exposure to high-risk, high-reward assets at the top).

The rise of behavioral finance has led to integrating these insights from BMT into market strategies as traditional theories alone have proved insufficient for predicting real-world investor behavior. The growing body of work in this field offers a more realistic understanding of the markets, where psychological factors are deeply intertwined with economic outcomes. In response, asset managers and financial professionals have increasingly used behavioral finance to inform their strategies, exploiting inefficiencies caused by such biases as overconfidence, anchoring, and herding.

COGNITIVE BIASES IN FINANCIAL DECISION-MAKING

Cognitive biases are systematic patterns of deviation from rationality that affect how individuals perceive, interpret, and respond to information. These biases are deeply rooted in human psychology and can significantly influence financial decision-making. Understanding these biases is crucial for developing models that more accurately reflect investor behavior.

Loss Aversion and Its Impact on Markets

Loss aversion is a central concept in behavioral finance. It refers to the tendency for individuals to prefer avoiding losses over acquiring equivalent gains. This bias is rooted in the psychological discomfort associated with losses, which is often more intense than the satisfaction derived from gains of the same magnitude.

In financial markets, loss aversion can lead to several behaviors that deviate from the predictions of traditional models. For instance, investors may hold on to losing stocks for too long in the hope that prices will recover, a behavior known as the *disposition effect*. Conversely, they may sell winning stocks too quickly to lock in gains, potentially missing out on further appreciation. These behaviors can lead to suboptimal portfolio performance and contribute to market anomalies.

Empirical studies have demonstrated that loss aversion plays a significant role during major financial crises, such as the GFC. According to research highlighted in Fabozzi, Focardi, and Jonas (2010), investors' heightened sensitivity to losses led to widespread panic selling during the crisis, exacerbating the downward spiral in asset prices. This behavior was particularly evident as market participants, facing the prospect of significant losses, sought to liquidate their positions to avoid further declines, thereby contributing to the overall market instability.

Loss aversion is also closely linked to "flight to quality," whereby investors shift their portfolios from risky assets to safer ones, such as government bonds or gold, during market turmoil. This shift is driven by the fear of loss and the desire to preserve capital, even if it means accepting lower returns. The impact of loss aversion on asset prices and market dynamics underscores the importance of incorporating this bias into financial models, particularly in stress testing and scenario analysis.

Investment managers can mitigate the impact of loss aversion by developing strategies that enforce discipline in portfolio management. For example, a precommitment strategy, such as automatic rebalancing, can help investors maintain their investment objectives and avoid the emotional pitfalls of loss aversion. Additionally, framing investment decisions in terms of long-term goals rather than short-term losses can help reduce the psychological impact of potential losses.

Overconfidence and Market Dynamics

Overconfidence is another pervasive cognitive bias that can significantly influence financial decision-making. Overconfident investors tend to overestimate their knowledge, underestimate risks, and believe they have more control over outcomes than they do. This bias can lead to excessive trading as overconfident investors think they can time the market or identify mispriced assets more accurately than others.

The impact of overconfidence on financial markets has been well documented, particularly in the context of market bubbles and crashes. Historical examples, such as the prelude to the Great Depression, highlight how overconfidence can lead to speculative bubbles. During periods of economic expansion, overconfidence among investors can result in inflated asset prices as they become overly optimistic about future returns. This optimism often leads to increased risk-taking and leverage, exacerbating the severity of subsequent market corrections.

One notable example of overconfidence contributing to a market bubble is the dot-com bubble of the late 1990s. During this period, investors were overly optimistic about the growth prospects of internet-related companies, leading to a dramatic rise in stock prices. When the bubble eventually burst, many investors experienced significant losses. Overconfidence also played a role in the housing market bubble of the mid-2000s, when investors underestimated the risks associated with subprime mortgages, leading to the GFC.

To mitigate the impact of overconfidence, investment managers can encourage a more measured approach to trading, emphasizing the importance of diversification and long-term investing. Stop-loss orders can also help limit potential losses by automatically selling assets when their prices fall below a certain threshold. By recognizing the signs of overconfidence, such as excessive trading volume or rapidly rising asset prices, investors and regulators can take steps to reduce the risk of market bubbles and crashes.

Anchoring and Its Effects on Investment Decisions

Anchoring is a cognitive bias that leads individuals to rely too heavily on the first piece of information they encounter (the "anchor") when making decisions. In financial markets, anchoring can manifest in various ways, such as investors basing their expectations for future asset prices on historical prices, even when current market conditions suggest otherwise.

Anchoring significantly influences the decision-making processes of both individual investors and market analysts. For example, when investors anchor on the purchase price of a stock, they may be reluctant to sell it at a lower price, even if the stock's fundamentals have deteriorated. This behavior can lead to inertia in investment decisions, where investors hold on to underperforming assets longer than they should.

Quantitative evidence from Fabozzi, Focardi, and Ma (2005) suggests that anchoring also affects market analysts' forecasts, leading to systematic biases in price targets. Analysts often base their future projections on historical performance without fully accounting for changes in a company's prospects or broader market conditions. This reliance on historical anchors can result in price targets that are either too optimistic or too pessimistic, contributing to mispricing in the market.

To counteract the effects of anchoring, investors and analysts can use objective criteria, such as that obtained from fundamental analysis or quantitative models, to guide their decision-making processes. Additionally, regularly revisiting and updating price targets based on current market conditions can help reduce the influence of anchoring on investment decisions.

Herding Behavior and Market Anomalies

Herding behavior occurs when individuals mimic the actions of a larger group, often leading to collective irrationality. In financial markets, herding can result in the formation of asset bubbles and subsequent crashes as investors pile into popular assets without thoroughly assessing the intrinsic value of those assets.

The impact of herding behavior on financial markets is particularly pronounced during periods of market exuberance or panic. For instance, the housing market bubble that preceded the GFC was significantly driven by herding behavior. According to Fabozzi, Focardi, and Jonas (2010), as housing prices continued to rise, more and more investors, including those with little experience in real estate, entered the market, driving prices even higher. This collective behavior created a self-reinforcing cycle of price increases, eventually leading to a dramatic market correction when the bubble burst.

Herding behavior is also evident in the context of financial contagion, where the actions of a few market participants can trigger widespread panic. During the GFC, the failure of major financial institutions led to a cascading effect, with investors rushing to sell assets to avoid further losses, thereby exacerbating the market decline. Fabozzi, Focardi, and Ma's (2005) insights provide a deeper understanding of how herding behavior can contribute to market anomalies and systemic risks.

Investment managers who recognize the influence of herding can develop contrarian strategies that exploit market inefficiencies created by this behavior. For example, value investing strategies focusing on undervalued assets can capitalize on mispricing when most investors chase overvalued assets. Additionally, maintaining a disciplined investment approach and avoiding the temptation to follow the crowd can help mitigate the risks associated with herding behavior.

MARKET ANOMALIES AND THE CHALLENGES TO TRADITIONAL FINANCE

Market anomalies are patterns in asset prices or returns that deviate from the predictions of traditional financial models. These anomalies challenge the efficient market hypothesis, which posits that asset prices fully reflect all available information and that it is impossible to consistently achieve higher-than-average returns without taking on additional risk. Behavioral finance explains many of these anomalies by highlighting the role of cognitive biases and psychological factors in driving investor behavior.

The Equity Premium Puzzle

The equity premium puzzle refers to the observation that historical stock returns have been significantly higher than traditional financial models would predict, given the level of risk involved. According to the efficient market hypothesis, the excess return of stocks over risk-free assets (such as government bonds) should be relatively small, as investors are assumed to be rational and risk-averse. However, empirical evidence shows that the equity premium has been much more significant than expected, leading to questions about the validity of traditional models.

Behavioral finance provides a potential explanation for the equity premium puzzle through the concept of loss aversion. Loss-averse investors are more sensitive to possible losses than gains, so they may demand a higher risk premium to compensate for the perceived risk of investing in stocks. This higher required return could explain the observed equity premium, suggesting that investor behavior is crucial in asset pricing, not just risk and return trade-offs.

In addition to loss aversion, overconfidence and optimism also contribute to the equity premium. As Focardi and Fabozzi (2014) discuss, overconfident investors may underestimate the risks associated with equities, leading them to accept a lower risk premium than rationally expected. Similarly, optimistic investors may overestimate the potential returns from equities, increasing their demand for stocks and driving up prices. These behavioral factors result in a higher equity premium as the market consistently prices in these biases over time.

Moreover, the equity premium puzzle can be further explored by considering the long-term impact of behavioral factors. Studies indicate that during periods of economic expansion, investors tend to become more optimistic and overconfident, further inflating stock prices and contributing to the equity premium. Conversely, loss aversion becomes more pronounced during economic downturns, leading to a greater demand for risk premiums to compensate for the increased risk perception. This cyclical behavior, driven by changing investor sentiment, is critical in maintaining the persistent equity premium observed in historical data.

The Momentum Effect

The momentum effect is another well-documented market anomaly whereby stocks that have performed well in the past continue to outperform in the future and stocks that have performed poorly continue to underperform. This pattern contradicts the efficient market hypothesis, which would predict that past performance should not affect future returns, as all available information should already be reflected in asset prices.

Behavioral finance suggests that cognitive biases such as overconfidence and herding may drive the momentum effect. Overconfident investors may believe that past trends will continue, leading them to buy winning stocks and sell losing ones. Herding behavior can also contribute to momentum as investors follow the crowd by purchasing assets already rising in value. Prices are pushed even higher as more investors pile into these assets, creating a self-reinforcing momentum cycle.

A deeper analysis of the momentum effect can be found by comparing its manifestation across different asset classes. Studies demonstrate that momentum is prevalent in equities, commodities, currencies, and bonds (Focardi & Fabozzi, 2012). However, the underlying behavioral drivers may differ across these asset classes. For instance, in commodity markets, momentum may be influenced more by speculative trading and less by fundamental valuation. In contrast, in equity markets, it might be driven by a combination of herding and overreaction to earnings reports.

Additionally, the momentum effect can be influenced by macroeconomic conditions. During periods of economic growth, the momentum effect tends to be stronger, as investor optimism and overconfidence are more prevalent. Conversely, momentum may weaken or reverse during recessions or market uncertainty as fear and loss aversion dominate. This cyclical nature of momentum suggests that it is not merely a result of market inefficiencies but is also closely tied to the behavioral tendencies of market participants.

Investment strategies that exploit the momentum effect, known as momentum investing, have gained popularity in recent years. However, momentum investing also carries risks as market trends can reverse suddenly, leading to significant losses. Understanding the behavioral drivers of momentum can help investors develop strategies that mitigate these risks, such as combining momentum with other factors, for example value or quality, to create more balanced portfolios.

The Disposition Effect

The disposition effect is a behavioral bias whereby investors are more likely to sell assets that have increased in value while holding on to assets that have decreased in value. This behavior is inconsistent with rational decision-making, which would suggest that investors should evaluate each asset based on its prospects rather than on its past performance.

The disposition effect can be explained by a combination of loss aversion and the tendency to avoid realizing losses. Investors may hold on to losing assets hoping that the prices will recover, thereby preventing the pain of a realized loss. Conversely, they may sell winning assets to lock in gains and prevent them from evaporating. This behavior can lead to suboptimal portfolio performance as investors may hold on to poorly performing assets while missing out on opportunities to invest in better-performing ones.

Behavioral finance research, such as that discussed by Shefrin and Statman (1985) and Odean (1998), suggests that the disposition effect is not uniform across different types of investors. For example, individual investors tend to exhibit stronger disposition effects than institutional investors, who may be more disciplined in their investment approach (Shapira & Venezia, 2001). Cultural differences also play a role as the disposition effect may be more pronounced in markets where loss aversion is culturally ingrained (Grinblatt & Keloharju, 2001).

Furthermore, the disposition effect can have broader market implications. When a significant number of investors hold on to losing stocks, it can result in price stagnation or even further declines as these stocks remain under pressure from selling. On the other hand, the premature selling of winning stocks can lead to missed opportunities for price appreciation, contributing to market inefficiencies. These inefficiencies are often exploited by contrarian investors, who take positions opposite the prevailing disposition-driven trends.

To address the disposition effect, investment managers can implement rules-based strategies that enforce discipline in portfolio management. For example, setting predefined criteria for selling assets, such as stop-loss orders or target prices, can help investors avoid the emotional pitfalls of the disposition effect. Additionally, using quantitative models that evaluate assets based on objective factors rather than past performance can help reduce the influence of this bias on investment decisions.

The Value Anomaly

The value anomaly indicates that stocks with low price-to-earnings (P/E) ratios or low price-to-book (P/B) ratios tend to outperform stocks with high P/E or P/B ratios. This phenomenon challenges the efficient market hypothesis, which would predict that stocks with low valuations should not consistently deliver higher returns as their lower prices should already reflect the risk of underperformance.

Behavioral finance offers several explanations for the value anomaly. One explanation is that investors may overreact to negative news or short-term earnings disappointments, leading them to undervalue stocks temporarily out of favor. This overreaction is driven by cognitive biases such as loss aversion and anchoring, whereby investors anchor their expectations on recent performance and fail to recognize the potential for recovery.

The expanded discussion in Fabozzi, Focardi, and Jonas (2014) looks at long-term studies that track the performance of value versus growth stocks, highlighting the persistence of the value premium across different market environments. These studies suggest that the value anomaly may be rooted in the long-term underestimation of recovery potential for undervalued stocks, an underestimation driven by investor pessimism and overreaction to short-term negative information.

Another explanation is that value stocks may be perceived as "boring" or "unexciting" compared to growth stocks, leading investors to overlook them in favor of more glamorous investments. This behavioral bias can create opportunities for value investors to capitalize on the mispricing of these stocks by buying them at a discount to their intrinsic value. However, the value premium has not been consistent across all market environments, and there have been periods in which value stocks have underperformed growth stocks, particularly during times of technological innovation or economic expansion.

Understanding the behavioral factors that drive the value anomaly can help investors develop more effective value investing strategies and avoid potential pitfalls. For example, combining value investing with other factors, such as quality or momentum, can help enhance returns while mitigating the risks of relying solely on the value factor.

INTEGRATING BEHAVIORAL FINANCE INTO QUANTITATIVE MODELS

Integrating behavioral finance into quantitative models represents a significant advance in finance as it allows a more accurate representation of investor behavior and market dynamics. Traditional financial models, such as the CAPM and Black-Scholes model, assume that investors are rational and markets are efficient. However, the insights from behavioral finance have shown that this is not always the case, and that cognitive biases and psychological factors can lead to systematic deviations from rationality. Researchers and practitioners have developed new models incorporating behavioral factors to address these limitations, leading to more realistic and robust frameworks for asset pricing, portfolio management, and risk assessment.

The Behavioral CAPM

One of the most significant contributions of behavioral finance to quantitative modeling is in the development of the behavioral CAPM. The model extends the traditional CAPM by incorporating investor psychology. In the traditional CAPM, the expected return on an asset is a function of its beta, which measures its sensitivity to market risk. However, the behavioral CAPM introduces a behavioral beta, which captures the impact of cognitive biases and sentiment on asset prices.

The behavioral beta in the behavioral CAPM accounts for factors such as loss aversion, overconfidence, and herding behavior, which can lead to deviations from the predictions of the traditional CAPM. For example, during periods of market euphoria, overconfident investors may bid up asset prices, leading to higher returns than expected based on those assets' traditional beta alone. Conversely, during periods of market panic, loss-averse investors may drive down prices, leading to lower returns.

According to the research discussed in Focardi and Fabozzi (2016), the behavioral CAPM can be further refined by incorporating additional behavioral factors, such as investor sentiment and market mood. These factors can be quantified using sentiment analysis tools that process large volumes of data from news articles, social media, and financial reports. By integrating these elements, the behavioral CAPM provides a more comprehensive view of market dynamics, capturing the psychological underpinnings of price movements that are not explained by traditional models (see Fabozzi, Focardi, & Ma, 2005).

Moreover, the behavioral CAPM can be applied across different market environments to assess its predictive power relative to the traditional CAPM. Comparative studies suggest that the behavioral CAPM is particularly effective in volatile markets, where investor behavior is more likely to deviate from rational expectations. For instance, during the dot-com bubble, behavioral beta provided a better explanation for the excessive valuations of tech stocks than the traditional beta. This observation highlights the importance of incorporating behavioral factors into risk management and portfolio optimization strategies, particularly in environments characterized by high levels of uncertainty and speculation.

PROSPECT THEORY AND ASSET PRICING

Prospect theory posits that individuals evaluate potential losses and gains relative to a reference point rather than in absolute terms and are more sensitive to losses than to gains. This theory has profound implications for asset pricing. For instance, loss-averse investors may demand a higher risk premium for assets perceived as having a greater likelihood of loss, even when the expected returns are identical to those of other assets. This insight helps explain the equity premium puzzle.

Prospect theory has important implications for asset pricing, suggesting that investors may require a higher risk premium for assets that carry a greater chance of losses—even when those assets have the same expected return as others. This can lead to asset mispricing as traditional models may underestimate the risk premium loss-averse investors require.

Incorporating prospect theory into asset pricing models has led to new frameworks that adjust the traditional utility function to account for the value function described by Kahneman and Tversky. As Fabozzi, Focardi, and Ma (2005) discuss, these models provide a more accurate representation of investor behavior, particularly in situations involving significant uncertainty or potential losses. For example, prospect theory–based models can explain the equity premium puzzle by showing that loss-averse investors require a higher premium to compensate for the perceived risk of investing in stocks, leading to higher observed returns over time.

Additionally, prospect theory has been used to develop models that better predict investor behavior during market downturns. During such periods, investors are likelier to exhibit loss aversion, resulting in a flight to safety and a reallocation of assets toward less risky investments. Prospect theory–based models can capture these behavioral shifts, providing insights into market dynamics that traditional models do not capture. By understanding how investors perceive risk and reward through prospect theory, financial professionals can develop more effective strategies for managing portfolios during periods of market stress.

Behavioral Portfolio Theory

Behavioral portfolio theory is another crucial framework that integrates insights from behavioral finance into quantitative models. BPT challenges the traditional mean-variance optimization framework, which assumes that investors are solely concerned with maximizing expected return for a given level of risk. Instead, BPT suggests that investors construct their portfolios based on a combination of goals and aspirations rather than purely on the trade-off between risk and return.

In BPT, investors are modeled as holding multiple "mental accounts," each corresponding to a different goal or aspiration. For example, an investor might have one mental account for retirement savings, another for a child's education, and a third for discretionary investments. Each mental account is associated with a different risk tolerance and return expectation level, leading to a portfolio that combines different subportfolios, each optimized for a specific goal.

Studies show that BPT provides a more realistic representation of how investors construct their portfolios. Traditional portfolio theory assumes investors are only concerned with the overall risk-return trade-off (see Fabozzi, Focardi, & Jonas, 2014). Still, BPT recognizes that investors often have multiple, sometimes conflicting goals influencing their investment decisions. For instance, an investor might be willing to take on more risk in a discretionary account while maintaining a conservative approach in a retirement account. By incorporating these behavioral considerations, BPT allows for creating more personalized investment strategies that better align with an investor's goals and risk preferences (see Fabozzi, Focardi, & Ma, 2005).

Furthermore, BPT has practical applications in developing customized investment solutions, such as target-date funds or goal-based investment portfolios. These products are designed to meet specific investor needs by considering the behavioral factors influencing how individuals approach saving and investing. By integrating BPT into the design of these products, financial institutions can offer more tailored solutions that better serve their clients' long-term financial objectives.

BEHAVIORAL FINANCE IN THE ERA OF BIG DATA AND POWERFUL ALGORITHMS

As big data and advanced algorithms revolutionize financial markets, they provide new opportunities to explore and quantify these behavioral patterns with unprecedented precision. However, before integrating big data and behavioral insights into finance, it is important to briefly revisit the foundational rationality and utility theories underlying traditional finance.

Rationality and the Foundations of Utility Theory

Rationality has long been a cornerstone of economic and financial theory, serving as the basis for models that assume individuals make decisions to maximize utility. The origins of utility theory can be traced back to the St. Petersburg paradox, a problem first articulated by Nicolas Bernoulli and later formalized by his cousin, Daniel Bernoulli. This paradox exposed the limitations of using expected monetary value as the sole criterion for rational decision-making and introduced the concept of utility as a more appropriate measure.

As Daniel Bernoulli introduced, utility captures the diminishing marginal value of wealth. This groundbreaking insight resolved the paradox by suggesting that individuals value additional increments of wealth differently depending on their initial level of wealth. The mathematical formulation of utility functions provided a framework for analyzing decisions under uncertainty and laid the groundwork for expected utility theory, which became a central tenet of modern finance.

Behavioral finance has revealed some of the limitations of utility theory. While utility theory assumes that individuals are rational and consistent in their preferences, empirical studies have highlighted deviations from this idealized behavior. Despite its limitations, utility theory remains a foundational financial concept, providing a benchmark against which deviations can be studied. Advances in behavioral finance and computational tools now allow researchers to explore these deviations more comprehensively, blending classical theories with new insights from data-driven approaches.

Behavioral Deviations from Rationality

While utility theory provides a foundational framework for understanding financial decision-making, behavioral finance has revealed significant deviations from these rational models. These deviations are driven by cognitive biases and emotional factors, which often lead individuals to act in ways that diverge from the predictions of traditional utility-maximizing frameworks.

Prospect theory is one of the most notable contributions to this field. Prospect theory challenges the notion that individuals evaluate outcomes based on final wealth levels. Instead, it demonstrates that individuals assess potential gains and losses relative to a reference point, often exhibiting loss aversion, where losses are perceived as more impactful than equivalent gains. This phenomenon explains why investors may avoid risks even when the potential rewards outweigh the possible losses.

Another important behavioral deviation is overconfidence, which can lead investors to overestimate their ability to predict market movements or manage risks. This bias is particularly prevalent in active traders, who may engage in excessive trading, eroding returns because of the higher transaction costs associated with frequent trading. Similarly, herd behavior—whereby individuals mimic the actions of others rather than relying on their own analysis—often drives irrational market bubbles and crashes.

These behavioral deviations underscore the importance of integrating psychological insights into financial models. By understanding how real-world decision-making diverges from theoretical predictions, behavioral finance provides a more nuanced and accurate lens through which to study market behavior. This sets the stage for exploring how modern tools, such as big data and algorithms, can enhance our ability to analyze and address these deviations.

Big Data and Behavioral Insights

The advent of big data has transformed the way behavioral finance investigates investor decision-making. Traditional behavioral models often relied on controlled experiments or limited datasets, constraining their ability to yield findings generalizable to real-world financial markets. In contrast, big data enables the analysis of vast quantities of transactional, demographic, and market information, uncovering patterns and insights that were previously inaccessible.

Big data enhances behavioral finance by offering a granular view of investor behavior on a large scale. For instance, data from trading platforms, credit card transactions, and social media interactions allow researchers to examine how cognitive biases such as overconfidence, loss aversion, and herd behavior manifest in real-time market conditions. These insights have validated earlier experimental findings and revealed new dimensions of behavioral biases that vary across demographics, geographies, and market conditions.

Moreover, the availability of big data facilitates the integration of advanced predictive tools, such as machine learning and natural language processing, into behavioral finance. These tools can process unstructured data, such as news articles or sentiments on social media, to predict market movements influenced by behavioral drivers. For example, sentiment analysis can quantify market optimism or fear, providing actionable insights into investor psychology during periods of volatility.

While integrating big data offers significant opportunities, it also presents challenges. The potential for overfitting models to historical data or misinterpreting correlations as causations underscores the need for rigorous methodological frameworks. Additionally, ethical concerns regarding data privacy and the unintended consequences of algorithmic bias remain critical considerations.

This intersection of big data and behavioral finance marks a paradigm shift in understanding investor behavior. By leveraging modern technologies, researchers and practitioners can move beyond traditional models to develop more robust, data-driven approaches to addressing behavioral biases in financial markets.

Deep Learning and Predictive Behavioral Models

As financial markets become increasingly complex, deep learning and other advanced machine learning (ML) algorithms have emerged as powerful tools for understanding and predicting investor behavior. Unlike traditional statistical models, which often rely on linear assumptions and predefined relationships, deep learning algorithms can process vast amounts of unstructured and high-dimensional data, uncovering hidden patterns and nonlinear interactions that drive market dynamics.

In the context of behavioral finance, deep learning models can analyze complex datasets, such as trading records, news articles, and social media sentiment, to identify behavioral biases on a large scale. For example, recurrent neural networks (RNNs) and long short-term memory (LSTM) networks have been used to capture temporal dependencies in financial data, enabling the prediction of market trends influenced by overconfidence, herd behavior, or loss aversion. Similarly, convolutional neural networks (CNNs) can process visual data, such as price charts, to detect patterns consistent with behavioral biases in technical trading.

One notable application of deep learning is in developing sentiment-driven market models. These models can quantify investor sentiment and its impact on asset prices by integrating textual data from news sources or social media. For instance, a surge in optimistic language during earnings season might signal overconfidence, while heightened pessimism during a crisis could indicate panic-driven market sell-offs.

Despite their promise, deep learning models also introduce challenges. Overfitting is a persistent risk, particularly when models are trained on historical data that may not reflect future market conditions. Additionally, the interpretability of deep learning models remains a significant limitation as their "black box" nature makes it difficult to understand the causal mechanisms driving predictions. These challenges highlight the need for hybrid approaches that combine the predictive power of deep learning with the theoretical rigor of behavioral finance. Integrating deep learning into behavioral finance represents a transformative shift in how researchers and practitioners approach market prediction and investor analysis. By leveraging these tools, financial professionals can develop more sophisticated strategies to mitigate behavioral biases and enhance decision-making processes in a rapidly evolving financial landscape.

Challenges and Ethical Considerations in Behavioral Finance and Big Data

While integrating big data and advanced algorithms into behavioral finance opens up new possibilities, it also introduces critical ethical, practical, and regulatory challenges that must be addressed.

One of the most pressing concerns is data privacy. Behavioral models often rely on sensitive personal information—such as trading histories, search behavior, or social media activity. If these data are used without proper consent or safeguards, it raises legal and ethical issues. Firms must ensure compliance with data protection regulations (e.g., GDPR, CCPA) and be transparent about how behavioral data are collected and used.

Another issue is algorithmic bias. Machine learning models trained on biased or incomplete data can reinforce stereotypes, exclude vulnerable groups, or misinterpret behavioral signals. This is especially problematic in finance, where predictive models may influence lending, investing, or hiring decisions. Ethical use of behavioral data requires that developers assess and test for bias throughout the model development process.

There is also concern about the manipulative use of behavioral insights. If firms use behavioral finance tools to exploit investor weaknesses—such as nudging toward excessive risk-taking or timing messages to trigger emotional decisions—they may cross ethical boundaries. Transparency, fairness, and intent are critical when applying behavioral findings in commercial settings.

Finally, as models grow more complex, there is an increasing need for governance and accountability. Financial institutions must put systems in place to audit models, explain their decisions when needed, and provide recourse to users affected by automated outputs. Without these safeguards, trust in data-driven finance may erode.

The application of big data and behavioral finance must be grounded not only in technological sophistication but also in ethical responsibility. As these tools become more influential in shaping financial decision-making, it is essential to prioritize trust, fairness, and transparency. Only by aligning innovation with strong ethical standards can the long-term credibility and impact of data-driven finance be sustained.

APPLICATIONS OF BEHAVIORAL FINANCE IN INVESTMENT MANAGEMENT

Behavioral finance has significantly influenced investment management by revealing how cognitive biases and psychological factors have an impact on investor behavior. This understanding enables investment managers to craft strategies that capitalize on market inefficiencies caused by these biases. As a result, behavioral insights are increasingly integrated into investment strategies, with "smart beta" strategies being a prominent example. These approaches allow investors to systematically capture excess returns while accounting for the psychological tendencies that often distort market pricing.

Smart Beta Strategies and Behavioral Insights

One application of behavioral finance in investment management is in the development of smart beta strategies, which seek to capture the benefits of factor investing while accounting for behavioral biases. Smart beta strategies typically involve weighing assets based on factors such as value, momentum, or quality rather than traditional market capitalization. By incorporating behavioral insights, these strategies can be designed to mitigate the impact of cognitive biases such as overconfidence or herding on portfolio performance. As discussed in Fabozzi, Focardi, and Jonas (2014), smart beta strategies that integrate behavioral finance principles are particularly effective in capturing excess returns while mitigating the risks posed by market inefficiencies caused by investor biases.

Smart beta strategies have become increasingly popular as investors seek to combine the systematic approach of passive investing with the potential for outperformance traditionally associated with active management. According to Fabozzi, Focardi, and Ma (2014), beta strategies can be enhanced by integrating behavioral finance principles, particularly when selecting and weighing factors. For instance, a value-focused smart beta strategy could capitalize on the value anomaly by systematically identifying and investing in undervalued stocks. Behavioral finance suggests that value stocks are often undervalued owing to overreaction to negative news driven by loss aversion and anchoring. By recognizing these biases, smart beta strategies can better exploit these mispricings.

Moreover, momentum-based smart beta strategies can be adjusted for the momentum effect, often driven by overconfidence and herding behavior. By understanding the psychological underpinnings of momentum, such as the tendency for investors to chase past performance, smart beta strategies can be designed to capture momentum while avoiding the pitfalls of buying into overextended trends. This can involve incorporating additional filters, such as valuation or risk measures, to ensure that momentum stocks are not overvalued and that the strategy remains robust across different market environments.

In addition, smart beta strategies can be tailored to address specific behavioral biases in certain investor groups. For example, strategies targeting retail investors might emphasize simplicity and transparency, as these attributes help mitigate the effects of overconfidence and loss aversion. By designing smart beta products that consider the behavioral tendencies of their target audience, investment managers can create more effective solutions that align with investor behavior and preferences.

Robo-Advisers and Behavioral Finance

Another application of behavioral finance is in the design of automated investment platforms, such as robo-advisers. Robo-advisers use algorithms to manage portfolios based on predefined rules and objectives, reducing the influence of emotions and biases on investment decisions. By incorporating behavioral finance principles, robo-advisers can provide personalized investment advice that considers an investor's risk tolerance, goals, and psychological preferences.

Robo-advisers represent a significant advance in democratizing financial advice, making it accessible to a broader range of investors. However, their effectiveness depends on how well they incorporate behavioral finance principles into their algorithms. As discussed in Focardi, Fabozzi, and Mazza (2020), robo-advisers can be designed to address specific behavioral biases that typically affect retail investors, such as loss aversion and short-term thinking. For instance, a robo-adviser that incorporates loss aversion into its algorithms might adjust its asset allocation recommendations based on an investor's sensitivity to potential losses. This approach can help create a portfolio that aligns with the investor's psychological profile, reducing the likelihood of panic selling during market downturns.

Robo-advisers can also use behavioral finance principles to encourage better investor behavior. For example, by framing investment decisions to emphasize long-term goals rather than short-term market fluctuations, robo-advisers can help reduce the impact of biases such as loss aversion. This can be achieved through personalized communication strategies that remind investors of their long-term objectives during periods of market volatility, thereby helping them stay the course and avoid making emotionally driven decisions.

Furthermore, robo-advisers can incorporate nudges—subtle prompts that encourage desirable behavior—based on insights from behavioral economics. For instance, automatic rebalancing features can be seen as a nudge that helps investors maintain their target asset allocation without managing their portfolios actively. By automating these decisions, robo-advisers reduce the cognitive load on investors and help prevent common behavioral mistakes.

As robo-advisers evolve, their ability to incorporate more advanced behavioral finance concepts will likely increase. For example, integrating ML and AI could allow robo-advisers to develop more sophisticated models that better predict investor behavior and market trends. These advances could lead to more personalized and adaptive investment strategies, further enhancing the role of behavioral finance in automated investment management.

Behavioral Finance in Risk Management

Behavioral finance also plays a crucial role in enhancing risk management practices in investment management. Traditional risk management models often assume that markets are efficient and that investors act rationally. By incorporating insights from behavioral finance, investment managers can develop more effective risk management strategies that take into account the psychological factors influencing investor behavior.

As discussed in Fabozzi, Focardi, and Jonas (2010), one of the key contributions of behavioral finance to risk management is in recognizing how cognitive biases can exacerbate market volatility. By understanding these dynamics, investment managers can develop risk management strategies more resilient to behavior-driven market disruptions.

One approach is to integrate behavioral risk factors into stress testing and scenario analysis. Traditional stress tests may not fully capture the impact of behavioral biases on market dynamics, particularly during extreme events. By incorporating scenarios that account for potential behavioral responses—such as widespread panic or overconfidence—investment managers can better prepare for adverse market conditions and develop contingency plans that mitigate the impact of these behaviors.

Another application of behavioral finance in risk management is in using behaviorally adjusted risk metrics. For example, incorporating investor sentiment or market mood measures into risk assessments can provide a more comprehensive view of potential risks. These metrics can be beneficial in identifying periods of market exuberance or fear, during which traditional risk measures might fail to capture the elevated risk levels fully.

Incorporating behavioral finance into risk management also involves adjusting communication and reporting strategies to align with investor psychology. For instance, during periods of market volatility, providing clear and concise information that focuses on long-term goals rather than short-term losses can help reduce investor anxiety and prevent reactive decisions. By understanding how investors perceive and respond to risk, investment managers can develop more effective communication strategies that help maintain investor confidence and encourage disciplined decision-making.

Behavioral Finance in Investment Strategy Design

Behavioral finance has also influenced the design of investment strategies that exploit market inefficiencies created by cognitive biases. By understanding how these biases influence investor behavior, investment managers can develop strategies that take advantage of mispricings and anomalies in the market.

Fabozzi, Focardi, and Jonas (2014) point out that one of the critical areas where behavioral finance has had an impact on strategy design is in the development of contrarian and value-based investing strategies. These strategies are often based on the premise that cognitive biases, such as overreaction and loss aversion, lead to the mispricing of assets. For example, value investing strategies focus on identifying undervalued stocks that have been overlooked or oversold owing to negative sentiment. By recognizing the behavioral drivers behind these mispricings, investment managers can capitalize on the eventual correction as market prices adjust to reflect the true value of the assets.

Similarly, contrarian strategies that go against prevailing market trends can be informed by behavioral finance. During periods of market euphoria, when herding behavior can lead to the overvaluation of certain assets, a contrarian approach would involve identifying and investing in assets that are undervalued owing to a lack of investor interest. Conversely, during market downturns, when fear and loss aversion dominate, contrarian investors might seek opportunities in assets that have been excessively sold off. By understanding the behavioral forces, investment managers can develop strategies that exploit these temporary inefficiencies for long-term gain.

Additionally, behavioral finance has influenced the development of factor-based investing strategies, in which specific factors, such as momentum, value, or low volatility, are used to build portfolios. These strategies often incorporate behavioral insights to enhance their effectiveness. For example, momentum strategies may be adjusted to account for the behavioral drivers of momentum, such as overconfidence or herding, ensuring that the strategy remains robust even when market trends reverse.

Overall, integrating behavioral finance into investment strategy design has led to the development of more sophisticated and adaptive approaches that are better aligned with real-world investor behavior. By recognizing the impact of cognitive biases on market dynamics, investment managers can create strategies that capitalize on market inefficiencies to provide a more personalized and psychologically informed approach to investing.

CASE STUDIES IN BEHAVIORAL FINANCE AND MARKET DYNAMICS

This section examines several case studies that highlight the role of cognitive biases and psychological factors in driving market behavior. These case studies illustrate the practical applications of behavioral finance in investment management and demonstrate how behavioral finance can provide a more comprehensive understanding of market dynamics, particularly during periods of market exuberance or crisis.

The Dot-Com Bubble

The dot-com bubble of the late 1990s and early 2000s was characterized by a rapid rise in the stock prices of internet and technology companies, followed by a sharp collapse. Traditional financial models, which assume that markets are efficient and that prices reflect all available information, failed to predict the bubble and its subsequent collapse. In contrast, behavioral finance models, which take into account the impact of cognitive biases and psychological factors on investors' decisions, provide a more accurate framework for understanding the dynamics of the dot-com bubble.

Fabozzi, Focardi, and Jonas (2014) explain that investors were overly optimistic about the growth prospects of internet-related companies, resulting in excessive valuations not supported by the underlying fundamentals. This overconfidence was fueled by the media and financial analysts, who frequently projected unrealistically high growth rates for these companies, further stoking investor enthusiasm.

Herding behavior was also a critical factor in the formation of the bubble. As more investors piled into internet stocks, driven by the fear of missing out (FOMO), prices continued to rise, creating a self-reinforcing cycle. This behavior was particularly evident among institutional investors, who felt pressure to invest in the booming tech sector to keep up with their peers. According to Fabozzi, Focardi, and Ma (2005), this collective irrationality contributed to the extreme overvaluation of tech stocks as traditional valuation metrics were largely ignored in favor of speculative bets on future growth.

When the bubble eventually burst, the psychological impact on investors was profound. Loss aversion led to widespread panic selling as investors sought to minimize their losses, exacerbating the market decline. The dot-com bubble is a cautionary tale about the dangers of cognitive biases in financial markets, highlighting the need for investment strategies that account for these biases and the potential for irrational exuberance.

2007–2008 Global Financial Crisis

The GFC of 2007–2008 exposed vulnerabilities in international markets, particularly regarding liquidity and systemic risk management. Many asset managers struggled to adapt their strategies to these new market realities, highlighting the limitations of traditional risk models that did not account for investors' behavioral biases (Fabozzi, Focardi, & Jonas, 2010).

One of the primary cognitive biases that contributed to the GFC was overconfidence, particularly among financial institutions and housing market investors. Fabozzi, Focardi, and Jonas (2014) discuss how overconfidence led to underestimating the risks associated with subprime mortgages and the overvaluation of mortgage-backed securities (MBS). Acting on the belief that housing prices would continue to rise indefinitely, investors took on excessive leverage, increasing their exposure to the housing market.

Loss aversion also played a significant role in the crisis. As housing prices began to decline, investors were reluctant to sell their declining assets, hoping for a recovery that never materialized. This reluctance to realize losses led to a prolonged period of market decline as investors held on to toxic assets, hoping to avoid further losses. The insights from the behavioral finance literature suggest that loss aversion contributed to the downward spiral in asset prices as selling pressure increased when it became clear that the housing market would not recover quickly.

Herding behavior was evident in the actions of financial institutions that continued to invest in high-risk MBS despite the warning signs of a market collapse. This behavior was driven by the belief that other institutions had superior information, leading to a collective misjudgment of the risks involved. The contagion effect, whereby the failure of one institution led to widespread panic and the eventual collapse of others, underscores the role of herding in amplifying the crisis.

The GFC highlighted the need for more comprehensive risk management models that account for the impact of cognitive biases on market behavior. In response to the crisis, financial institutions and regulators have implemented various measures to strengthen risk management practices, including integrating behavioral finance principles into stress testing and scenario analysis.

The Impact of High-Frequency Trading on Market Stability

High-frequency trading has become dominant in modern financial markets, accounting for a significant share of the trading volume on major exchanges. High-frequency trading uses algorithms to execute trades at extremely high speeds, often in milliseconds or microseconds, to exploit small price discrepancies across markets. While high-frequency trading has been credited with increasing market liquidity and reducing transaction costs, it has also been associated with increased market volatility and the potential for flash crashes.

The May 6, 2010, flash crash serves as a case study of the potential dangers of high-frequency trading and the role of cognitive biases in exacerbating market instability. During this event, a large sell order in the futures market triggered a cascade of selling across multiple asset classes, leading to a rapid and severe price decline. As discussed in Focardi, Fabozzi, and Mazza (2020), high-frequency trading algorithms, designed to capitalize on short-term market movements, contributed to the extreme volatility by executing trades based on rapidly changing price signals without considering the broader market context.

Herding behavior by high-frequency trading algorithms can lead to the emergence of extreme events such as flash crashes, where prices deviate significantly from their fundamental values. These algorithms, programmed to react to the same market signals, can amplify market movements as they simultaneously execute similar trades. This collective behavior can result in a feedback loop whereby price movements become increasingly exaggerated, leading to sudden, sharp market declines.

Behavioral finance provides insights into the impact of high-frequency trading on market stability, particularly the role of cognitive biases in driving market behavior. For example, investors' tendency to rely on automated trading systems without fully understanding their potential risks can lead to overconfidence in their stability. Fabozzi, Focardi, and Jonas (2014) suggest that relying on high-frequency trading has introduced new forms of systemic risk that traditional models may not fully capture, requiring new risk management approaches that consider the behavioral dynamics of automated trading.

The flash crash highlighted the need for regulatory measures to mitigate the risks associated with high-frequency trading. In response, regulators have implemented circuit breakers and other safeguards to prevent similar events from occurring in the future. These measures, informed by behavioral finance principles, aim to reduce the likelihood of extreme market volatility by addressing the cognitive biases that can drive automated trading behavior.

The Housing Market Bubble and Subsequent Crisis

Another illustrative case is the housing market bubble that preceded the GFC. The housing market bubble was fueled by cognitive biases, including overconfidence, herding, and loss aversion, which were critical in driving the market dynamics that ultimately led to the crisis.

Overconfidence in the continued appreciation of home values characterized the housing market bubble. As discussed in Fabozzi, Focardi, and

Jonas (2010), this overconfidence was not limited to individual homebuyers but extended to financial institutions, investors, and regulators. The widespread belief that housing prices would never decline led to aggressive lending practices, the proliferation of subprime mortgages, and the creation of complex financial products, such as MBS, based on the assumption of ever-increasing home values.

Herding behavior was evident as more and more investors, including those with little experience in real estate, entered the housing market, driving prices even higher. This behavior was motivated by the perception that others were making significant profits in the housing market. This led to a FOMO that encouraged even more speculative buying. The insights from Fabozzi, Focardi, and Ma (2005) suggest that this collective irrationality played a significant role in inflating the housing bubble as traditional housing affordability and risk were mainly ignored.

Loss aversion also played a critical role in the housing market bubble and its subsequent collapse. As housing prices began declining, homeowners and investors were reluctant to sell their properties at a loss, hoping prices would eventually recover. This behavior, driven by the desire to avoid realizing losses, contributed to the prolonged downturn in the housing market as sellers held on to properties for more extended periods, exacerbating the oversupply of homes on the market.

The housing market bubble and subsequent crisis underscore the importance of incorporating behavioral finance principles into risk management and investment strategy design. By understanding the cognitive biases that drive market behavior, financial institutions can develop more effective strategies to prevent asset bubble formation and manage the risks associated with market downturns.

CRITICALLY REVISITING BEHAVIORAL FINANCE

As discussed in previous sections, the conceptual underpinning of behavioral finance is prospect theory, developed by Daniel Kahneman and Amos Tversky. Prospect theory is a theory of decision-making under uncertainty. Based on many controlled experiments, Kahneman and Tversky identified that psychological and cognitive biases influence human decision-making. Prospect theory asserts that people assess losses and gains asymmetrically. This theory has been used in many fields, including economics and political studies, and later gave rise to several research streams in psychology based on understanding and eventually exploiting psychological biases.

Prospect theory and behavioral finance oppose the rational decision-making theory, which von Neuman and Morgenstern put forward thirty-five years earlier, in 1944. According to rational decision-making, investors maximize expected utility. Behavioral finance claims investors are not entirely rational because they have psychological and cognitive biases. Therefore, investors do not choose to maximize their expected utility.

Both theories have a fundamental weakness: people do not know the future perfectly, not even in a probabilistic sense. The ability to make forecasts based on past data is limited for both humans and machines. Muth (1961) proposed the concept of rational expectations. Since then, the idea of rationality has included perfect probabilistic forecasts. Rationality claims that agents know all available information and can make perfect probabilistic forecasts. The same idea is the basis of the efficient market hypothesis: prices reflect all available information.

"All available information" is misleading phrasing. It is well known that pure data do not exist; data are "theory laden." This concept is well known in the philosophy of science and applies to economics. For example, inflation and volatility are two terms that depend on the models used to compute them. Above all, even assuming we have true data at time t, we need models to project these data at time $t+1$. Information gathered today does not include future data.

It is far from evident that we can perfectly forecast the future. First, future data might be utterly unforecastable because it is impossible to know at time t probability distributions at time $t+1$. Let's state explicitly that knowledge of the probability of an outcome at a future date differs from knowledge of the probability distribution of outcomes.

Classical physics was deterministic up until the discovery of chaos. Quantum mechanics is inherently probabilistic, but probability distributions can, in principle, be determined. However, complex systems, the subject of chapter 5, might be inherently probabilistic and eventually totally unpredictable. There are different possible reasons for unpredictability. There might be laws that we do not know. However, the simplest explanation of unpredictability is complexity itself. Computation might take too long, eventually infinitely long. Complex systems such as modern economies or financial markets might be unpredictable.

Equating rationality with predictability, even at a probabilistic level, is not supported by any theoretical or empirical evidence. Not only humans but even computer algorithms are not able to produce sure forecasts or estimate future probability distributions with certainty.

Investors do have psychological biases concerning their evaluation of probability distributions. However, the key point is that their estimates of probability distributions might be simply wrong because it is impossible to know the true probability distribution. The true probability distribution might not even exist if we evaluate unique events. For example, the results of a presidential election might not be predictable in any sense because a presidential election is a unique event.

In summary, the notion that rational agents with access to all relevant information make decisions by choosing the highest expected value of their utility is an idealization that does not correspond to reality. Neither human agents nor machines can know with certainty the future distribution of probability. Similarly, labeling agents as irrational solely because they exhibit psychological and cognitive biases overlooks the deeper issue—that uncertainty about future outcomes is a fundamental and unavoidable feature of real-world decision-making. The eventual impossibility of forecasting events or probability distributions is an objective characteristic of economies.

Herbert Simon objected to the notion of rational behavior and rational decision-making because any agent, human or machine, has access only to a finite set of information and therefore cannot be sure of probabilistic forecasts (Simon, 1957). Agents do not optimize because probability distributions are unknown, and true optimization might be too demanding from a computational point of view. Simon replaced rational agents with boundedly rational agents with access to a finite information set and showed they can make only uncertain forecasts. These agents do not optimize but use heuristics to make decisions.

Simon's theory has not gained the same popularity as behavioral finance has because it is much more challenging to apply. Ultimately, behavioral finance accepts the basic tenets of rationality: agents could be rational if they were not psychologically biased. However, biases cause only small perturbations of rational behavior. Biases can be reduced by coaching investors and supporting them with appropriate tools.

On the other hand, representing the behavior of boundedly rational agents requires a theory of how agents make forecasts and decisions. It is tough to rationalize the behavior of boundedly rational agents with a parsimonious theory. Only multiagent systems have been able to implement Simon's ideas. However, multiagent systems are complex systems that allow simulations.

We must distinguish between two forms of behavioral finance. One form is the active management of portfolios. With the diffusion of quantitative algorithms, it seems reasonable to predict that the price formation mechanism will be increasingly determined by the interplay of algorithms and less by human interventions. The other form of behavioral finance is given by individual investors' decisions as to where to allocate their discretionary funds. Understanding how people are planning their finances, how to counsel them, and the effect of aggregate investors' decisions on prices will require considerations of behavioral finance.

The impact of big data and algorithms, such as deep learning tools, is an open question. Will these tools drastically improve forecastability, and if yes, what will be the consequences? As noted above, objective limits to the forecastability of economies and financial markets might exist. Processing the huge amount of data now available might benefit forecastability only marginally.

If big data and powerful algorithms, perhaps powered by quantum computing, significantly improve the ability to forecast economic events, then the entire organization of financial relationships will change. Uncertainty is fundamental to the organization of our economies. For example, the entire insurance business is based on uncertainty. Rewarding risk is one of the major tasks of financial markets. The planning of personal lives is primarily based on uncertainty. Eliminating uncertainty will fundamentally change our lives. It seems unlikely, but we still need to consider that reducing uncertainty is not surely beneficial.

In chapters 8 and 9, we critically revisit the foundations and limitations of behavioral finance, contrasting it with classical finance and decision-making models such as prospect theory and rational expectations theory. The discussion there highlights that while behavioral finance has made significant contributions by acknowledging human biases, it may still fall short in addressing the inherent unpredictability of financial markets. Chapter 8 argues that both classical and behavioral models rely on assumptions about the predictability of future events, but this assumption may not hold in complex systems such as financial markets. The chapter also emphasizes the contributions of Herbert Simon's theory of bounded rationality, which suggests that decision-makers work with limited information and use heuristics rather than optimal strategies. Finally, it raises the question of whether big data and advanced algorithms might enhance the predictive power of financial models. Still, it cautions that uncertainty may remain a fundamental characteristic of financial systems.

SUMMARY

This chapter examined the profound impact behavioral finance has had on our understanding of financial markets. Traditional finance has long been grounded in the assumption that investors are rational actors who make decisions based on all available information. However, behavioral finance challenges this view by incorporating psychological factors and cognitive biases into financial models. This approach reveals that investor behavior often deviates from the rational ideal, leading to market outcomes that classical financial theories cannot fully explain.

We discussed various cognitive biases influencing financial decision-making, including loss aversion, overconfidence, anchoring, and herding behavior. Loss aversion, for instance, leads investors to hold on to losing stocks for too long or to sell winning stocks prematurely, resulting in suboptimal portfolio performance. Overconfidence can drive excessive trading and contribute to market bubbles, as seen in the dot-com bubble of the late 1990s. Anchoring causes investors to rely too heavily on initial information, such as the purchase price of a stock, which can lead to inertia in decision-making. Herding behavior, in which investors mimic the actions of others, can exacerbate market anomalies and lead to asset bubbles and crashes, as illustrated by the housing market bubble that preceded the 2007–2008 GFC.

The integration of behavioral finance into quantitative models represents a significant advance in the field of finance. However, new models such as the behavioral CAPM and prospect theory–based frameworks provide a more accurate representation of market dynamics by incorporating behavioral insights. These models take into account cognitive biases and psychological factors, leading to more realistic assessments of risk and return. For instance, the behavioral CAPM introduces a behavioral beta that reflects the impact of investor sentiment on asset prices. At the same time, prospect theory–based models adjust the traditional utility function to better capture investor behavior under uncertainty.

We also highlighted the practical applications of behavioral finance in investment management, mainly through developing smart beta strategies and robo-advisers. Smart beta strategies use factor-based investing to mitigate the effects of cognitive biases on portfolio performance. At the same time, robo-advisers incorporate behavioral principles to provide personalized investment advice that aligns with an investor's psychological profile.

3 Toward a Comprehensive Economic Framework: The Role of Causal Models

UNDERSTANDING CAUSALITY IN ECONOMIC AND FINANCIAL SYSTEMS

Causality has always been a fundamental concern in finance and economics as understanding causal relationships informs policy development and decision-making processes, particularly in managing investments. In this chapter, we introduce an innovative perspective on causal modeling in financial markets and economics, founded on three core principles: (1) the recognition that modern economies are evolving into complex systems that operate under increasing environmental constraints; (2) the adoption of a forward-looking, engineering-oriented approach to developing new causal frameworks and equations; and (3) the necessity for causal models to coexist alongside noncausal economic theories. These principles align with the argument that while mathematical models in economics are reasonably effective, they are not as empirically rigorous as those in the physical sciences. Focardi and Fabozzi (2009) argue that the complexity of economic systems—human-designed and governed by multiple variables—imposes limitations on the predictive power of mathematics. The unique uncertainties and human-driven innovations in economies make mathematical models more descriptive and less prescriptive than physics models.

The foundations of causal modeling in econometrics were established through pioneering work in simultaneous equations, probability-based approaches, and the study of selection bias and treatment effects. The simultaneous equations models by Frisch (1934) helped capture the interdependent relationships between variables in economic systems, while Haavelmo

(1944) introduced a probability-based approach to distinguish correlation from causation. Heckman's (1979) work on selection bias and treatment effects advanced the practical applications of causal modeling, and McFadden's (1974) contributions to discrete choice modeling expanded its relevance for real-world decision problems.[1]

The ideas discussed in this chapter are drawn from the discussion in Fabozzi, Focardi, and Simonian (2024) of integrating empirical, theoretical, and real-time qualitative information to build comprehensive causal models. López de Prado, Lipton, and Zoonekynd (2024) provide a similar critique in their call for causal factor investing, emphasizing the need to transition from associational models to causal inference in financial analysis.

Current methods for causal discovery typically begin by analyzing the joint probability distribution of various variables, looking for conditionally independent variables. This form of causal inquiry aims to deepen our understanding of the underlying mechanisms through models that distinguish causality from mere correlation. However, this approach diverges from how causality is treated in scientific and technological disciplines, where causal models often stem from fundamental laws and describe systems where manipulating input variables leads to predictable output changes.

In this chapter, we argue that economics and finance should adopt this more pragmatic approach to causal modeling. It is essential to recognize that causal modeling must work in tandem with economic theories, which are not inherently causal but provide the necessary descriptive frameworks for modern economies. Causal models, by contrast, represent interventions and adjustments within these theoretical frameworks.

A challenge highlighted by Robert Lucas, a Nobel laureate in economics, is that economic theory and decision-making cannot be entirely separated (Lucas, 1976). Economies and financial markets are self-reflective, meaning that agents adjust their behavior in anticipation of policy changes, which can neutralize the effectiveness of these interventions. However, the complexities of modern economies suggest that the purely rational, equilibrium-based models that Lucas advocated are insufficient. Herbert Simon, another Nobel laureate, introduced the concept of bounded rationality, arguing that real-world decision-making often results in "satisficing" rather than in optimal outcomes (Simon, 1953). This perspective suggests that more flexible, multidisciplinary approaches are necessary for dealing with the complexities of modern economies.

Artificial intelligence (AI) offers new methods for managing vast datasets and mimicking human decision-making processes. AI systems designed to work with causal models can predict the outcomes of interventions such as investment decisions or policy changes, although the predictions are inherently uncertain. Future generations of these systems will likely need to incorporate feedback mechanisms to account for the evolving responses of the systems they model.

Two broad families of causal models are relevant to this discussion. The first family includes models based on the laws of physics, which are widely applied in science and engineering. The second family includes causal models derived from data, representing systems in which only one real-world instance is observed, such as economies and financial markets. Unlike in physical systems, in the systems described by these models, interventions and counterfactuals play a significant role. The growing interest in data-driven causal models, particularly their integration with AI, has propelled the development of "causal AI" and expanded their application to such fields as finance, economics, and business.

We begin by placing causal systems within a broad scientific framework and discussing causation, scientific explanation, paradigm shifts, and causal models. We then apply these concepts to economics and asset management, proposing the necessary paradigm shift to align asset management with modern economic realities.

CAUSATION, SCIENCE, AND CAUSAL MODELS

This section explores the concepts of causation and scientific explanation, and the role of causal modeling. In the physical sciences, causality is not inherent to fundamental laws; however, causal models that adhere to these laws are widely used. Similarly, causal models can be developed in finance and economics from empirical data, providing a basis for decision-making, while economic theories offer broader descriptive frameworks.

Causation

Causation has been a central theme in philosophy since ancient times, with thinkers like Plato and Aristotle laying the groundwork for understanding the nature of cause and effect. Aristotle's theory of causation profoundly influenced scientific thought for centuries. He proposed four types of causes:

- the material cause (what something is made of),
- the formal cause (its shape or form),
- the efficient cause (the agent or process that brings something into being), and
- the final cause (the purpose or end goal of the thing).

This deeply metaphysical construct sought to explain how and why things happen. It provided a holistic view of nature according to which every phenomenon could be understood in terms of its purpose and inherent qualities. For centuries, this understanding of causation guided both scientific inquiry and philosophical thought, with scholars focusing on the underlying reasons for natural events.

The Enlightenment brought a significant challenge to this view. In the eighteenth century David Hume, a key figure in modern empiricism, famously critiqued the traditional concept of causality. Hume (1739) proposed that what we call "causation" is not an inherent connection between events but rather a mental habit of observing regular associations. According to Hume, we assume a causal link when we see one event consistently followed by another, such as a match being struck and a flame appearing. Yet we do not directly observe a "cause" itself; we only witness a sequence of events. He contended that causation is not a necessary feature of the world but a product of the human mind's tendency to infer connections based on repeated experience. His skepticism laid the groundwork for modern empirical science, which focuses on observable data and regular patterns rather than invoking unseen metaphysical forces.

This shift in thinking was crucial as it aligned with the development of modern science in the seventeenth century. Prior to Galileo's publication of *The Assayer* (Galilei, 1623) and Newton's *Principia Mathematica* (Newton, 1687), scientific inquiry focused on mathematical descriptions of natural phenomena. Galileo emphasized the importance of measurement and experimentation, arguing that nature could be understood through mathematics. Newton took this further by formalizing laws of motion and gravitation and expressing them in the language of calculus. Newton's laws provided a predictive framework that did not rely on metaphysical concepts of purpose or inherent qualities. Instead, mathematical relationships and forces could explain such phenomena as the planets' motion or an apple's falling. These laws shifted science's focus from seeking the "why" of Aristotle's final causes to understanding the "how" of physical processes through quantitative analysis.

The emergence of differential equations and their use in modeling complex systems further cemented this shift. Scientists could now describe dynamic processes from planetary orbits to fluid dynamics without appealing to metaphysical causes.[2] Instead, they could rely on precise mathematical formulations to predict and explain the behavior of these systems. This mathematical approach became the foundation of modern physics and the broader scientific method, moving the concept of causality away from metaphysical speculation and toward relationships governed by universal laws, relationships that could be measured and observed.

In this way, Hume's critique of causation and Galileo's and Newton's mathematical advances marked a fundamental turning point in the philosophy of science. Causality was no longer viewed as attributable to a metaphysical force or explanation but as a tool to describe systems where input variables control output variables. This transformation laid the groundwork for the modern scientific approach, which replaces metaphysical accounts with the use of empirical evidence and mathematical reasoning to predict how things happen.

Differential equations do not imply causality. The deductive-nomological (D-N) principle of scientific explanation, introduced by Carl Hempel and Paul Oppenheim in 1948, describes how scientific explanations are based on logical deductions from general laws, initial conditions, and boundary constraints (Hempel & Oppenheim, 1948). This principle, which forms the basis for simulations and is widely accepted in physics and applied sciences, is operationalized to understand how scientific explanations work, particularly in the natural sciences. It explains events by showing how they logically follow general laws and specific conditions. The term "deductive-nomological" can be separated into its parts: "deductive," meaning involving logical reasoning, and "nomological," meaning related to the laws of nature.

In simple terms, the D-N model explains an event by demonstrating that it is predictable given certain laws and facts. For example, if we want to explain why a pot of water boils at 100°C, we can refer to the laws of physics (such as the law that water boils at 100°C under normal atmospheric pressure) and the specific fact that the water was heated to that temperature. The explanation shows that the event (boiling) had to happen because it logically followed the combination of the general law (the boiling point of water) and the specific condition (the water being heated to 100°C).

The D-N principle emphasizes that scientific explanations are like logical arguments. In these arguments, we start with some known laws of nature and specific facts about a situation, and then we deduce or derive the outcome. This makes scientific explanations different from mere descriptions: they tell us what happened and why it had to happen according to the laws of nature. This approach is helpful in many areas of science because it helps clarify how events can be understood as part of a broader system governed by rules. However, the D-N model has also been critiqued for not accounting well for explanations in such fields as biology or the social sciences, where outcomes might not always be strictly determined by laws in the same way as in physics or chemistry. Despite its limitations, the D-N principle remains an important idea in the philosophy of science for understanding how we explain natural phenomena.

Quantum Mechanics and the Challenge to Deterministic Causality

Quantum mechanics, unlike classical mechanics, does not operate on deterministic laws but rather on probabilistic principles. In classical physics, every event can be explained as a predictable deduction from the laws of nature, which fits neatly within the D-N model. For example, the trajectory of a thrown ball can be predicted and explained using Newton's laws of motion. In quantum mechanics, however, this certainty breaks down.

Probabilities govern quantum phenomena, and events at the subatomic level cannot be predicted with certainty. For instance, the famous Heisenberg uncertainty principle states that we cannot simultaneously know a particle's precise position and momentum. Quantum mechanics operates on wave functions, which provide probabilities of where a particle might be but not where it definitively will be.[3] This introduces a fundamental uncertainty in how we explain events at this scale, challenging a deterministic view of science.

In this context, causality is not straightforward. For example, the phenomenon of quantum entanglement suggests that two particles can become connected in such a way that the state of one instantly affects the state of the other, even at a distance, without a clear causal mechanism as understood in classical terms.

The challenges quantum mechanics poses to classical causality echo earlier critiques from philosophers like Ernst Mach and Bertrand Russell, who questioned the notion of causality in the physical sciences. Mach, an influential philosopher of science, was skeptical of the metaphysical underpinnings of causality. He argued that scientific explanations should focus on observable phenomena rather than on unseen causal forces. For Mach, science aimed to describe regularities and patterns in nature without invoking cause-and-effect reasoning, which he saw as unnecessary or even misleading in some cases (Mach, 1883).

Russell (1913) took this critique further in the early twentieth century, famously stating that "the law of causality, like much that passes muster among philosophers, is a relic of a bygone age, surviving, like the monarchy, only because it is erroneously supposed to do no harm." Russell considered that modern physics, especially with the advent of the theory of relativity and quantum mechanics, did not need the traditional concept of causality. Instead of explaining events through causal chains, physics had become a science of describing relations between events—what happens under certain conditions—without invoking the necessity of one event causing another in a classical sense.

Despite these critiques, causality remains a useful concept in many areas of science, particularly when discussing systems that we need to control eventually making uncertain decisions. For example, we often still use causal models to explain phenomena in classical mechanics, chemistry, and biology. However, quantum mechanics has shifted the philosophical understanding of causality, particularly at the level of fundamental particles.

Some philosophers and scientists suggest that we rethink causal models as they apply to the micro level of reality. Instead of viewing causality strictly deterministically, causality might be reinterpreted probabilistically. Here, events are not strictly caused by prior conditions but are influenced by them in terms of probabilities. For example, we might say that a quantum event is more likely to occur given certain initial conditions, but we cannot predict the exact outcome with certainty.

This probabilistic approach to causality aligns better with the framework of quantum mechanics, where outcomes are described in terms of the likelihood of different possibilities rather than a single determined outcome. In this sense, the D-N model is modified to account for probabilistic causality, especially in fields where uncertainty and probability play a central role.

Scientific Explanation

The D-N principle remains the cornerstone of scientific explanation in physics. It asserts that the behavior of any physical system can be explained through deductions from general laws and initial conditions. This principle's effectiveness in describing complex phenomena, such as tornadoes, highlights the power of mathematics in science, as Eugene Wigner famously discussed (Wigner, 1960).

Economics, however, has yet to achieve the same empirical rigor as the physical sciences. While general equilibrium models provide mathematical descriptions of economic rationality, they are often highly idealized and difficult to test empirically. Multiagent systems, which simulate economies as collections of interacting agents, come closer to providing logical simulations, though they still lack the empirical grounding of econometric models.

Based on differential equations, physical laws are not inherently causal, as setting initial conditions does not constitute a causal intervention. Nonetheless, causal systems can be constructed by engineering the internal structures that allow for control over outputs, as seen in technologies like engines or flight simulators.

Causal Systems and Models

Causal systems are defined by their ability to control outputs through interventions. For example, pressing the brake pedal of a car constitutes an intervention that changes the car's speed. A causal relationship exists when changes to one variable (the input) lead to predictable changes in another (the output), but not vice versa. This principle extends to more complex systems, from home appliances to airplanes.

Discovering causal structures in unique economic and social systems that cannot be replicated for experimental testing is challenging. Economies and financial markets represent such systems, whereas causal modeling requires assumptions about uncertainty and probability. While physical systems allow repeated experiments to be conducted, economic systems require models that account for their singularity and the nonexperimental nature of data.

This chapter also introduces the concepts of interventions and counterfactuals, which are essential to understanding causal systems not governed by physical laws. Interventions in economics involve changing policy variables, such as interest rates, while counterfactuals explore how systems behave under different historical conditions.

Causal Models in Economics and Finance

To tackle the complexities of modern economies and financial markets, causal models offer a powerful framework for understanding the underlying relationships between variables. These models are particularly valuable because they describe correlations and identify causal pathways, which are essential for making reliable predictions and policy interventions. However, as noted by Focardi and Fabozzi (2009), the effectiveness of these models in economic and financial contexts is constrained by the complexity of the systems being studied. Unlike the physical sciences, where fundamental laws govern behavior, economic systems are human-designed artifacts that evolve and change based on human decision-making processes. Thus, while causal models provide a useful tool for understanding these relationships, they must be viewed as limited in their ability to predict complex, multivariable systems such as economies.

Such econometricians as Ragnar Frisch and Trygve Haavelmo laid the groundwork for distinguishing causality from correlation. Frisch's simultaneous equations models addressed the challenges of interdependent variables (Frisch, 1934), while Haavelmo formalized the probability approach, emphasizing the importance of structural models for identifying causal relationships James Heckman's work on correcting selection bias and estimating treatment effects in nonexperimental settings further expanded the practical applications of causal modeling (Heckman, 1979).

Fabozzi, Focardi, and Simonian (2024) discussed the critical role of causal models in investment decision-making because they integrate causal relationships between market variables and real-time qualitative information. Contributions from various disciplines, including economics and data science (particularly AI), have shaped the evolution of these models.

The Role of Probability in Causal Models

In economics, probability plays a crucial role in dealing with uncertainty, particularly in developing causal models to predict and understand economic and financial systems. Simonian (2023) applied a double machine learning (ML) approach to analyze market contagion, which yielded a more precise understanding of how shocks in one market propagate to others. This approach isolates the causal relationships between market events while addressing biases introduced by confounders, making it a robust tool for studying causal dynamics in high-dimensional settings.

In their analysis of mathematical modeling, Focardi and Fabozzi (2009) propose that economic systems, being complex and influenced by human behavior, are subject to higher levels of unpredictability than physical systems. This inherent uncertainty limits the effectiveness of traditional probabilistic models based on assumptions of repeatability and stationarity, concepts that often do not hold in financial markets and economies.

John Maynard Keynes introduced a critical approach to probability in economics in his *Treatise on Probability*. In it, he proposed that probability should be seen as an intermediate truth value rather than as something strictly true or false (Keynes, 1921). This was a departure from the classical view of probability, which tended to treat it as either a certainty or a mere lack of knowledge about an event.

Keynes's approach to probability differs because it focuses on uncertainty around beliefs or expectations rather than just measurable events. For instance, a Keynesian might use probability to represent our confidence that an economic policy will result in growth, even if we don't have complete data. This is helpful when there isn't enough concrete information, but decisions must be made. Keynes's framework helps economists estimate the likelihood of uncertain outcomes—such as predicting the impact of an interest rate cut—without relying on precise historical data.

The framework of Andrey Kolmogorov, widely used today, is a deductive axiomatic probability theory. It needs an interpretation to be applied (Kolmogorov, 1956). The usual interpretation looks at probabilities as relative frequencies. Relative frequency is not a formal definition of probability. There is no way to extract certainty from probabilistic statements. It is most effective when there is a lot of data. For example, economists use Kolmogorov's framework to analyze past stock prices and predict future trends. This method works well when large datasets are available to calculate the likelihood of different outcomes. Unlike Keynes's flexible approach, which deals with uncertainty and beliefs, Kolmogorov's method focuses on objective data, making it perfect for risk assessment and forecasting based on historical information.

In Kolmogorov's system, probability is often applied to systems with multiple realizations—events or data points that can occur many times and can be averaged over time to estimate probabilities. With this framework, stock prices, interest rates, or GDP growth rates can be modeled using probabilistic methods. Because we can collect data over many time periods or across different companies, we can estimate the likelihood of various outcomes, making it useful for forecasting and risk assessment. More precisely, by applying data transformations such as differencing, we can obtain stationary data. Assuming ergodicity, that is, the possibility of exchanging time averages with probabilistic means, we can apply probabilistic concepts.

While Kolmogorov's probabilistic framework has been widely adopted in economics and finance, it presents challenges when applied to unique systems, such as entire financial markets or economies. These systems don't have multiple realizations that allow cross-sectional averaging. Data cannot be averaged over time with singular, evolving systems with only one historical trajectory. This is where traditional probability models can face limitations.

For instance, in financial markets, you have only one realization of the past performance of the stock market. This means that applying traditional probabilistic models requires certain assumptions, such as *stationarity* (the idea that the statistical properties of the system remain constant over time) or *ergodicity* (the belief that the system's time averages are equivalent to its ensemble averages across different realizations). Financial markets and economies are often nonstationary, being subject to shocks, structural changes, and evolving dynamics, which complicates the use of traditional probability models. As a result, economists must usually introduce assumptions about the system's behavior or incorporate more flexible probabilistic methods to account for these unique challenges.

The contrast between Keynes's approach and Kolmogorov's highlights an important tension in how probability is used in causal models. Keynes's framework is more adaptable to systems where information is incomplete and probabilities represent degrees of belief about the likelihood of various outcomes. It is particularly useful in cases where causal relationships are uncertain or evolving. For example, in economic forecasting, where future outcomes depend on many uncertain factors, Keynes's interpretation of probability allows for more nuance in assessing the likelihood of different scenarios.

On the other hand, Kolmogorov's framework, with its well-defined rules and reliance on objective frequencies, is more suited to systems where outcomes can be repeated and measured over time. This makes it ideal for econometrics, where large datasets allow calculating statistical probabilities based on historical patterns. However, in contexts such as financial markets or macroeconomic systems, where each trajectory is unique and unrepeatable, this approach may require careful assumptions and adjustments to ensure that the models accurately reflect the system's complexity.

Keynes's ideas are well-suited to dealing with uncertainty in unique, complex systems, while Kolmogorov's framework offers a more formal structure for analyzing systems with repeatable, measurable outcomes. Both approaches continue to shape how economists model uncertainty, causality, and prediction to understand and forecast economic behavior.

Advances in Causal Modeling

Over the past three decades, the field of causal modeling has transformed, driven mainly by the work of researchers such as Judea Pearl and the team at Carnegie Mellon University. In addition, Laudy, Denev, and Ginsberg (2022) introduced a framework for building probabilistic causal models using natural language processing (NLP) applied to large text datasets. Their method leverages collective intelligence to automatically extract causal links between economic and financial variables, constructing Bayesian networks that represent real-time causal relationships. This approach helps address biases in expert-driven models and provides a data-driven method for uncovering causal mechanisms in financial systems.

Further advances came from Joshua Angrist, Guido Imbens, and David Card, corecipients of the 2021 Nobel Prize in Economics, who developed methods for using natural experiments and instrumental variables to estimate causal effects.[4] Their "local average treatment effect" framework allows economists to infer causality from observational data, in this way providing a robust approach for evaluating policy interventions in complex economic systems.

These advances have reshaped how we understand the nature of cause-and-effect relationships in complex systems. At the heart of these developments is the recognition that causation and correlation, while often related, are fundamentally distinct concepts. Correlation measures the strength of a relationship between two variables, but it does not imply that one variable causes the other. Modern causal models seek to uncover these deeper causal connections, even in the presence of confounding factors or complex interactions.

Pearl's contributions, particularly his development of the structural causal model (SCM), have provided a robust framework for identifying and reasoning about causality (Pearl, 2000). SCMs are built around the idea that systems can be represented by structural equations in which each endogenous variable (a variable determined by the system) is explained by other variables within the system. These relationships are causal, meaning that changing one variable directly affects another. What sets SCMs apart from simpler statistical models is their incorporation of the direction of these relationships and their explicit acknowledgment of how interventions (such as changing a variable) affect the system as a whole.

A central tool in SCMs is directed acyclic graphs (DAGs), which are visual representations of the causal relationships between variables. The nodes represent variables in these graphs and the directed edges (arrows) indicate causal influence. The acyclic nature of these graphs is crucial as it ensures no feedback loops—in which one variable might influence another, which in turn influences the original variable—making it possible to trace the cause-and-effect pathways. Under certain conditions, this structure helps clarify which variables are independent of others and allows more rigorous reasoning about the system's causal dynamics.

A key challenge in causal modeling is that while correlations can offer clues about potential causal relationships, they cannot, on their own, definitively establish causality. For instance, two variables might be highly correlated, but this could be due to the influence of a third, hidden variable. To overcome this limitation, causal models rely on additional assumptions, one of the most critical being conditional independence. This principle suggests that, given knowledge of certain variables, other variables may become independent—an insight that helps disentangle causal relationships from mere statistical associations.

In practical terms, conditional independence allows researchers to "control" the effects of certain variables and test whether the remaining relationships hold up under these conditions. For example, if two variables—say, A and B—are correlated, one might check whether this correlation remains when controlling for a third variable, C. If the correlation disappears, it suggests that C might be the actual cause, with A and B merely correlated through their relationship to C.

The power of SCMs and DAGs lies in their ability to systematically apply such assumptions, using graphical techniques and formal rules to derive conclusions about the likely causal structure. This process is known as causal inference and is especially valuable in fields such as economics, medicine, and the social sciences, where controlled experiments are often impractical or impossible to conduct. Instead, researchers rely on observational data and causal models to infer the underlying mechanisms.

As discussed in the next section, these advancements have practical applications in various economic and financial contexts.

APPLICATIONS IN ECONOMICS AND FINANCE

The shift toward using causal models in economics and finance represents a significant departure from traditional approaches that primarily rely on correlations between variables, such as asset returns, interest rates, or macroeconomic indicators. While these traditional methods have long been the foundation of financial and economic analysis, they often fail to account for the underlying causal relationships between variables. Economists and financial analysts can examine the effects of their actions or external factors on economic systems, providing a more comprehensive framework for decision-making.

In traditional economic and financial models, correlations are often used to forecast future trends based on historical data. For example, a central bank might observe a correlation between inflation and interest rates and use this relationship to inform monetary policy decisions. However, this approach assumes that past relationships will hold in the future and does not account for how the system might change when interventions, such as adjusting interest rates or enacting fiscal policies, are made. Causal models address this gap by predicting how the economy or financial markets will respond to specific actions, such as a change in tax policy or a large-scale capital investment in a particular sector.

This shift toward causal reasoning is significant in the context of interconnected global economies and financial markets, which are increasingly susceptible to systemic risks. For instance, understanding the causal impact of a government's fiscal stimulus on unemployment, consumer spending, and inflation is critical for shaping effective economic policies. Instrumental variables, operationalized in a method formalized by Haavelmo, have become a key tool in isolating exogenous variation in economic variables. Angrist and Imbens (1944) further advanced this approach by developing the local average treatment effect framework, which estimates the causal impact of policies using natural experiments. David Card's work in labor economics, particularly in evaluating the causal effects of minimum wage policies on employment, provides a practical example of how these tools can be applied to real-world economic questions (Card, 1991).

Fabozzi, Focardi, and Simonian (2024) highlight similar applications of causal models in asset management, where causal analysis can guide investment strategies in response to macroeconomic shocks. Similarly, in finance, causal models allow analysts to predict how investor behavior and market liquidity might change in response to policy changes or macroeconomic shocks, such as a financial crisis or a pandemic. This is further evidenced in the work of López de Prado, Lipton, and Zoonekynd (2024), who demonstrate that misspecified factor models in asset management, particularly those relying on associational analysis, can lead to systematic underperformance. They argue that correctly specified causal models are critical for avoiding systematic losses and better predicting investment outcomes.

By incorporating causal models, economists and financial professionals can also evaluate the broader effects of economic decisions, including social and environmental impacts. With this ability to forecast the direct and indirect consequences of policies and investments, causal modeling is a valuable tool for decision-making in today's complex and dynamic financial and economic environments.

Interventions and Counterfactuals in Economics and Finance

A key feature of causal models is their ability to analyze interventions—actions that deliberately change the input of a system to observe the effects. In economics, interventions often take the form of policy changes, such as adjusting interest rates, altering tax rates, or implementing fiscal stimulus programs. Causal models help economists predict how these interventions will affect critical macroeconomic variables such as inflation, unemployment, GDP growth, and market stability. For instance, central banks frequently rely on causal models to understand the potential impacts of interest rate cuts on economic growth and inflation, ensuring that policy decisions are based on past data and anticipated future effects.

What sets causal models apart from traditional statistical approaches is their ability to simulate the outcomes of specific interventions in ways that go beyond mere correlations. These models allow economists to consider the ripple effects of a policy decision throughout an economy. For example, increasing government spending may lead to higher aggregate demand, reducing unemployment and increasing inflationary pressure. Causal models can capture these multifaceted dynamics, giving policymakers a more comprehensive understanding of any intervention's trade-offs.

Another essential concept in causal analysis is counterfactuals. Counterfactual reasoning allows economists and policymakers to ask "what if" questions about alternative scenarios, exploring how different policies or actions might have led to different outcomes. Simonian (2022) builds on this by introducing a decision-making framework for investment decisions under almost complete causal ignorance. He argues that portfolio managers can identify robust investment strategies across various possible causal scenarios by measuring causal distance, minimizing risk even when the precise causal mechanisms driving market events are unknown. López de Prado, Lipton, and Zoonekynd (2024) similarly endorse using counterfactual analysis in asset management, where such reasoning can help investors understand how alternative investment strategies might perform under different market conditions. This approach enables the design of more resilient strategies that account for potential systemic risks.

For example, a counterfactual analysis might investigate how the global economy could have evolved had governments adopted different fiscal policies during the 2007–2008 Global Financial Crisis (GFC). Specifically, economists could explore whether implementing a more aggressive budgetary stimulus earlier might have resulted in a faster economic recovery. By comparing the actual recovery to this hypothetical scenario, analysts could better understand the policies' impact on reducing unemployment and stabilizing financial markets. Fabozzi, Focardi, and Simonian (2024) similarly argue for using counterfactuals in asset management to understand the impacts of interventions and inform investment strategies. This type of analysis provides valuable insights into the consequences of policy decisions, allowing the development of improved techniques to mitigate future risks and enhance decision-making.

Counterfactuals are particularly valuable when examining large-scale economic events with complex causal pathways. For instance, in evaluating the impact of a fiscal stimulus package, a counterfactual model might estimate how the economy would have performed if no stimulus had been implemented, helping to quantify the policy's contribution to economic recovery. This type of analysis is beneficial for understanding the immediate effects of interventions, evaluating long-term consequences, and refining future policy decisions.

While causal models offer powerful tools for understanding economic systems, it is crucial to recognize that not all correlations support causal interventions. The philosopher Hans Reichenbach emphasized that correlations between variables can arise for different reasons. Sometimes one variable directly causes the other, while in other cases a third unseen factor influences both variables (Reichenbach, 1956). This distinction is critical in economic policymaking, where acting on correlated variables without understanding their causal structure can lead to ineffective or harmful outcomes.

For example, a correlation might be observed between increased government spending and higher inflation. However, if both are caused by a third variable, such as a sudden surge in commodity prices, increasing government spending further might not directly affect inflation, and intervening in spending might not alleviate inflationary pressures. Causal models help policymakers distinguish between genuine causal relationships and spurious correlations, ensuring that interventions are targeted at the right variables to achieve the desired economic outcomes.

This distinction becomes particularly important in complex economic systems where multiple factors interact nonlinearly. Economists and policymakers can avoid the pitfalls of mistaking correlation for causation by relying on causal models and counterfactual reasoning. Thus they can craft more effective policies that address the root causes of economic issues rather than merely responding to surface-level correlations.

TOWARD A NEW PARADIGM IN ECONOMIC AND FINANCIAL THEORY

Causal models are powerful tools for understanding the structure and dynamics of economic systems; they also play a crucial role in shaping the development of new economic theories. As global economies become more complex, interconnected, and subject to rapid technological change, traditional economic models based on variables such as growth, inflation, and productivity often fall short of capturing the full picture of modern economic phenomena. This growing complexity highlights the need for a paradigm shift in economic theory that embraces causal reasoning and accommodates a broader range of factors influencing economic outcomes.

A central challenge in developing causal models for these intricate systems is identifying and defining new variables that more accurately reflect the evolving nature of economic activity. Traditional economic metrics, such as GDP for growth or the Consumer Price Index (CPI) for inflation, offer valid but incomplete views of the economy. For instance, GDP measures the total market value of goods and services produced. Still, it does not account for the qualitative changes in the composition of output, environmental impacts, or the broader social consequences of production and consumption. Likewise, inflation measures may fail to capture the true cost of living in an economy where the quality of goods and services, and even their symbolic value, can change rapidly owing to technological innovation and shifting consumer preferences. Fabozzi, Focardi, Ponta, and others (2022) and Focardi and Fabozzi (2023) discuss how modern economies should consider qualitative growth as genuine growth. The authors create a formal theory of qualitative growth based on defining abstract variables to represent quantity and quality.

Economists must rethink the relationship between economic theory and empirical observation to address these limitations. Traditionally, economic theories have been constructed based on assumptions that lead to testable hypotheses using observable variables. However, as economic systems grow more complex, many important variables may not be directly observable or easily quantified. For example, factors such as digitalization, sustainability, and the social impact of economic activity are becoming increasingly relevant but are not adequately captured by traditional models.

Redefining Economic Variables in the Context of Causal Models

One of the most significant insights derived from causal models in economics is the realization that traditional variables, which have long been the foundation of economic theory, may not fully capture the intricate realities of modern economies. By focusing on the relationships and mechanisms through which variables influence one another, causal models push economists to reconsider how vital economic indicators are defined, measured, and understood. This shift is crucial for developing more accurate models that reflect the complexities of the global economy, which is increasingly shaped by technological advances, environmental challenges, and shifting societal dynamics.

Traditional economic models often rely on a limited set of well-established variables, such as GDP, inflation rates, and unemployment levels, to assess the health and performance of an economy. While these indicators have been helpful, they tend to provide a narrow view of economic activity, primarily focusing on measurable outcomes such as output and consumption. Causal models, however, emphasize the importance of the underlying pathways that lead to these outcomes. This broader perspective reveals the need for new variables for assessing sustainability, societal well-being, and inequality, which are becoming increasingly important in the twenty-first century.

In the context of economic growth, traditional models typically focus on output levels, often measured by GDP. While GDP has long been the go-to indicator for economic performance, it falls short of capturing the full range of factors that contribute to sustainable, equitable growth. Causal models highlight the importance of integrating variables related to environmental sustainability into growth models. For instance, in an era of climate change, measuring the impact of production processes on natural resources and ecosystems is essential for understanding long-term economic health. Growth that depletes natural resources or damages the environment may lead to short-term gains in GDP but could have long-term negative consequences, which traditional models often overlook.

Similarly, causal models encourage economists to incorporate measures of wealth distribution into assessments of growth. GDP growth does not account for how wealth is distributed across different segments of society, meaning that rising GDP may coexist with increasing inequality. Economists can better understand the societal impacts of growth and design policies that promote inclusive economic development by including variables that track the distribution of wealth and income. For example, a causal model might reveal that certain policies aimed at boosting economic growth disproportionately benefit the wealthy, leading to greater inequality and potentially destabilizing the economy in the long run.

Another critical factor often overlooked in traditional growth models is societal well-being. While GDP measures the market value of goods and services produced, it does not capture the quality of life experienced by citizens. Causal models open the door to integrating variables that reflect social outcomes, such as health, education, and overall life satisfaction. For example, rapid economic growth in some regions may lead to environmental degradation, overwork, or a decline in mental health, which GDP alone would not reflect. Causal models provide a more holistic view of economic progress by including social well-being indicators.

Inflation is another area in which causal models can help redefine traditional economic variables. Traditional inflation measures, such as the CPI, focus on the price levels of a fixed basket of goods and services over time. However, as economies evolve and digital goods, services, and global supply chains become more dominant, these measures may not fully capture the changing nature of inflation.

One challenge is the changing quality of goods and services. In many industries, products and services improve in quality over time, making direct price comparisons difficult. For example, the price of a smartphone today may be higher than that of a phone ten years ago, but the features, performance, and capabilities have dramatically increased. Traditional inflation measures may register the cost difference as price inflation, even though consumers get more value for their money. Causal models encourage economists to develop new measures that adjust for quality changes, ensuring that inflation data reflect not just price increases but also improvements in product quality.

Additionally, the rise of digital and nontangible products presents challenges for traditional inflation measures. Many digital products, such as software, media, or online services, may have very different pricing structures than physical goods, often involving subscription models, premium services, or platform-based pricing. These changes complicate measuring inflation, as the products' value and cost structures do not fit neatly into traditional economic categories. Causal models that account for the shifting nature of digital goods and services can help economists develop more accurate inflation measures that reflect the realities of modern consumption.

The globalization of supply chains also complicates inflation measurement. In a globalized economy, the prices of goods and services are influenced by factors worldwide, from production costs in emerging markets to currency fluctuations and international trade policies. Traditional inflation measures may miss these nuances, leading to incomplete or misleading conclusions about the sources of inflationary pressure. Causal models incorporating global supply chain dynamics can offer a more precise understanding of how inflation is transmitted through the economy, allowing policymakers to make better-informed decisions about monetary policy.

The need to redefine economic variables in the context of causal models reflects a broader trend in economic theory toward more comprehensive and nuanced models. As economies become more interconnected and complex, traditional indicators such as GDP and CPI provide only a partial view of economic performance. Causal models push economists to think beyond these conventional measures and develop new variables that capture the broader forces shaping modern economies.

This shift has important implications for both economic theory and policy. Causal models provide a more complete picture of economic dynamics by incorporating variables related to environmental sustainability, wealth distribution, societal well-being, and the changing nature of goods and services. This in turn enables policymakers to design interventions that promote sustainable, equitable growth and respond more effectively to such challenges as climate change, inequality, and technological disruption.

The Duhem-Quine Thesis and Its Implications for Economic Theory

The shift toward more complex causal modeling in economics aligns closely with the Duhem-Quine thesis, a significant philosophical concept in the philosophy of science. The Duhem-Quine thesis, formulated by Pierre Duhem (1954) and W. V. O. Quine (1951), posits that scientific theories must be tested globally. In other words, when empirical data contradict a prediction, that does not necessarily falsify a single variable or hypothesis but could reflect a problem anywhere within the theoretical framework. This insight has profound implications for how economic theories are developed, tested, and refined, particularly in light of the growing complexity of global economic systems.

In economic theory, the Duhem-Quine thesis implies that a single prediction or variable does not determine the success or failure of a theory, which instead rests on how well the entire theoretical structure accounts for observed phenomena. This holistic approach forces economists to recognize that models are composed of interconnected assumptions about variables, relationships, and mechanisms. If a model fails to predict an outcome accurately, it might not be because of a single faulty assumption but rather the result of a misalignment or incompleteness within the broader framework. This perspective underscores the need for robust models incorporating a wide range of assumptions and variables to capture the full complexity of modern economies.

Rethinking Economic Models in the Context of Causality

Traditionally, economic models have focused on a limited set of well-established, observable variables, such as interest rates, asset prices, GDP, inflation, and unemployment rate. These models, while helpful, often oversimplify the economy's intricate workings and fail to account for more abstract factors that influence economic behavior. Causal models challenge this traditional approach by emphasizing the importance of understanding the mechanisms and pathways through which variables affect each other, even when those variables are challenging to observe directly. This shift encourages economists to broaden the scope of their models to include more nuanced and often abstract elements that play critical roles in economic outcomes.

For instance, in analyzing the causes and effects of financial crises, traditional models might focus on easily measurable variables such as interest rates, stock market indices, and credit availability. While these variables are crucial, they often fail to capture more profound and complex forces, such as market sentiment, systemic risk, and network effects among financial institutions. Though less tangible, these factors play an essential role in the propagation of economic shocks, as seen in the GFC. Market sentiment, for example, can shift rapidly as a result of various factors, amplifying panic and exacerbating crises. Likewise, the interconnectedness of financial institutions can lead to cascading failures when one key institution faces liquidity issues, triggering a systemic collapse that would be missed in models that took into account only isolated, observable variables.

Abstract and Unobservable Variables in Economic Theory

The Duhem-Quine thesis encourages economists to embrace the fact that not all critical variables are directly observable or easily measurable. In modern economies, many significant forces—such as technological innovation, systemic risk, and ecological sustainability—may not be captured by traditional economic metrics but are crucial for understanding economic outcomes. Causal models help bridge this gap by incorporating abstract variables into the analysis, allowing a more comprehensive understanding of how economies function.

For instance, when economists want to develop theories of economic growth, traditional models tend to focus on such factors as capital accumulation, labor productivity, and GDP growth. However, causal models show that this narrow focus misses critical long-term growth drivers, such as technological innovation and human capital development. Technological innovation is inherently difficult to measure because its impacts are often spread across different sectors and time periods. It requires economists to consider not only the rate of technological advancement but also how it diffuses through industries and interacts with other economic factors. Similarly, human capital, though somewhat more measurable, can encompass abstract qualities such as creativity, problem-solving skills, and adaptability, which are difficult to quantify but critical to sustained economic progress.

Furthermore, in today's global challenges, ecological sustainability is another unobservable factor that must be integrated into growth theories. The traditional focus on output growth without considering the environmental costs of production is increasingly seen as inadequate. Causal models can incorporate environmental variables such as resource depletion, pollution, and climate change, recognizing that long-term economic growth cannot be sustained without accounting for ecological impacts. This broader understanding of growth aligns with the holistic approach emphasized by the Duhem-Quine thesis, which suggests that economic theories must evolve to include variables beyond simple measurements of output and productivity.

Implications for Policy and Prediction

Integrating abstract and unobservable variables into causal models has significant economic policy and prediction implications. One of the critical advantages of causal models is their ability to simulate the effects of interventions, such as monetary or fiscal policy changes. For example, a causal model might predict the long-term effects of a government's investment in green technologies on GDP and environmental sustainability. Traditional models might only capture the immediate boost to GDP from the investment. In contrast, a causal model could trace the more complex feedback loops between technology adoption, productivity improvements, and environmental outcomes.

Additionally, causal models incorporating variables such as market sentiment and network effects are crucial for designing effective regulatory frameworks addressing systemic risks in financial markets. Understanding the causal pathways that link financial institutions, market conditions, and investor behavior can help policymakers develop regulations that prevent the amplification of small shocks into full-blown crises. This aligns with the Duhem-Quine thesis by recognizing that economic models must be evaluated according to their ability to predict single variables such as GDP or inflation and by how well they capture the complex interplay of forces that drive economic behavior.

Toward a New Theoretical Paradigm

In light of the Duhem-Quine thesis, economic theory must evolve to embrace a more comprehensive, flexible, and holistic framework that reflects the interconnected nature of modern economies. Causal models provide the tools to achieve this by encouraging economists to rethink traditional variables, incorporate abstract factors, and build models that can accommodate the complexities of economic systems. These models enable a deeper understanding of how different variables influence each other, how shocks propagate through the economy, and how policy interventions can have immediate and long-term effects.

This shift represents a move from purely descriptive models to a new paradigm in which economic theories are predictive and explanatory, allowing more informed decision-making in an increasingly complex world. By recognizing the limitations of traditional models and embracing the insights offered by causal modeling, economists can develop more robust theories that better capture the realities of economic systems and provide valuable guidance for policymakers facing the challenges of the twenty-first century.

MOVING BEYOND EMPIRICISM: BRIDGING THEORY AND OBSERVATION

As economic theories evolve to include more complex causal relationships, the relationship between empirical data and theoretical modeling will also need to be reexamined. In traditional economics, empirical observation has often been used to validate theories with data collected on measurable variables. However, as causal models incorporate new and abstract variables, there may be a greater reliance on proxies or inferred relationships that are not directly observable.

For instance, in finance, systemic risk is a critical variable in understanding market stability, yet it cannot be easily measured, unlike interest rates or stock prices. Causal models allow economists to analyze systemic risk by analyzing the relationships between observable variables—such as the interconnectedness of financial institutions and the flow of capital—while recognizing that systemic risk remains an abstract concept. This shift represents a move away from a purely empirical approach and toward a model that balances theoretical insight with data-driven analysis.

The future of economic theory lies in its ability to provide a coherent descriptive framework that supports causal modeling, allowing economists to understand and predict the effects of various interventions and policy decisions. This framework must be flexible enough to incorporate many variables, including abstract or difficult-to-measure ones, while providing meaningful insights into how economies function. Theories must account for the complexities of modern economies, such as the effects of climate change, socioeconomic inequality, technological disruption, and globalization, and how these factors interact with traditional economic variables such as growth and inflation.

Consequently, as causal models become increasingly integral to economic analysis, they will shape the development of new economic theories to better reflect the complexities of modern economies. By expanding the range of variables and relationships considered and embracing a more flexible approach to theory and empirical observation, economists can create models that explain economic phenomena more accurately and provide actionable insights for addressing the challenges of the twenty-first century.

INTEGRATION WITH DESCRIPTIVE ECONOMIC THEORIES

While causal models provide a framework for understanding the dynamics of economic systems, they must be integrated with descriptive economic theories that explain how economies function. This integration is essential because causal models alone cannot capture all the nuances of economic behavior, particularly in systems where agents have bounded rationality and make decisions based on incomplete information.

For example, multiagent models, which simulate the interactions of various economic actors, often reveal emerging behaviors that traditional equilibrium-based models cannot easily predict. These models are crucial for understanding how individual decisions aggregate to produce macroeconomic outcomes. Still, they must be grounded in sound economic theory to provide useful insights for policy and decision-making.

New economic theories will likely need to incorporate elements of causal reasoning to account for how economic agents interact with and influence the system. This interaction between causal modeling and economic theory will be significant as policymakers face the challenge of managing increasingly complex economies.

In this chapter, we have argued for a paradigm shift in economics and finance through causal models. As modern economies evolve into increasingly complex systems, traditional economic theories—based on simplified assumptions and correlations—fail to capture financial markets' intricate, dynamic nature. Causal models, which integrate theoretical insights and data-driven approaches, offer a promising way to manage investments in this challenging environment.

THE LIMITATIONS OF TRADITIONAL MODELS IN ASSET MANAGEMENT

The chapter to this point has discussed the broader applications of causal models in economics and finance. As financial markets become more interconnected and complex, traditional asset management models face increasing limitations.

Causal models offer a promising alternative to traditional models by focusing on the dynamic cause-and-effect relationships between market variables. Fabozzi, Focardi, and Simonian (2024) support this shift toward causal modeling and emphasize the importance of incorporating qualitative, forward-looking views in investment decisions. The following discussion highlights how causal models can address these challenges and enhance asset management strategies. López de Prado, Lipton, and Zoonekynd (2024) highlight similar limitations in traditional factor investing models, showing that brute force p-hacking[5] and overfitting[6] can result in models that appear robust but ultimately fail under real market conditions. They advocate a shift toward causal inference methods to avoid these specification errors and to improve long-term performance in asset management. They further emphasize that the future of asset management lies in causal factor investing, where models are rigorously tested for causal validity rather than mere statistical significance. They argue that factor investing will continue to suffer from systematic errors and underperformance without this shift.

López de Prado (2023) argues that much of the existing factor investing literature relies on associational rather than causal claims, leading to systematic errors and overfitting. He contends that factor investing research often fails to identify causal graphs consistent with observed phenomena, justify model specifications in causal terms, or propose experiments to falsify causal mechanisms. Without a causal theory, he suggests, many findings will likely be incorrect owing to backtest overfitting and incorrect specification choices.

Traditional asset management relies heavily on correlation-based approaches such as modern portfolio theory (MPT) and capital asset pricing models (CAPM). These models assume a static market structure in which risks and returns are optimized based on historical data. However, they need to account for the evolving nature of economic variables and the systemic effects of large-scale interventions. Moreover, these models assume rational market behavior, ignoring the complex interplay between human decisions and market dynamics.

In contrast, causal models emphasize the effects of interventions, allowing asset managers to simulate how large-scale investment decisions or policy shifts might affect the broader market. These models address the inherent limitations of traditional models by focusing on cause-and-effect relationships rather than on simple correlations.

There are four reasons why causal models are essential for modern asset management. First, causal models allow asset managers to simulate the effects of market interventions, such as monetary policy changes or large-scale investment shifts. By predicting the outcome of these actions, causal models can inform better decision-making in real time. Second, as financial markets become more intertwined with global economic, social, and environmental factors, causal models help disentangle these variables' complex relationships. Third, traditional models measure risk in isolation, often ignoring the systemic impact of decisions on the broader economy. Causal models incorporate these broader effects, leading to a more holistic understanding of risk. Finally, many causal models integrate insights from behavioral finance, accounting for investor biases such as loss aversion and overconfidence. These models provide a more realistic representation of market behavior, particularly in volatile or irrational environments.

As AI and ML use continues to grow, causal models are poised to play a more significant role in financial markets. AI can enhance causal models by identifying patterns and relationships that are not readily apparent to human analysts. Additionally, integrating big data can further refine these models, enabling more accurate predictions of market behavior.

The next generation of causal models will likely incorporate more abstract economic variables, such as investor sentiment, market psychology, and social trends. These variables are difficult to quantify using traditional models but are essential for understanding the underlying drivers of market movements in today's interconnected world.

To navigate the complexity of modern financial markets, asset managers must adopt more sophisticated tools that go beyond traditional, correlation-based approaches. Causal models, which focus on the impact of interventions and account for the evolving nature of markets, offer a more comprehensive framework for decision-making. As economic systems become more interdependent, integrating causal models into asset management strategies will become increasingly important. Simonian (2021) introduced a robust framework that leverages causal networks and the noisy-or model to address uncertainties in financial decision-making. The noisy-or model is a probabilistic method used in causal inference to represent situations where multiple independent causes can each trigger an effect, and where the presence of one cause does not negate the contribution of others. This framework helps portfolio managers assess risk and improve decision-making by integrating multiple sources of evidence into causal probability assessments."

This chapter underscores the need for a paradigm shift in asset management in which causal models coexist with and complement traditional economic theories.

As Focardi and Fabozzi (2009) emphasize, the unique nature of economic systems—shaped by human innovation and decision-making—means that, while helpful, causal models face inherent limitations regarding their predictive power. Unlike the physical sciences, where immutable laws govern behavior, economics operates in a world of complex and evolving human-made systems. Thus models must explain past behavior and adapt to ever-changing dynamics, making the quest for causality an ongoing challenge."

SUMMARY

This chapter has explored the evolution and application of causal models in economics and finance, contrasting them with traditional models, which rely heavily on correlations between variables. Causal models, which consider how variables influence each other through causal, independent mechanisms, offer a more dynamic and comprehensive framework for analyzing complex economic systems. These models provide a forward-looking approach, allowing economists to predict outcomes of policy interventions while incorporating modern variables such as sustainability and societal well-being.

The discussion began with an overview of causation, tracing its philosophical roots and modern science's shift toward probabilistic explanations, primarily through quantum mechanics. This laid the foundation for understanding why causal models are necessary in economics, a field increasingly required to deal with uncertainties and complex systems that deterministic models cannot easily explain.

Causal models in economics have significant practical implications, particularly in forecasting and policy evaluation. Traditional economic models, such as those that focus on GDP and inflation, often fail to predict how systems will respond to such interventions as fiscal or monetary policy changes. In contrast, causal models incorporate market sentiment and systemic risk, providing a more accurate picture of how economies and financial markets will evolve in response to these interventions.

A strength of causal models lies in their ability to analyze interventions and counterfactuals, exploring not just what happens but what could have happened under different circumstances. For example, a counterfactual analysis might evaluate how different fiscal policies could have affected the recovery from the GFC. This capability makes causal models particularly valuable for policymakers who need to understand their decisions' direct and indirect effects.

The chapter also touched on the Duhem-Quine thesis, which suggests that economic models must be evaluated as part of a larger framework of assumptions rather than in isolation. This holistic approach requires economists to embrace abstract, sometimes unobservable variables, such as systemic risk or technological innovation, which are crucial to understanding modern economies. Causal models help bridge the gap between theory and observation, accommodating these complex variables.

The chapter argued for a paradigm shift in economic theory leading to a central role for causal models. Traditional economic models fall short as global economies grow more complex and interconnected. Causal models offer a more robust economic and financial analysis and policy development framework by focusing on the underlying relationships between variables and incorporating modern factors such as environmental and social considerations. This approach will be essential for managing the evolving challenges of the twenty-first century.

The development of causal modeling owes much to the foundational contributions of econometricians who formalized methods for distinguishing causation from correlation, addressing endogeneity, and correcting for selection bias, and of economists, who have advanced the field of causal modeling through their work on natural experiments and instrumental variables, providing practical tools for inferring causal relationships from observational data.

4 The Integration of Complexity Science into Financial Modeling

EMBRACING COMPLEXITY IN FINANCIAL SYSTEMS

In response to the shortcomings of traditional financial models, complexity science has emerged as a robust framework for understanding financial markets. Complexity science views financial systems as complex adaptive systems in which numerous interacting agents, each with their own objectives and strategies, create a network of interdependencies that gives rise to unpredictable and often nonlinear outcomes. This perspective shifts the focus from the assumption of market equilibrium to understanding markets as constantly evolving systems that adapt to changing conditions.

Complexity science also introduces the concept of emergence, where the interactions between agents give rise to new patterns and behaviors that cannot be predicted by analyzing the system's components in isolation. This is particularly relevant in financial markets, where collective behaviors such as herding can lead to such phenomena as asset bubbles and crashes. The adaptive nature of financial markets means that agents continually adjust their strategies based on the evolving environment, further complicating predicting market outcomes (Fabozzi, Focardi, Ponta, et al., 2022).

The adoption of complexity science in financial modeling has led to the development of new tools and methodologies that better capture the realities of financial markets. Agent-based models (ABMs), for example, simulate the interactions of individual agents to explore how complex market dynamics emerge from the bottom up. Network theory provides another valuable tool for analyzing the interconnections within financial systems and assessing systemic risk. These approaches significantly depart from traditional models, offering a more nuanced and realistic understanding of market behavior.

As financial markets evolve and become more interconnected, the need for models that embrace the principles of complexity science will only grow. The traditional models that have dominated financial theory for decades are increasingly seen as inadequate for addressing the challenges posed by modern markets. By incorporating the insights of complexity science, financial modeling can move beyond the limitations of equilibrium-based theories and provide a more robust framework for understanding and managing the complexities of today's financial systems. This chapter explores the various ways complexity science is being integrated into financial modeling, highlighting the benefits and challenges of this new approach.

COMPLEX ADAPTIVE SYSTEMS AND FINANCIAL MARKETS

Complex adaptive systems (CAS) are a central concept in complexity science, offering a powerful lens through which to view financial markets. Numerous interacting agents operate according to individual rules and objectives in a CAS. Yet their interactions collectively produce emerging patterns and behaviors that are not easily predicted by examining each agent in isolation. This starkly contrasts with traditional financial models, which often assume that markets move toward a stable equilibrium. Financial markets are far from equilibrium; they are dynamic, constantly evolving, and driven by the complex interplay of market participants.

One of the most critical characteristics of CAS is the presence of feedback loops. In financial markets, feedback loops occur when agents' decisions feed back into the system becoming inputs to future decisions. For example, a sudden drop in asset prices might prompt a wave of selling by investors, further driving down prices and potentially triggering a market crash. This positive feedback loop can amplify initial shocks, leading to significant market volatility. Conversely, negative feedback loops can stabilize markets, such as when falling prices attract buyers who see an opportunity, thus supporting the market.

Emergence is another defining feature of complex adaptive systems. Emerging phenomena arise when the collective behavior of individual agents produces outcomes that are not directly predictable from any single agent's actions. In financial markets, this can manifest in various ways, such as in the formation of asset price bubbles or market crashes. These phenomena are often challenging to predict because they result from the interactions of numerous agents, each responding to their own incentives and information. The emerging nature of financial markets challenges the traditional view that market outcomes can be fully understood or predicted by simply aggregating individual decisions.

The adaptive nature of CAS also means that financial markets constantly change in response to new information and evolving conditions. Agents in these markets are not static; they learn from their experiences, adapt their strategies, and influence the market environment. This ongoing adaptation can lead to complex dynamics whereby past behaviors may not reliably predict future outcomes. For instance, a trading strategy that works well in one market environment may fail in another as agents adapt and the market landscape shifts.

Feedback Loops and Emerging Phenomena

The role of feedback loops in financial markets cannot be overstated. Positive feedback loops, where subsequent actions amplify an initial change, are particularly significant in understanding market volatility. For instance, during periods of market euphoria, rising prices can lead to increased buying, further driving up prices and potentially leading to an asset bubble. Conversely, during periods of fear, falling prices can lead to panic selling, exacerbating market declines and potentially causing a crash. These feedback loops illustrate how individual actions, when aggregated across the market, can lead to far more extreme outcomes than any single agent's actions would suggest.

Negative feedback loops, on the other hand, play a crucial role in stabilizing markets. For example, if asset prices fall to a level perceived as undervalued, buyers may enter the market, providing support and preventing further declines. This balancing effect helps to moderate market fluctuations and can contribute to the overall stability of the financial system. Understanding these feedback mechanisms is essential for developing models that accurately capture the dynamics of financial markets.

Emerging phenomena, such as market bubbles and crashes, are the most striking examples of the complexity inherent in financial markets.[1] These events arise from the collective behavior of market participants, often in unexpected and difficult-to-predict ways. For instance, the dot-com bubble of the late 1990s was fueled by widespread speculation in internet-related stocks, leading to unsustainable, dramatic price increases. When the bubble burst, it resulted in significant losses for investors and highlighted the dangers of herd behavior and speculative excess.

The concept of emergence challenges the traditional view of markets as rational and predictable. Instead, it suggests that markets are driven by complex interactions among agents, each with their own motivations and information. This complexity can give rise to behaviors not easily anticipated by traditional models, which often rely on simplifying assumptions about market dynamics. Complexity science provides a more realistic framework for understanding markets' unpredictable and usually nonlinear behavior by recognizing the emerging nature of financial markets.

Examining specific examples of market bubbles and crashes helps illustrate the concepts of feedback loops and emerging phenomena in action. The housing bubble of the mid-2000s and the subsequent GFC serve as influential case studies. During this period, a combination of easy credit, speculative investment, and complex financial instruments fueled a dramatic increase in housing prices. Positive feedback loops were evident as rising home prices encouraged more borrowing and investment, further inflating the bubble.

However, when the housing market peaked and prices declined, the feedback loops reversed. Falling prices led to a wave of foreclosures, which further depressed home values and triggered significant losses in mortgage-backed securities. The interconnectedness of financial institutions, through complex derivative products, spread the crisis across the global financial system, demonstrating the systemic risks inherent in a highly interconnected market.

This illustration highlights how feedback loops and emerging phenomena can lead to extreme market outcomes that are difficult to predict or manage using traditional financial models. It underscores the importance of developing models that can account for the complex dynamics of financial markets, including the potential for sudden and severe disruptions.

In addition to understanding feedback loops and emergence, network theory provides a valuable tool for analyzing the interdependencies within financial systems. Network analysis provides critical insight into how shocks can propagate through financial systems.

In summary, the study of CAS provides crucial insights into the behavior of financial markets. By recognizing the role of feedback loops, emergence, and network interdependencies, we can develop more sophisticated models that better capture the realities of financial market dynamics. These models can improve our understanding of market behavior, enhance risk management practices, and ultimately contribute to a more stable and resilient financial system. As financial markets evolve, integrating complexity science into financial modeling will be essential for navigating the challenges of an increasingly complex global economy.

Is Complexity Science an Empirical Science?

Earlier, we discussed the critical points of modern empirical science and asked whether economics is or will be an empirical science. We recall here that scientific explanation is based on general laws such that logical deductions from basic principles can represent any "object" or process. Science explains by creating general laws. More specifically, the key points are:

1. Empirical sciences are based on observations. However, observations are not pure data but depend on the theory.
2. Theories are made of general laws that apply to every phenomenon in a given domain.
3. General laws include abstract terms defined through the theory itself.
4. Scientific explanation consists of representing all phenomena in a given domain as deductions from general laws, plus initial and boundary conditions.
5. General laws are hypotheses. There is no way to generalize with certainty from a finite set of observations to the entire universe.
6. An empirical science such as physics responds globally to the empirical test; individual statements can always be made true.
7. Science progresses through significant, discrete changes that implement paradigm shifts in the sense that both laws and the descriptive framework change.
8. New theories are generally incommensurable with old theories.

Does the theory of complexity satisfy all these principles? First, there is no single all-encompassing theory of complexity. There is no unified theory of complex systems. CAS share several properties, as detailed in the previous sections.

CAS are made of many interacting agents. A CAS typically exhibits emerging properties, a behavior that cannot be explained by the individual agents' properties and interactions.

This fact does not mean we cannot study the global behavior of complex systems. For example, we can study macroeconomic theory, but we cannot derive macroeconomic behavior from the behavior of individual agents. In addition, macroeconomic laws will generally be nonlinear and exhibit areas of unpredictability (Fabozzi, Focardi, Ponta, et al., 2022).

The mathematician Warren Weaver anticipated the modern development of complexity science by distinguishing three types of scientific approaches: the science of trajectories, primarily classical dynamics; the science of disorganized complexity, notably statistical physics; and, as he foresaw in 1948, the emerging science of organized complexity (Weaver, 1948). The physicist Philip Anderson, corecipient with Sir Neville Francis Mott and John Hasbrouck Van Vleck of the 1977 Nobel Prize in Physics, criticized the idea of universal reductionism. Anderson (1972) claims that there is a hierarchy of sciences characterized by different levels of complexity,

Does a CAS obey the same principles of scientific explanation? As we observed, though a CAS generally exhibits emerging properties, its high-level properties can be formulated as general laws. This statement might be vague, as some sciences, such as psychology, cannot be formulated concisely and axiomatic. For these sciences, the deductive-nomological (D-N) principle discussed in the previous chapter might be difficult to apply. However, suppose we restrict our analysis to economics. In that case, we might say that we should be able to study macroeconomics using the principles of science even if macroeconomics cannot be reduced to microeconomics.

AGENT-BASED MODELS IN FINANCIAL MARKETS

Agent-based models have emerged as one of the most innovative tools in studying financial markets within the frame of complexity science. Unlike traditional models, which often rely on aggregate variables or assume a representative agent, ABMs simulate the interactions of numerous heterogeneous agents, each with distinct characteristics, objectives, and decision-making rules. These agents operate within a virtual environment where they interact with each other and adapt their behavior based on their experiences and the evolving state of the market.

ABMs offer a bottom-up approach to understanding market dynamics, capturing how the microlevel behaviors of individual agents aggregate to produce macrolevel phenomena such as market bubbles, crashes, and contagion. This modeling approach is particularly well-suited for exploring scenarios where traditional equilibrium-based models fall short, such as during periods of financial stress or when market conditions are highly volatile. By focusing on the decentralized interactions of agents, ABMs provide a more nuanced and realistic representation of how financial markets operate.[2]

One of the main strengths of ABMs is their ability to model emerging phenomena, where complex patterns arise from simple rules governing individual agents. For instance, an ABM might simulate how different trading strategies, risk preferences, and information asymmetries among agents can lead to the formation of asset price bubbles. These bubbles emerge not from any single agent's actions but from the collective behavior of many agents acting in their own self-interest. Similarly, ABMs can capture how market panics and crashes occur when these bubbles burst, leading to widespread selling and the rapid devaluation of assets.

Applications and Challenges of ABMs

Central banks and financial regulators might use ABMs to simulate the effects of different policy interventions on market stability, helping them to identify potential risks before they materialize. ABMs can also be used by hedge funds and asset managers to test and optimize trading strategies under various market conditions, providing a competitive edge in an increasingly complex financial landscape.

Despite their potential, ABMs also present several challenges. One of the primary difficulties lies in accurately calibrating these models to reflect real-world market conditions. Unlike traditional models, which often rely on historical data to estimate parameters, ABMs require detailed assumptions about the behavior of individual agents and the rules governing their interactions. This makes calibration complex and resource-intensive, requiring extensive data and computational power.

The validation of ABMs poses another significant challenge. Given the stochastic nature of these models and the complexity of the systems they aim to replicate, it can be difficult to determine whether an ABM accurately reflects real-world market behavior. This challenge is compounded by the fact that financial markets are constantly evolving, meaning that a model validated under one set of conditions may not perform as well under different circumstances.

Researchers are exploring several approaches to addressing these challenges. One promising avenue is using machine learning (ML) techniques to improve the calibration and validation of ABMs. By analyzing large datasets and identifying patterns in agent behavior, ML algorithms can help refine the rules governing agent interactions, leading to more accurate and reliable models. Additionally, advances in computational power are making it possible to run more complex simulations, allowing researchers to explore a broader range of scenarios and better understand the dynamics of financial markets.

A compelling example of the insights offered by ABMs can be found in the study of the flash crash of May 6, 2010. On that day, the U.S. stock market experienced an unprecedented and rapid decline, with the Dow Jones Industrial Average plummeting nearly 1,000 points in minutes, only to recover most of the losses shortly afterward. This event, one of the most significant anomalies in recent market history, was initially difficult to explain using traditional financial models.

ABMs, however, have provided valuable insights into the dynamics that led to the flash crash.[3] By simulating the interactions of various market participants, including high-frequency traders, institutional investors, and market makers, researchers have been able to reconstruct the conditions that triggered the crash. The model revealed how the rapid execution of large sell orders and the actions of high-frequency trading algorithms created a positive feedback loop that exacerbated the initial price decline. As prices fell, more algorithms triggered additional sell orders, further driving down prices and leading to a temporary liquidity crisis.

This example highlights the power of ABMs to capture the complex and often nonlinear interactions that characterize modern financial markets. By providing a detailed, agent-level view of market dynamics, ABMs offer a unique perspective on how market anomalies can arise and propagate, offering valuable lessons for risk management and regulatory oversight.

Challenges in the Implementation of ABMs

While the potential of ABMs is clear, implementing them in real-world financial settings is challenging. The complexity of these models, combined with the need for extensive computational resources, makes them difficult to deploy on a large scale. Furthermore, the stochastic nature of ABMs means that their outcomes can vary significantly depending on the initial conditions and assumptions used in the model. This introduces uncertainty that can be difficult to manage, particularly in high-stakes environments such as financial markets.

Another challenge lies in interpreting the results generated by ABMs. Because these models are highly complex and involve numerous interacting agents, the outcomes can be challenging to analyze and understand. This raises the risk of misinterpreting the results or overlooking important insights. To mitigate these risks, researchers and practitioners need to develop robust methods for analyzing and interpreting the output of ABMs, ensuring that the models provide meaningful and actionable insights.

Additionally, using ABMs in financial decision-making requires a shift in mindset from traditional approaches. Financial professionals must become comfortable with the idea that markets are inherently complex and unpredictable and that traditional models may not always provide reliable guidance. However, by embracing the insights offered by ABMs, they can gain a deeper understanding of market dynamics and develop more effective strategies for managing risk and navigating uncertainty.

The Future of ABMs in Financial Markets

Looking ahead, the future of ABMs in financial markets is promising. As computational power continues to increase and data become more readily available, the accuracy and reliability of these models are expected to improve. This will enable researchers and practitioners to explore more complex scenarios and gain deeper insights into the behavior of financial markets.

Moreover, integrating ABMs with advanced technologies, such as ML and artificial intelligence (AI), holds significant potential. These technologies can help automate the calibration and validation of ABMs, making it easier to develop and deploy these models in real-world settings. They can also enhance the ability of ABMs to adapt to changing market conditions, providing a more dynamic and responsive tool for financial decision-making.

ABMs represent a powerful and versatile approach to understanding the complexities of financial markets. By capturing the interactions of individual agents and exploring the emerging phenomena that arise from these interactions, ABMs offer a more realistic and nuanced view of market dynamics. While challenges remain in implementing them and interpreting the results, the potential benefits are substantial, making ABMs an increasingly important tool in the toolkit of financial professionals. As complexity science continues to evolve, ABMs will likely play a central role in shaping the future of financial modeling and risk management.

NETWORK THEORY AND FINANCIAL INTERDEPENDENCIES

Network theory offers a robust framework for understanding the intricate connections that characterize modern financial systems.[4] At its core, network theory studies the relationships between entities—nodes—and the connections between them, known as links or edges. In financial markets, nodes can represent various entities, such as financial institutions, investors, and market instruments, while the links represent the financial relationships or transactions between these entities.

Applying network theory to finance allows analyzing how interconnectedness among financial entities can influence market behavior and stability. By mapping the structure of financial networks, researchers and practitioners can identify key players within the system, understand the flow of capital, and assess the potential for systemic risk. The concept of "too interconnected to fail" emerges from network theory, emphasizing that the failure of a critical node in a highly interconnected network can produce a cascade of effects throughout the entire system, leading to widespread financial instability (Focardi & Fabozzi, 2004b).

One of the fundamental insights of network theory in finance is the importance of network topology—how the nodes and links are arranged. Different topological structures can have different implications for the resilience or fragility of the financial system. For example, a highly centralized network, in which a few nodes are connected to many others, may be efficient under normal conditions but highly vulnerable to the failure of these central nodes. On the other hand, a decentralized network, in which connections are more evenly distributed, may be more resilient to localized shocks but less efficient in disseminating information and capital.

The study of financial networks also involves understanding the roles of various types of connections, such as direct versus indirect links, and the strength of these connections. Direct links represent direct financial relationships, such as loans between banks, while indirect links represent relationships mediated through other entities. The strength of a connection can be measured by the volume of transactions or the level of exposure between entities. Understanding these nuances is crucial for assessing the risk of contagion, that is, the degree to which distress in one part of the network spreads to other parts, potentially leading to a systemic crisis.

Systemic Risk and Network Structures

Systemic risk is one of the most critical concerns in financial markets, and network theory provides a valuable lens for assessing and managing this risk. Systemic risk arises when the failure of a single entity or a small group of entities triggers a chain reaction that leads to the collapse of other entities and, ultimately, the broader financial system.[5] The GFC is a stark example of systemic risk: the interconnectedness of financial institutions through complex financial instruments led to a rapid and widespread contagion of financial distress.

Network theory helps identify which financial network nodes are most critical to maintaining stability. These nodes, often called "systemically important financial institutions" (SIFIs), are those whose failure would significantly affect the network. By analyzing the network structure, regulators and policymakers can focus on monitoring and supporting these key nodes to prevent systemic collapse.

The structure of financial networks also plays a crucial role in determining the speed and extent of contagion.[6] In a highly interconnected network, distress can spread rapidly as the failure of one entity quickly affects others to which it is connected. Conversely, in a less interconnected network, the contagion spread may be slower or more contained, allowing more time to implement corrective measures. Network theory thus provides insights into how the architecture of financial systems influences their susceptibility to systemic risk.

Moreover, network theory allows exploring scenarios in which the failure of seemingly insignificant nodes can lead to significant systemic effects. These scenarios often involve "hidden" risks that are not immediately apparent but become critical under certain conditions, such as during extreme market stress. Understanding these hidden risks is essential for developing more robust risk management strategies and regulatory policies.

Resilience of Financial Networks

Resilience in financial networks refers to the ability of the system to absorb shocks and recover from disruptions without a systemic crisis ensuing. Network theory offers valuable tools for assessing and enhancing the resilience of financial systems. Two critical factors influencing resilience are the diversity and redundancy of connections within the network. A network with diverse connections is less likely to be destabilized by the failure of a single node as other connections can absorb the impact. Similarly, redundancy, or the existence of multiple pathways for financial flows, can help maintain the system's functionality even when some connections are disrupted.

Network theory also suggests that certain structural features can enhance resilience. For example, the presence of "buffer" nodes—entities that can absorb and mitigate shocks—can prevent the spread of contagion. These buffer nodes often act as intermediaries that can isolate distressed nodes from the rest of the network, thereby containing the impact of a failure. Additionally, feedback loops within the network can contribute to resilience by allowing the system to self-correct and adapt to changing conditions.

Another critical aspect of resilience is the network's ability to reconfigure itself in response to disruptions. In a resilient financial network, nodes can adjust their connections and strategies to maintain stability. This adaptability is essential in the face of systemic shocks, where the ability to reestablish connections and restore functionality quickly can make the difference between a contained disruption and a full-blown crisis.

The study of resilience also involves understanding the trade-offs between efficiency and stability in financial networks. While highly interconnected networks may be efficient regarding capital flow and information dissemination, they may also be more vulnerable to systemic risk. Conversely, less interconnected networks may be more stable but less efficient. Network theory helps researchers and policymakers navigate these trade-offs by identifying the optimal balance between efficiency and resilience, guiding the design of financial systems that can withstand shocks while maintaining functionality.

The GFC provides a powerful case study of how network theory can be applied to understand systemic risk and resilience in financial markets. In the years leading up to the crisis, the financial system became increasingly interconnected through complex financial instruments such as mortgage-backed securities (MBS) and collateralized debt obligations (CDOs). These instruments linked banks, investment firms, and other financial institutions in a web of financial dependencies, creating a highly centralized network with significant systemic risks.

When the U.S. housing market began to decline, the value of MBS and CDOs plummeted, leading to massive losses for institutions exposed to these instruments. The financial system's network structure played a crucial role in the rapid spread of this distress. As critical nodes—such as Lehman Brothers—failed, the effects quickly cascaded through the network, leading to a global financial meltdown.

Network theory helps explain how the financial system's interconnectedness amplified the crisis's impact. The failure of a few central nodes caused a chain reaction that destabilized the entire network. Moreover, the network's lack of diversity and redundancy meant the system had few pathways to absorb the shocks, leading to widespread contagion.

In the aftermath of the crisis, regulators and policymakers have increasingly had recourse to network theory to assess systemic risk and enhance the financial system's resilience. For example, stress testing and the designation of SIFIs are strategies informed by network theory aimed at identifying and mitigating systemic vulnerabilities. The crisis underscored the need for a more comprehensive understanding of financial networks and the importance of designing systems that can withstand systemic shocks.

Policy Implications and Future Directions

The insights gained from network theory have significant implications for financial regulation and policy. Policymakers can use network analysis to identify systemic risks and implement measures to strengthen the financial system's resilience. These might include enhancing the transparency of financial networks, promoting diversity and redundancy in connections, and monitoring the activities of SIFIs more closely.

Future research and policy development could focus on refining network models to capture the complexities of modern financial systems better. As financial markets evolve, accurately modeling and understanding network dynamics will be crucial for preventing future crises and ensuring the global financial system's stability.

Network theory provides a critical framework for understanding the interconnectedness of financial markets and the systemic risks that can arise from these connections. By applying the principles of network theory, researchers and policymakers can gain valuable insights into the structure and dynamics of financial systems, leading to more effective strategies for managing risk and enhancing resilience. As the financial landscape continues to grow in complexity, integrating network theory into financial modeling and regulation will be essential for maintaining stability and preventing systemic crises.

COMPLEXITY SCIENCE IN RISK MANAGEMENT AND REGULATORY POLICY

Traditional risk management strategies in financial markets have long assumed that risks can be quantified, controlled, and diversified away through established techniques such as portfolio diversification, hedging, and financial derivatives. These strategies typically rely on models that assume a normal distribution of returns, linear relationships between variables, and the ability to measure risk through metrics such as value at risk (VaR). However, the financial crises of the past few decades, particularly the GFC, have exposed significant flaws in these traditional approaches (Focardi & Fabozzi, 2003).

One of the most glaring challenges is that traditional risk management models often fail to account for the complex, nonlinear interactions that can lead to extreme market events. The assumption of normal distributions underestimates the likelihood of "black swan" events—rare, unexpected occurrences that have a disproportionate impact on markets. For instance, the failure of Lehman Brothers in 2008 and the subsequent cascade of financial institution failures were events that traditional risk management models were ill-equipped to predict or manage.

Moreover, these models typically focus on individual risks in isolation without considering the systemic risks that arise from the interconnectedness of financial institutions and markets. This siloed approach overlooks the potential for small, localized shocks to propagate through the financial system, leading to widespread instability. While a popular risk measure, VaR has also been criticized for providing a false sense of security as it measures only potential losses under normal market conditions and fails to take into account tail risks. These extreme losses occur during periods of market turmoil.

The shortcomings of traditional risk management approaches have led to a growing recognition that financial markets are better understood as CAS where risks are emerging properties of the interactions between and among numerous agents. This perspective requires a fundamental shift in managing risk, away from the use of static models and toward a more dynamic, holistic approach that takes into account the complexity of financial systems.

Adaptive Risk Management Strategies

Adaptive risk management strategies recognize that financial markets are constantly evolving and that risks can change rapidly in response to new information, shifts in market sentiment, and the actions of market participants. These strategies emphasize the importance of flexibility, resilience, and the ability to adapt to changing conditions.

One of the critical components of adaptive risk management is stress testing and scenario analysis. Unlike traditional risk measures, which assume that the future will resemble the past, stress testing involves simulating various adverse scenarios to assess how a portfolio or financial institution would perform under different conditions. These scenarios can include market shocks, economic downturns, geopolitical events, and other factors that could lead to significant financial stress. Financial institutions can identify potential vulnerabilities and develop strategies to mitigate them by exploring these scenarios.

Scenario analysis, a related tool, involves exploring multiple potential future scenarios based on different assumptions about market conditions and the behavior of market participants. This approach recognizes that there is no single "right" prediction for the future and that financial markets are inherently uncertain. By considering a range of possible outcomes, scenario analysis helps institutions prepare for unexpected events and make more informed decisions in the face of uncertainty.

Another aspect of adaptive risk management is building resilience within financial systems. Resilience refers to the ability of a system to absorb shocks and recover from disruptions without leading to systemic failure. In financial markets, resilience can be enhanced through diversification, buffers (such as capital reserves), and the development of contingency plans for managing crises. Complexity science suggests that resilience is not about avoiding risk altogether but about being prepared to manage and adapt to risks when they arise.

Implications for Regulatory Policy

The insights gained from complexity science have significant implications for regulatory policy in financial markets. Traditional regulatory frameworks have often assumed that markets are self-correcting and risks can be managed through transparency, market discipline, and regulatory oversight. However, the GFC revealed the limitations of this approach and the need for a more proactive and comprehensive regulatory framework that can address the complexities of modern financial markets.

The macroprudential policy has emerged as a vital tool in the regulatory response to systemic risk. Unlike microprudential regulation, which focuses on the safety and soundness of individual institutions, macroprudential policy is concerned with the financial system's stability. This approach recognizes that the failure of one or more institutions can have systemic consequences, particularly in a highly interconnected financial network. Macroprudential tools include countercyclical capital buffers, leverage ratios, and systemic risk surcharges, all designed to reduce the buildup of systemic risk during periods of financial expansion and to enhance resilience during downturns.

Stress testing has also become a central component of regulatory policy, with regulators requiring financial institutions to conduct regular stress tests to assess their ability to withstand adverse economic conditions. These stress tests are designed to identify vulnerabilities in the financial system and ensure institutions have sufficient capital and liquidity to absorb losses in a crisis. The results of these stress tests are often used to inform regulatory actions, such as requiring institutions to raise additional capital or to reduce their exposure to certain risks.

Regulatory policy has also increasingly focused on the interconnectedness of financial institutions and the potential for contagion. As discussed in the previous section, network analysis has become an essential tool for regulators in assessing systemic risk. By mapping out the connections between institutions and markets, regulators can identify key nodes within the financial network that are critical to maintaining stability and can take steps to mitigate the risks associated with these connections.

Dynamic Regulatory Tools and Future Directions

The integration of complexity science into regulatory policy will likely continue to evolve, driven by technological advances and the increasing complexity of financial markets. One area of focus is the development of dynamic regulatory tools that can adapt to changing market conditions in real time. Traditional regulatory approaches often rely on static rules and regulations that may become outdated as markets evolve. In contrast, dynamic tools use real-time data and advanced analytics to monitor market conditions, identify emerging risks, and adjust regulatory requirements accordingly.

For example, real-time monitoring of market transactions using big data and ML algorithms can help regulators detect early signs of market stress or the buildup of systemic risk. These tools can provide regulators with a more granular and up-to-date understanding of market dynamics, enabling them to take proactive measures to prevent crises. Additionally, using ML and AI in stress testing and scenario analysis can enhance the accuracy and reliability of these tools, allowing more effective risk management.

Another important direction for regulatory policy is the development of frameworks that address the global nature of financial markets. As financial markets become increasingly interconnected across borders, contagion and systemic failure risks are no longer confined to individual countries or regions. Global coordination among regulators is essential to ensure that systemic risks are managed effectively and that financial stability is maintained globally. This may entail the harmonization of regulatory standards, the sharing of information across jurisdictions, and the development of global contingency plans for managing financial crises.

Complexity science provides a valuable framework for understanding and managing risk in financial markets. Financial institutions and regulators can better navigate the complexities of modern financial systems by recognizing the limitations of traditional risk management approaches and embracing adaptive, resilient strategies. Integrating complexity science into risk management and regulatory policy is essential for building a more stable and robust financial system capable of withstanding the challenges of an increasingly complex and interconnected global economy. As we move forward, the continued development and application of these principles will be critical in ensuring the stability and resilience of financial markets.

INVESTMENT STRATEGIES IN COMPLEX FINANCIAL MARKETS

This section explains how investors can design effective strategies for navigating complex and evolving financial markets. Particular attention is given to the critical roles of diversification and adaptability in managing uncertainty and achieving long-term performance.

The Importance of Diversification and Adaptability

In complex financial markets, traditional investment strategies that rely solely on diversification and static asset allocation have proved inadequate in the face of rapid and often unpredictable market changes. Diversification, which involves spreading investments across various assets to reduce risk, remains a fundamental principle of portfolio management. However, in complex markets characterized by interconnectedness and emerging behaviors, the effectiveness of diversification can be compromised. During systemic stress, correlations between assets often increase, reducing the benefits of diversification and exposing portfolios to more significant risks.

In response to these challenges, investment strategies in complex markets must prioritize adaptability alongside diversification. Adaptability refers to adjusting investment strategies in response to changing market conditions, new information, and evolving risks. This requires a dynamic approach to portfolio management in which asset allocations are regularly reviewed and adjusted based on market developments. Adaptive strategies recognize that financial markets are not static and that the relationships between assets can change rapidly, especially during market turbulence.

One approach to achieving adaptability is through tactical asset allocation, whereby portfolio managers make short-term adjustments to asset allocations based on market conditions and forecasts. Tactical asset allocation allows investors to take advantage of short-term opportunities and mitigate risks that may not be captured by a traditional, long-term strategic asset allocation. Additionally, flexible investment vehicles, such as exchange-traded funds, can facilitate rapid adjustments to portfolio composition, enhancing the ability to respond to market changes.

Another critical aspect of adaptability is integrating scenario analysis and stress testing into the investment process. By simulating various market scenarios, including extreme events, investors can assess the potential impact on their portfolios and develop strategies to mitigate adverse outcomes. This proactive approach to risk management enables investors to remain resilient in the face of market shocks and to capitalize on opportunities that may arise from market dislocations.

The Role of Machine Learning and AI in Investment Strategies

The increasing complexity of financial markets has also driven the adoption of advanced technologies such as ML and AI in investment strategies. These technologies offer significant advantages in processing large datasets, identifying patterns, and making data-driven decisions in real time. ML algorithms, for example, can analyze vast amounts of historical and real-time data to detect subtle correlations and market signals that may not be apparent to human analysts.

In portfolio management, ML and AI can enhance various aspects of the investment process, from asset selection to risk management. For instance, predictive models based on ML can forecast asset price movements with a higher degree of accuracy by incorporating a wide range of variables, including macroeconomic indicators, market sentiment, and alternative data sources such as social media and news feeds. These models can help portfolio managers identify mispriced assets and optimize their portfolios for better risk-adjusted returns.

AI-driven portfolio optimization tools can also automate rebalancing portfolios in response to market changes. These tools use advanced algorithms to continuously monitor market conditions and adjust asset allocations in real time, ensuring that portfolios remain aligned with investment objectives and risk tolerance levels. This level of automation improves efficiency and reduces the potential for human error in decision-making.

Moreover, AI and ML can be crucial in enhancing risk management practices. AI-driven models can provide early warning signals of potential market disruptions by analyzing historical market data and identifying patterns associated with market downturns or systemic risks. This allows investors to take preemptive measures, such as adjusting asset allocations, hedging positions, or increasing liquidity, to protect their portfolios from significant losses.

Integrating ML and AI into investment strategies also supports the development of more sophisticated and adaptive investment models with which to navigate the complexities of modern financial markets. These models can learn from new data and continuously improve their predictions and recommendations, making them well-suited to dynamic and uncertain market environments.

Incorporating Behavioral Finance and ESG Factors

Another critical development in investment strategies in complex financial markets is the incorporation of behavioral finance insights and environmental, social, and governance (ESG) factors. As explained in chapter 2, behavioral finance recognizes that investors are not always rational and that cognitive biases, emotions, and social influences can have an impact on investment decisions. These biases can lead to systematic errors, such as overconfidence, herding, and loss aversion, affecting market outcomes and portfolio performance.

By incorporating insights from behavioral finance, investors can develop strategies that account for these biases and improve decision-making processes. For example, recognizing the tendency for herding behavior during market rallies, investors might adopt a contrarian strategy, reducing exposure to overvalued assets and seeking opportunities in undervalued ones. Similarly, understanding the impact of loss aversion on investor behavior can lead to implementing risk management techniques that help mitigate the emotional impact of market downturns.

ESG factors have also become increasingly important in developing investment strategies as investors recognize the long-term value of sustainable and socially responsible investing. Integrating ESG factors into decision-making entails evaluating companies' environmental practices, social responsibility commitments, and governance standards, alongside traditional financial metrics. This approach not only aligns investments with ethical and sustainability goals but also identifies companies better positioned to manage risks related to regulatory changes, environmental impacts, and social issues.

Incorporating ESG factors into investment strategies can enhance portfolio resilience by reducing exposure to companies with poor sustainability practices or weak governance structures. Additionally, ESG-focused investments have been shown to deliver competitive financial returns while contributing to positive societal and environmental outcomes. As ESG considerations become more central to investment decision-making, they represent a crucial element in the broader framework of complexity science and adaptive investment strategies.

A notable example of the successful integration of ESG factors into investment strategies can be seen in the response to the growing risks associated with climate change. As awareness of climate-related risks has increased, investors have increasingly sought to align their portfolios with companies that are proactive in managing their environmental impact and are committed to sustainability.

One approach to integrating ESG factors is to use "green" investment strategies, which focus on companies that are leaders in renewable energy, energy efficiency, and sustainable practices. These strategies reduce exposure to the risks associated with carbon-intensive industries and position investors to benefit from the growth of the green economy. In the context of complexity science, this approach recognizes the interconnectedness of environmental, economic, and financial systems. It seeks to build portfolios resilient to the systemic risks posed by climate change.

Furthermore, the development of ESG indices and ratings has supported the integration of ESG factors into investment strategies. These tools provide investors with the means to assess companies' sustainability performance, enabling them to make more informed decisions and align their portfolios with sustainability goals.

The evolution of investment strategies in complex financial markets reflects a growing recognition of the need for adaptability, the incorporation of advanced technologies, and the integration of behavioral and ESG factors. By embracing these developments, investors can better navigate the complexities of modern markets, manage risks more effectively, and achieve their financial and sustainability objectives. As financial markets continue to evolve, adapting investment strategies to changing conditions will be essential for achieving long-term success and resilience.

THE FUTURE OF FINANCIAL MODELING IN AN AGE OF COMPLEXITY

As financial systems grow more interconnected and volatile, the tools used to model them must evolve accordingly. Here we examine how financial modeling is adapting to this complexity and how emerging technologies are being integrated to enhance decision-making and risk assessment.

Integration of Emerging Technologies

As financial markets continue to grow in complexity, the future of financial modeling will be increasingly shaped by integrating emerging technologies such as ML, AI, and quantum computing. These technologies have the potential to revolutionize the way financial models are developed, tested, and applied, offering new tools for understanding and managing the intricate dynamics of global markets.

ML and AI are poised to play a central role in the evolution of financial modeling. These technologies allow vast amounts of data to be analyzed, identifying patterns and correlations often missed by traditional models. ML algorithms can be trained on historical data to develop predictive models that are more accurate and adaptable to changing market conditions. As these algorithms learn from new data, they become increasingly effective at forecasting market movements, identifying potential risks, and optimizing investment strategies.

AI-driven models also offer the advantage of continuous improvement. Unlike static models, which often require manual updates, AI models can evolve in real time as they process new information. This dynamic nature makes AI an invaluable tool for navigating the uncertainties and rapid changes that characterize modern financial markets. Furthermore, the ability of AI to process unstructured data, such as news articles, social media posts, and other nontraditional sources of information, yields a more comprehensive view of market sentiment and potential drivers of market behavior.

Quantum computing, while still in its early stages, holds promise for transforming financial modeling by tackling problems beyond the reach of classical computation. Quantum computers can process and analyze complex datasets at unprecedented speeds, making it possible to solve optimization problems that are too complex for traditional computing methods. In financial modeling, quantum computing could optimize large portfolios, simulate market scenarios with a higher degree of accuracy, and enhance the precision of risk management models.

The integration of these emerging technologies into financial modeling is not without challenges. One of the primary obstacles is the need for expertise in both finance and technology. Developing effective models requires a deep understanding of financial markets and the ability to design and implement advanced algorithms. Additionally, the adoption of these technologies raises concerns about transparency and interpretability. In particular, AI and ML models are often described as "black boxes" because their decision-making processes can be challenging to understand. Ensuring that these models are transparent and that human analysts can interpret their outputs will be crucial for their successful integration into financial practice.

Despite these challenges, the potential benefits of integrating emerging technologies into financial modeling are significant. As these technologies continue to advance, they will enable the development of more sophisticated, accurate, and adaptable models that can better navigate the complexities of modern financial markets. This not only will enhance the ability of financial institutions to manage risk and optimize returns but also will contribute to the overall stability and resilience of the global financial system.

Challenges and Opportunities Ahead

The future of financial modeling will be shaped by challenges and opportunities. One of the most significant challenges is developing models robust enough to handle global financial markets' increasing complexity and interconnectedness. As financial systems become more integrated, the potential for systemic risk increases, making it more critical to develop models to identify and mitigate these risks (Fabozzi, Focardi, & Jonas, 2017).

Another challenge lies in the ethical concerns around using AI and ML in financial modeling. These technologies raise important questions about fairness, accountability, and transparency. For example, if an AI-driven model makes a decision that leads to significant financial losses, who is responsible? Ensuring that these models are used ethically and that their decision-making processes are transparent will be critical to gaining the trust of regulators, investors, and the public.

In addition to these challenges, there are significant opportunities for innovation in financial modeling. The increasing availability of data, combined with technological advances, provides an unprecedented opportunity to develop more accurate, adaptive, and comprehensive models. For example, integrating ESG factors into financial modeling is an area of growing interest. As investors become more focused on sustainability, there is a growing demand for models that can assess the long-term impact of ESG factors on financial performance. By incorporating these factors into financial models, investors can make more informed decisions that align with their values and long-term goals.

Furthermore, the rise of decentralized finance (DeFi) presents both a challenge and an opportunity for financial modeling. DeFi, which operates on blockchain technology, is transforming the financial landscape by offering new ways to borrow, lend, trade, and invest without traditional financial intermediaries. This shift requires the development of new models that can account for the unique characteristics and risks associated with DeFi platforms. At the same time, DeFi offers the opportunity to create more transparent, efficient, and inclusive financial systems, providing access to financial services for underserved populations.

As the financial landscape continues to evolve, the future of financial modeling will be shaped by the ability to adapt to new challenges and seize emerging opportunities. Integrating complexity science and technological advances provides a robust framework for developing models that can navigate the uncertainties and complexities of modern financial markets. By embracing these innovations, financial institutions can enhance their ability to manage risk, optimize returns, and contribute to the stability and resilience of the global financial system.

The Role of Collaboration and Interdisciplinary Approaches

As financial modeling becomes increasingly complex and technology-driven, collaboration and interdisciplinary approaches will be essential for success. The development of advanced financial models requires expertise not only in finance but also in mathematics, computer science, data analytics, and behavioral economics. By bringing together experts from these diverse fields, financial institutions can develop more sophisticated and practical models that leverage the latest advancements in technology and theory.

Collaboration between academia and industry is also critical. Academic researchers can provide the theoretical foundations and innovative ideas that drive the development of new models. At the same time, industry practitioners can offer practical insights and real-world data that ensure these models are applicable and useful. Joint research initiatives, conferences, and workshops that bring together academics, industry professionals, and regulators can facilitate the exchange of knowledge and the development of best practices in financial modeling (Fabozzi, Focardi, & Jonas, 2010).

Moreover, collaboration with regulators will be increasingly important as financial models become more complex and impactful. Regulators ensure that financial models are used responsibly and do not introduce new risks into the financial system. By working closely with regulators, financial institutions can ensure that their models comply with regulatory requirements and contribute to the stability and integrity of financial markets.

The future of financial modeling will also benefit from interdisciplinary approaches integrating insights from psychology, sociology, and environmental science. For example, behavioral economics can provide valuable insights into how cognitive biases and emotions influence investor behavior, insights that can be incorporated into financial models to improve accuracy. Similarly, environmental science can inform the development of models that take into account the long-term impacts of climate change on financial markets.

By embracing collaboration and interdisciplinary approaches, the future of financial modeling will be more innovative, inclusive, and effective. These approaches will enable the development of models that are better equipped to navigate the complexities of modern financial markets, manage emerging risks, and capitalize on new opportunities.

Building a Resilient and Adaptive Financial System

Integrating complexity science and emerging technologies into financial modeling will be essential for building a resilient and adaptive financial system. The challenges posed by the increasing complexity and interconnectedness of global financial markets require innovative approaches beyond those available through traditional models. By embracing the potential of ML, AI, quantum computing, and interdisciplinary collaboration, financial institutions can develop models that are more accurate, adaptive, and capable of managing the risks and uncertainties of the modern financial landscape.

The future of financial modeling is not just about predicting market movements or optimizing returns; it is about creating a resilient, inclusive, and sustainable financial system. This requires a commitment to continuous innovation, ethical practices, and collaboration across disciplines and industries. By doing so, we can build a financial system that not only withstands future challenges but also contributes to society's and the environment's well-being.

The future of financial modeling holds tremendous promise, but it also comes with significant responsibilities. As we navigate this rapidly evolving landscape, we must remain focused on the principles of complexity science, the potential of emerging technologies, and the importance of collaboration. By doing so, we can ensure that financial modeling continues to be a powerful tool for managing risk, optimizing returns, and building a better, more resilient financial system for the future.

SUMMARY

This chapter has discussed the profound implications of complexity science for financial markets and modeling. As financial systems have become increasingly intricate and interconnected, traditional models relying on equilibrium and rational behavior assumptions have often failed to accurately capture these systems' true dynamics. The chapter began by introducing the concept of financial markets as CAS, where the interactions of numerous agents, feedback loops, and emerging phenomena create patterns that cannot be easily predicted. The limitations of conventional models were highlighted, and a shift toward approaches that recognize the complexity and adaptive nature of financial markets was advocated.

Much of the chapter discussed ABMs and their role in financial modeling. Unlike traditional models, ABMs simulate the interactions between and among diverse agents with different strategies and decision-making processes. ABMs make it possible to model emerging behavior, such as asset price bubbles or financial contagion, a capability critical to understanding market dynamics during periods of stress. Network theory is another tool for analyzing the interdependencies in financial systems, providing insights into systemic risk and the resilience of financial networks. The chapter underscored the importance of these advanced tools in identifying systemic vulnerabilities and enhancing the stability of financial markets.

We further examined the application of complexity science principles in risk management and regulatory policy. Traditional risk management approaches, which assume that risks can be quantified and managed through diversification and other techniques, are increasingly seen as inadequate in the face of the nonlinear dynamics and emerging behaviors in complex financial markets. We emphasized the need to adopt adaptive and resilient strategies, such as stress testing and macroprudential policies, which are better suited to managing the uncertainties inherent in these systems. Regulatory frameworks that take into account the interconnectedness of global financial markets and the potential for systemic risks to spread rapidly across borders will be necessary in the future.

Finally, we discussed the future of financial modeling in an era of complexity, highlighting the growing importance of integrating complexity science with emerging technologies such as ML, AI, and quantum computing. These technologies offer new opportunities to develop more accurate and adaptive models to better navigate the complexities of modern financial markets. We advocate the continuous innovation in financial modeling to create a more resilient and sustainable financial system that can effectively navigate the challenges of an increasingly complex global economy.

5 The Role of Mathematical Modeling and New Economic Thinking in Modern Finance

CHARTING A NEW COURSE FOR FINANCIAL MODELS

The interplay between mathematical modeling and economic thought has long been a central theme in the development of modern finance. From the early days of quantitative finance to the present era of big data and machine learning (ML), mathematical models have served as the bedrock on which much of financial theory and practice has been built. These models have provided the tools to quantify risk, optimize portfolios, and price complex financial instruments. However, the effectiveness of these models has not gone unchallenged.

The global financial crises of the early twenty-first century exposed significant flaws in the traditional approaches, prompting a reevaluation of the role that mathematical models should play in finance. Central to this reevaluation is a deeper understanding of these models' assumptions, such as normal distribution of asset returns, constant volatility, and rational market behavior. These assumptions often fail under real-world conditions, where financial markets exhibit heavy tails, volatility clustering, and behavioral biases. Recognizing and addressing these limitations is essential for improving the robustness of future models.

At the heart of this reevaluation is the recognition that financial markets are complex, adaptive systems whose operations deterministic models cannot fully capture. Theories that once dominated economic thought, such as the efficient market hypothesis and rational expectations, have been questioned. Evidence shows that irrational behavior, feedback loops, and emerging phenomena often drive markets. This has led to the rise of alternative theories, such as behavioral economics and complexity economics, which offer new ways of thinking about market dynamics.

Moreover, the increasing interconnectedness of global financial markets has given rise to novel risks that traditional models are ill-equipped to handle. These risks, ranging from cyberattacks to climate change, present unique challenges for risk management and require innovative approaches beyond those afforded by the standard finance tools. As these risks evolve, so must the financial decision-making models and theories.

This chapter explores the evolution of quantitative finance from its early beginnings to its current state, and discusses the challenges and opportunities that lie ahead. We begin by examining the role of mathematical modeling in finance, tracing its development from early theoretical frameworks to the sophisticated algorithms used today. We delve into the assumptions underlying these models, their strengths, and their limitations.

We also explore the integration of behavioral finance into quantitative models, highlighting how cognitive biases and psychological factors can influence market behavior. This is followed by a discussion of the risks associated with quantitative models, particularly model risk and data quality issues.

The chapter considers how mathematical modeling and economic thought can be integrated to understand better and navigate modern finance's complexities. By synthesizing insights from three foundational works, we aim to comprehensively analyze how these elements can be used to build more resilient financial systems. We begin by examining the historical evolution of mathematical models in economics and finance, exploring their strengths and limitations. Next, we delve into the coexistence of conflicting economic theories, discussing how these theories can be reconciled through the lens of complexity and systems thinking.

In doing so, this chapter seeks to contribute to the ongoing dialogue on the future of finance. We propose that a balanced approach that integrates the rigor of mathematical models with the insights of new economic thought is essential for addressing the multifaceted challenges of today's financial markets. Through this interdisciplinary lens, we hope to offer a roadmap for integrating diverse perspectives and methodologies to build a more adaptive and resilient financial system.

To understand the evolution of these challenges, we must first describe the origins of mathematical finance and the foundational models that shaped the field.

THE ORIGINS OF MATHEMATICAL FINANCE

The history of mathematical modeling in economics and finance can be traced back to the early twentieth century, when economists first began to formalize economic theories using mathematical notation. One of the earliest and most influential contributions to this field was Paul Samuelson's *Foundations of Economic Analysis* (Samuelson, 1947). Samuelson's work laid the groundwork for applying mathematical methods to a wide range of economic problems, from consumer choice to market equilibrium. His approach was based on the idea that economic behavior could be understood as the solution to an optimization problem in which agents seek to maximize utility or profit subject to constraints.

In the following years, mathematical models became increasingly sophisticated, driven by advances in calculus, linear algebra, and probability theory. The development of game theory by John von Neumann and Oskar Morgenstern in the 1940s provided a new framework for analyzing strategic interactions between rational agents, leading to important insights into competitive behavior, bargaining, and market structure (von Neumann & Morgenstern, 1944). Meanwhile, the introduction of stochastic processes into finance by Louis Bachelier in the early twentieth century paved the way for the development of modern financial models, including the famous Black-Scholes-Merton model for option pricing (Black & Scholes, 1973; Merton, 1973).

Modern Portfolio Theory and Asset Pricing

In the 1950s and 1960s, finance began to take shape as a rigorous academic discipline. This period saw the development of modern portfolio theory by Harry Markowitz, who introduced the concept of mean-variance optimization. Markowitz's work provided a framework for constructing portfolios that balanced risk and return based on the statistical properties of asset returns (Markowitz, 1952).

Building on Markowitz's work, William Sharpe developed the capital asset pricing model (CAPM) in the 1960s (Sharpe, 1964). The CAPM introduced the concept of systematic risk and provided a theoretical basis for asset pricing. The model posits that the expected return on an asset is a function of its sensitivity to market risk, as measured by its beta coefficient. The CAPM became a cornerstone of modern finance, offering a simple yet powerful framework for understanding the relationship between risk and return.

The concepts introduced by Markowitz and Sharpe laid the foundation for developing more advanced portfolio theories, such as the arbitrage pricing theory (APT) developed by Stephen Ross (Ross, 1976). The APT is a multifactor model that generalizes the CAPM by allowing multiple sources of systematic risk rather than a single market factor. It provides a more flexible framework for asset pricing as it does not rely on the assumption of a single risk factor and allows the inclusion of various factors.

The development of these models has had a significant impact on the investment management industry, leading to the widespread adoption of quantitative methods for portfolio construction and risk management. For example, the use of factor models has become standard practice in portfolio management, with investment managers using these models to identify and exploit sources of risk and return.

The success of these models also led to an overreliance on mathematical formalism in economics and finance. As mathematical models became more complex and abstract, they often lost touch with the underlying economic reality they were meant to represent. This disconnect was particularly evident during the 2007–2008 Global Financial Crisis (GFC), when highly sophisticated models failed to predict or prevent the collapse of major financial institutions. The crisis exposed the limitations of mathematical models that rely on assumptions of market efficiency, rational behavior, and normally distributed risks.

The Rise of Option Pricing Models

The development of the Black-Scholes option pricing model in 1973 with a simultaneous contribution by Robert Merton, marked a significant milestone in the evolution of mathematical finance. The model provided a closed-form solution for pricing European call and put options, relying on assumptions such as constant volatility and normally distributed returns.

The success of the Black-Scholes model largely owed to its elegant mathematical formulation, which made it possible to hedge options positions and manage risk more effectively. However, one of the key assumptions of the Black-Scholes model is that volatility remains constant over time. Market volatility fluctuates, particularly during periods of financial stress, as evidenced during events like the 1987 stock market crash.

While the Black-Scholes model has been highly influential, it too has limitations. One of the most important criticisms is its assumption of constant volatility. Volatility tends to change over time, particularly during periods of market stress. In response, more advanced models have been developed to better reflect observed market behavior, including stochastic volatility models and jump-diffusion models. The jump-diffusion model extends the standard option pricing framework by incorporating sudden, discrete jumps in asset prices in addition to continuous price movements. These jumps account for real-world phenomena such as earnings surprises, market crashes, or geopolitical shocks that cannot be captured by models assuming smooth, continuous price changes. The model combines a standard diffusion process with a Poisson jump process to better reflect the observed behavior of asset returns.

Moreover, empirical studies that show the presence of skewness and kurtosis in asset returns have challenged the assumption of normally distributed returns, indicating that extreme events are more likely than the model predicts. Despite these limitations, the Black-Scholes model has had a profound impact on the field of finance, revolutionizing the pricing of options and other derivative instruments.

The Evolution of Risk Management Models

Risk management has become an increasingly important area of focus in quantitative finance, particularly in the wake of the GFC. The crisis highlighted the limitations of traditional risk models, which often relied on assumptions of normality and constant volatility and failed to capture the full extent of the risks facing financial institutions.

In response to these challenges, new risk management models have been developed that account for the complexities and uncertainties of financial markets. Traditional risk models, such as value at risk (VaR) models, often assume normally distributed returns and constant volatility. Yet real-world financial markets demonstrate fat tails and clustering of extreme events, contradicting these assumptions. The failure to account for such behavior was one factor contributing to the underestimation of risk during the GFC.

While VaR modeling has become a widely used risk management tool, it has significant limitations. One key criticism of VaR modeling is its inability to account for tail risks—the risk of extreme events that occur with low probability but can have catastrophic consequences. This limitation arises because VaR modeling focuses only on the maximum expected loss over a given time frame for a specified confidence level, ignoring what happens in the worst-case scenarios beyond that threshold. For example, during the

GFC, many financial institutions relied on VaR models that severely underestimated the risks of extreme market conditions, leading to massive losses.

Alternative risk measures have been developed to address these shortcomings. Conditional value at risk (CVaR), also known as expected shortfall, offers a more comprehensive way to assess risk by focusing on the tail end of the loss distribution. Unlike VaR, which provides a cutoff at a particular percentile, CVaR estimates the average loss in the worst-case scenarios beyond the VaR threshold. This provides a better understanding of potential losses during extreme events, making CVaR more suited for managing risks in markets characterized by fat tails and heavy-tailed distributions (Artzner et al., 1999). These alternative models emphasize the need for financial institutions to move beyond simple probabilistic approaches and consider the deeper implications of systemic risks, especially when dealing with highly interconnected and volatile markets.

Using fat-tailed distributions is not the only innovation in risk management. The structure of the market connections also plays an important role in understanding risk. Focardi and Fabozzi (2005) show how autoregressive conditional duration models can help model the evolution of credit losses.[1] Focardi and Fabozzi (2004b) proposed the use of a market connectivity measure based on percolation theory as a risk factor.[2] Fabozzi, Focardi, and Jonas (2010) discuss how market perception of risk changed after the GFC.

CASE STUDIES IN THE EVOLUTION OF MATHEMATICAL FINANCE

To illustrate the strengths and limitations of mathematical modeling in finance, we examine several case studies of models both succeeding and failing.

The Black-Scholes-Merton Model and the 1987 Stock Market Crash

The stock market crash of October 19, 1987, "Black Monday," was one of the most significant market events of the twentieth century. Global stock markets experienced unprecedented declines in a single day. The crash was triggered by a combination of factors, including the widespread use of portfolio insurance strategies based on dynamic hedging models.

These models, which relied on the Black-Scholes option pricing framework, assumed that markets were liquid and that transactions could be executed without affecting prices. However, during the crash, the sheer volume of sell orders overwhelmed the market, leading to a liquidity crisis and a cascade of selling. The 1987 crash highlighted the limitations of quantitative models that rely on assumptions of market efficiency and constant volatility, and it underscored the need for more robust risk management strategies.

The Global Financial Crisis and Risk Management Models

The 2007–2008 GFC was another significant market event that exposed the limitations of traditional financial models. The crisis was triggered by the collapse of the U.S. housing market and widespread defaults on subprime mortgages, leading to a liquidity crisis and the failure of major financial institutions.

One key factor contributing to the crisis was the widespread use of complex financial instruments, such as non-agency residential mortgage-backed securities (MBS), real estate related asset-backed securities (ABS), collateralized debt obligations (CDOs), and structured investment vehicles (SIVs). These instruments were priced using quantitative models that failed to capture the full extent of the risks. These models often relied on historical data and assumptions of normality, which did not take into account the extreme tail risks associated with the housing market collapse.

The crisis underscored the need for more sophisticated risk management models that can take into account tail risks and the potential for systemic crises. In response to the crisis, regulators and financial institutions implemented a range of measures to strengthen risk management practices, including stress testing and scenario analysis to assess the impact of extreme market events.

The crisis also revealed the risks of misapplied financial innovation. One widely used tool, the Gaussian copula, was designed to model the joint default risk in complex instruments like CDOs. While mathematically elegant, it relied on assumptions such as stable (time-invariant) joint distributions that broke down under stress. What appeared to be a breakthrough in risk modeling instead contributed to systemic underestimation of credit risk, highlighting how innovations can obscure fragility when used without a full understanding of their limitations.

The Rise of High-Frequency Trading

High-frequency trading has become a dominant force in modern financial markets, accounting for a significant share of trading volume in major exchanges. High-frequency trading involves using algorithms to execute trades at extremely high speeds, often in milliseconds or microseconds, and to take advantage of small price discrepancies across markets.

While high-frequency trading has been credited with increasing market liquidity and reducing transaction costs, it has also been associated with increased market volatility and the potential for flash crashes. For example, on May 6, 2010, a flash crash was triggered by a large sell order in the futures market, which led to a cascade of selling across multiple asset classes.

The rise of high-frequency trading has highlighted the need for models that can account for the impact of algorithmic trading on market stability. This has led to the development of new models incorporating high-frequency trading dynamics and the potential for feedback loops that can amplify market movements.

EFFECTIVENESS OF MATHEMATICAL MODELING IN ECONOMICS AND FINANCE

Quantitative finance has transformed the financial industry by providing powerful tools for analyzing markets, pricing assets, and managing risk. As noted earlier, the roots of quantitative finance can be traced back to the mid-twentieth century. These models introduced a rigorous, mathematical approach to finance, replacing intuition and experience with data-driven decision-making.

The adoption of these models revolutionized the way financial markets operated. Suddenly, investment decisions could be made based on quantifiable metrics rather than subjective judgments. This shift toward quantification was part of a broader trend across many fields during the twentieth century, when advances in mathematics, statistics, and computing began to influence everything from economics to engineering.

However, as quantitative models spread, their limitations also became apparent. A major source of these limitations is the underlying assumptions of the models. For instance, as noted earlier, both the Black-Scholes option pricing model and the CAPM assume that asset returns follow a normal distribution. However, numerous empirical studies, including that by Cont

(2001) on "stylized facts," have shown that financial markets exhibit fat tails and volatility clustering, which deviate significantly from the normal distribution. This raises critical concerns about the reliability of models that fail to account for these extreme events.

The GFC exposed some of these models' flaws, particularly their reliance on assumptions that did not hold true under extreme conditions. This crisis led to a reevaluation of the models that had become the foundation of modern finance and prompted the development of new models that could better account for the complexities of real-world markets. Focardi and Fabozzi (2009, 2014) argue that extreme, unpredictable events, or "black swans," challenge the applicability of traditional mathematical models in finance. They suggest that while such models can offer insights into normal market conditions, they often fail to capture the complexity and nonlinearity of financial systems, which can lead to catastrophic outcomes during rare extreme events.

Behavioral Economics and Challenges to Rational Models

As explained in chapter 2, one key area where traditional models fall short is their rational behavior assumption. Behavioral economics challenges these assumptions, offering insights into how real-world decision-making deviates from the predictions of rational models.

Behavioral economics has challenged the long-standing assumptions of traditional models such as the CAPM and the efficient market hypothesis, which assume that market participants are fully rational and that prices reflect all available information. These rational models have been foundational to modern finance, forming the basis for asset pricing, portfolio management, and risk assessment. However, behavioral economists have demonstrated that cognitive biases, emotional responses, and social influences significantly affect decision-making, leading to deviations from the predictions of rational models.

Key contributions from behavioral economics, such as heuristics and biases, show how mental shortcuts such as the availability or representativeness heuristic can lead to systematic errors. Investors often overestimate the likelihood of recent events or expect future outcomes to mimic past ones. Biases such as overconfidence, whereby investors overestimate their ability to predict markets, and loss aversion, which gives more weight to avoiding losses than to achieving gains, further complicate decision-making. These behaviors result in suboptimal investment choices, such as holding on to losing stocks or trading too frequently.

Behavioral insights have led to the development of alternative models, such as the behavioral CAPM, which, as explained in chapter 2, incorporates investor biases into the traditional framework. Behavioral finance has also influenced the design of financial products and services, introducing "nudges" to encourage individuals to save more or diversify their portfolios and addressing cognitive biases that can lead to poor financial decisions.

Despite the advances brought about by behavioral economics, rational models remain central to finance because of their simplicity and testability. However, the increasing evidence of market complexities suggests that these models need to be revised or extended to better reflect real-world behavior and market dynamics.[3]

Challenges of Assuming Normality in Financial Returns: Implications for Portfolio and Risk Management

Over the past sixty years, many theoretical and empirical finance models have assumed that financial asset returns follow a normal (Gaussian) distribution. However, most studies since the 1960s have found little evidence supporting this assumption. Instead, empirical research shows that financial return distributions are often heavy-tailed and potentially skewed. The "tails" represent extreme values, and in financial markets, these extreme events—such as crashes and booms—occur more frequently than predicted by a normal distribution. This deviation is a theoretical concern and a practical issue for market participants who rely on models to assess risk. Sharp downturns in equity markets, for example, expose the limitations of traditional risk models, leading to skepticism about the robustness of statistical methods in finance.

Benoit Mandelbrot (1963), who first highlighted the phenomenon of fat tails, rejected normality as a valid model for asset returns and instead proposed stable Paretian distributions. Mandelbrot's findings were later supported by Eugene Fama (1965), who reinforced that financial returns exhibit heavy tails. These early challenges to Gaussian models raised significant concerns in the finance community, with such scholars as Paul Cootner (1964) questioning the validity of much of the econometric work published up to that point. He warned that if stable distributions more accurately described asset returns, much of the past research could be rendered irrelevant.

Economists' and physicists' models and computer simulations have since supported the concept of fat tails in financial markets as they replicate the statistical properties observed in real-world returns. Although simplified, these models provide a structured way to analyze return distributions and highlight the importance of addressing extreme events in financial risk assessments.

Failing to account for these deviations from normality has significant implications for risk management. For example, VaR, a risk measure we discuss earlier, may underestimate tail risks, leading to a false sense of security for investors unprepared for extreme market events. When returns exhibit fat tails, the probability of large losses increases, and models built on normal distribution assumptions, may fail to capture these risks accurately (Cont, 2001). This misjudgment of risk can lead to underhedging in portfolios, exposing investors more to extreme market movements than anticipated.

Advanced Risk Management Models and Techniques

From a risk management perspective, the normality assumption can misguide asset allocation decisions. Traditional asset allocation strategies often use standard deviation as a proxy for risk, if returns cluster around the mean. However, when returns are non-normal, these strategies may fail to diversify risks adequately. For instance, asset classes that appear uncorrelated in normal market conditions may show strong correlations during extreme market stress, further magnifying losses. Portfolio managers, therefore, need to incorporate alternative models that better reflect the fat-tailed, skewed nature of returns. Methods such as extreme value theory, generalized autoregressive conditional heteroskedasticity models, and stress-testing frameworks play crucial roles in capturing tail risks more effectively by focusing on the unique characteristics of extreme market events.

Extreme Value Theory Extreme value theory (EVT) is a branch of statistics specifically developed to model the extreme deviations from the median or mean in a distribution, particularly focusing on the behavior of the tails.[4] Traditional models, such as those based on normal distributions, capture the central tendencies of data and assume that most observations cluster around the mean. However, these models often fail to account for the rare but impactful events that occur in the distribution's tails, making them inadequate for assessing tail risks.

On the other hand, EVT is uniquely suited to analyzing these rare events by concentrating on the extreme values, which often cause severe financial market disruptions. For example, during market crashes or periods of extreme volatility, the assumptions of normal distribution often break down, leading to significant underestimation of risk. EVT provides a more accurate framework for assessing the probability and magnitude of such extreme market movements. By focusing on the distribution's tails, EVT enables portfolio and risk managers to better estimate the likelihood of large, unexpected losses, providing more precise risk limits and stress tests. This allows financial institutions and investors to develop more effective risk management strategies and design portfolios more resilient to extreme market conditions.

In practical application, EVT can assess the risk of extreme downside events, such as portfolio drawdowns or crashes, and guide asset managers in adjusting their positions or hedging strategies to mitigate these risks. It is particularly useful for long-term risk assessment in scenarios where extreme events could have catastrophic consequences for portfolio value.

Generalized Autoregressive Conditional Heteroskedasticity Models Generalized autoregressive conditional heteroskedasticity (GARCH) models offer another powerful tool for understanding tail risks by modeling how volatility evolves over time.[5] Unlike simpler models, which assume constant volatility, GARCH models account for the volatility clustering frequently observed in financial markets, in which similar episodes of heightened market activity often follow periods of high volatility. This clustering reflects that market conditions do not remain stable but exhibit alternating periods of calm and turbulence. By capturing this dynamic behavior, GARCH models provide a more detailed view of volatility than models with constant variance, such as the classic variance-covariance approach.

GARCH models also allow a more robust estimation of future volatility. Since volatility is not static but changes over time based on recent market movements, the ability to predict these fluctuations makes GARCH models especially effective for risk management. For instance, during periods of market stress, GARCH models can forecast an increase in volatility, enabling investors to make informed decisions about their portfolio exposure to risky assets. This is particularly relevant for estimating tail risks, which refer to extreme market events' probability. Such risks are often magnified in volatile conditions, making GARCH models essential for forecasting potential losses during crises.

In terms of practical application, the predictive capabilities of GARCH models can assist investors in refining their portfolio strategies. By incorporating real-time volatility predictions into their decision-making processes, investors can adjust their asset allocations to hedge against anticipated market downturns or capitalize on expected periods of stability. This adaptability enhances the investor's ability to manage portfolio risk in alignment with their risk tolerance and investment horizon. Additionally, GARCH models are instrumental in stress testing and scenario analysis, where investors simulate the impact of extreme market conditions on their portfolios to better prepare for potential tail risks.

Finally, GARCH models contribute to a more comprehensive understanding of the leverage effect, which refers to the tendency of volatility to increase as asset prices decline. This asymmetric behavior, in which negative market shocks lead to higher volatility than positive shocks of the same magnitude, is another aspect of tail risk that GARCH models can capture. Through this enhanced risk assessment, GARCH models enable portfolio and risk managers to manage exposure to extreme events better, improving their ability to preserve capital during market downturns (Cont, 2001).

Stress-Testing Frameworks Stress-testing frameworks take a more direct approach by simulating the impact of extreme market events on a portfolio. Unlike statistical models that rely on assumptions about return distributions, stress tests apply historical or hypothetical scenarios, such as financial crises, interest rate spikes, or sudden geopolitical shocks, to evaluate how a portfolio would perform under extreme conditions (Jorion, 2007). For example, risk managers might assess the potential effects of the GFC or an unexpected surge in inflation to understand how assets would react to similar disruptions in the future. This method allows a tailored examination of vulnerabilities that may not be captured by traditional risk models such as those reliant on the VaR because as noted earlier this metric often assumes normal distributions that fail to account for extreme tail events.

One of the strengths of stress testing is its ability to highlight specific risks that could lead to large losses, particularly during periods of market stress. These tests often include "what if" scenarios that expose weaknesses in diversification strategies, liquidity assumptions, or exposure to leverage, giving risk managers a clear view of where their portfolio might falter. By identifying these potential weak points, stress testing helps managers prepare for worst-case outcomes, providing a clearer understanding of the risks posed by rare but highly disruptive events, such as market crashes or systemic financial contagion.

By regularly applying stress tests, institutions can adjust their risk exposure, enhance capital buffers, or reallocate assets to mitigate the potential impact of market shocks. Ultimately, stress testing helps risk managers assess the robustness of portfolios, make proactive adjustments, and develop strategies to protect against severe losses (Duffie & Singleton, 2003).

MATHEMATICS AS A TOOL

Despite the limitations just noted, mathematics remains an indispensable tool in economics and finance. The power of mathematical models lies in their distillation of complex phenomena into a set of equations that can be analyzed and manipulated to derive insights. For example, the Black-Scholes-Merton model, despite its simplifying assumptions, provided a breakthrough in the pricing of options and other derivatives, enabling the growth of a multitrillion-dollar market for financial products.

However, the effectiveness of mathematical models depends on the accuracy of the assumptions underlying them. In the case of the Black-Scholes-Merton framework, as noted earlier, the assumption of constant volatility and normally distributed returns has been widely criticized for failing to capture the fat tails and volatility clustering observed in real financial markets. Similarly, the CAPM's assumption of a single market factor has been challenged by the development of multifactor models such as the Fama-French three-factor model, which includes size and value factors in addition to market risk (Fama & French, 1993).

One of the key challenges in using mathematical models in finance is the trade-off between simplicity and realism. Simple models, such as the CAPM, are easy to understand and apply, but they may omit important aspects of market behavior. More complex models, such as those based on stochastic differential equations or agent-based simulations, can capture a wider range of phenomena but are often difficult to calibrate and interpret.

As a result, there is a constant tension between the desire for analytical tractability and the need for empirical accuracy.

Mathematics also plays a crucial role in the development of new financial products and markets. Advances in mathematical modeling and computational techniques made possible the creation of MBS, CDOs, and other complex derivatives. These products have allowed financial institutions to manage risk more effectively and to create new sources of revenue. However, they have also introduced new risks and complexities that are not always well understood.

The GFC highlighted the dangers of relying too heavily on mathematical models without fully understanding their limitations. Many of the risk management models used by banks and financial institutions were based on historical data that did not account for the possibility of extreme market events. When these events occurred, the models failed to provide adequate warnings, leading to massive losses and the collapse of major institutions.

The crisis also underscored the importance of model validation and stress testing. Financial institutions now routinely subject their models to a range of scenarios, including worst-case events, to ensure that they are robust under a variety of conditions. This practice has led to the development of more sophisticated models that incorporate elements of behavioral finance, network theory, and other interdisciplinary approaches.

Applications of Stochastic Processes and Monte Carlo Simulation

One of the key developments in mathematical finance has been the application of stochastic processes to model the evolution of asset prices over time. The use of stochastic calculus, particularly Itô calculus, has allowed the development of models that can account for the random nature of price movements and the impact of volatility.

Itô calculus is a branch of mathematics that deals with stochastic processes and provides the tools necessary to model the continuous-time dynamics of financial markets. It has become a fundamental component of modern financial theory, underpinning models such as the Black-Scholes model and the Cox-Ross-Rubinstein binomial model (Cox, Ross, & Rubinstein, 1979).

Another important development has been the use of Monte Carlo simulation techniques to model the behavior of financial assets under different scenarios. Monte Carlo methods involve the use of random sampling to estimate the probability distribution of outcomes in a stochastic system.

These techniques have been particularly useful in the valuation of complex derivatives and in risk management, where they allow for the modeling of a wide range of possible future scenarios.

Monte Carlo simulation has become a standard tool in quantitative finance. It is used to estimate a portfolio's VaR, assess the potential impact of market shocks, and optimize asset allocation. The flexibility and power of Monte Carlo methods make them well-suited for modeling the complexities of financial markets and developing robust risk management strategies.

INTEGRATION WITH ECONOMIC THOUGHT

Integrating mathematical modeling with economic thought is essential for developing more accurate and reliable models of financial markets. Traditional economic theories, such as those based on the efficient market hypothesis and rational expectations, provide a valuable foundation for understanding market behavior. However, these theories must be updated and refined to take into account the complexities and uncertainties of real-world markets.

One approach to integrating mathematical modeling with economic thought entails incorporating insights from behavioral economics into traditional models, as explained in chapter 2. For example, the CAPM can be extended to include behavioral factors, such as overconfidence and loss aversion, to provide a more accurate representation of investor behavior. Similarly, models of market efficiency can be adjusted to account for the impact of psychological biases on price formation.

Another approach is to adopt a more interdisciplinary perspective, drawing on insights from fields such as complexity theory, network theory, and agent-based modeling, as described in chapter 4. These approaches recognize that financial markets are complex, adaptive systems that deterministic models cannot fully capture. These models provide a more realistic representation of how markets evolve over time by incorporating elements of randomness, nonlinearity, and feedback loops.

Integrating mathematical modeling with economic thought also requires a greater emphasis on empirical validation and model testing. Models should be subjected to rigorous testing using historical data and regularly updated to reflect changing market conditions. This continuous validation and refinement process is essential for ensuring that models remain relevant and reliable in a rapidly changing financial environment.

CONFLICTING THEORIES IN ECONOMICS AND FINANCE

The field of economics has long been characterized by a lack of unified theory, with competing schools offering divergent explanations for market behavior and policy outcomes. This section examines how such theoretical pluralism shapes both economic thought and financial practice.

Theoretical Pluralism in Economics

The coexistence of multiple, often conflicting, theories in the field of economics reflects the diversity of approaches to understanding complex economic phenomena. Theoretical pluralism acknowledges that different models and theories may offer valid insights depending on the context in which they are applied. This perspective is particularly relevant in finance, where the dynamics of markets can vary significantly based on factors such as investor behavior, market structure, and regulatory environment.

One of the most prominent examples of theoretical pluralism in economics is the debate between Keynesian and monetarist approaches to macroeconomic policy. Keynesian economics, rooted in John Maynard Keynes's work, emphasizes the role of government intervention in stabilizing the economy, particularly during recessions. Keynesians argue that fiscal and monetary policy can be used to manage aggregate demand and mitigate the effects of economic downturns.

In contrast, monetarist economics, championed by Milton Friedman, emphasizes the importance of controlling the money supply to achieve economic stability. Monetarists argue that inflation is primarily a monetary phenomenon and that maintaining a consistent growth rate in the money supply is the best way to ensure stable prices. This approach is more skeptical of government intervention, advocating for limited fiscal policy and focusing on monetary rules.

Both Keynesian and monetarist theories have influenced economic policy, and their coexistence highlights the complexity of macroeconomic management. In practice, policymakers often draw on elements of both approaches, depending on their specific economic conditions. For example, during the GFC, many governments adopted Keynesian-style stimulus measures to boost demand, while central banks implemented monetarist-style quantitative easing to manage the money supply.

Theoretical pluralism also extends to microeconomics and finance. Traditional models, such as the efficient market hypothesis and rational expectations, assume that markets are efficient and that prices reflect all available information. However, the rise of behavioral economics has challenged these assumptions, proving that markets are often driven by irrational behavior and psychological biases.

Behavioral economics has introduced new theories that explain market anomalies and investor behavior that cannot be accounted for by traditional models. For example, as explained in chapter 2, prospect theory, developed by Daniel Kahneman and Amos Tversky, describes how individuals evaluate potential losses and gains in ways that deviate from rational expectations. This theory has been used to explain phenomena such as the disposition effect, or the greater likelihood that investors will sell winning stocks rather than losing ones, even when doing so is not rational.

The coexistence of these conflicting theories has led to a richer understanding of financial markets, but it has also created challenges for policymakers and financial professionals. The presence of multiple valid theories raises questions about which model to use in each situation and how to reconcile conflicting insights. This is particularly relevant in risk management, where different models may provide different estimates of the same risk. Phoa, Focardi, and Fabozzi (2007) discuss how conflicting economic theories can, in practice, coexist.

Behavioral versus Rational Models

The conflict between traditional rational models and newer behavioral approaches is one of the most significant debates in modern economics and finance. Rational models, such as the efficient market hypothesis and CAPM, assume that market participants are fully rational and that prices reflect all available information. These models have been the foundation of much modern finance, providing the basis for asset pricing, portfolio management, and risk assessment.

However, as explained in more detail in chapter 2, behavioral approaches challenge these assumptions by arguing that investors are not always rational and that markets are inefficient. Behavioral economists have documented numerous examples of cognitive biases, emotional responses, and social influences that affect decision-making in ways that deviate from the predictions of rational models.

One of behavioral economics' key contributions is the identification of heuristics and biases that influence investor behavior. Heuristics are mental shortcuts that individuals use to make decisions more quickly, but they can lead to systematic errors in judgment. For example, the availability heuristic leads individuals to overestimate the likelihood of easily recalled events, such as recent market crashes. The representativeness heuristic leads individuals to assume that future events will resemble past events, even when there is no rational basis for this assumption.

Biases such as overconfidence and loss aversion further complicate decision-making. Overconfidence makes investors overestimate their ability to predict market movements, while loss aversion causes them to place greater weight on avoiding losses than on achieving gains. These biases can lead to suboptimal investment decisions, such as holding on to losing stocks for too long or trading too frequently.

The conflict between rational and behavioral models has significant implications for financial practice. Traditional models, such as the CAPM, assume that investors are rational and that markets are efficient. These models calculate the expected return on an asset based on its risk and form the basis for portfolio optimization and risk management strategies.

However, behavioral models suggest that these assumptions may not hold in practice. If cognitive biases and emotional responses influence investors, prices may deviate from their fundamental values, and markets may become inefficient. This has led to the development of alternative models incorporating behavioral factors, such as the behavioral CAPM, which adjusts the traditional model to account for investor biases.

Behavioral models have also influenced the design of financial products and services. For example, "nudges" are behavioral interventions that encourage individuals to make better financial decisions, such as saving more for retirement or diversifying their investments. These interventions are based on insights from behavioral economics and are designed to address the cognitive biases that lead to suboptimal behavior.

Despite the advances made by behavioral economics, rational models continue to play a central role in finance. This is partly due to their simplicity, elegance, and ability to provide clear and testable predictions. However, the growing body of evidence from behavioral economics suggests that these models may need to be revised or extended to capture real-world markets' complexities better.

Complexity Theory and Systems Thinking

As the limitations of traditional economic models have become increasingly apparent, interest has grown in alternative approaches that embrace the complexity and dynamism of financial markets. As explained in the previous chapter, complexity theory and systems thinking offer new ways of understanding how markets function, emphasizing the interactions between agents, the emergence of collective behavior, and the importance of feedback loops.

Complexity theory views financial markets as complex adaptive systems in which the whole system's behavior cannot be easily predicted from the behavior of individual agents. This perspective challenges the reductionist approach of traditional models, which often focus on individual decision-making in isolation. Instead, complexity theory emphasizes the importance of understanding the network of relationships between agents and how these relationships give rise to emerging phenomena, such as market bubbles and crashes.

One of the key insights of complexity theory is that small changes in one part of the system can lead to significant and unpredictable outcomes elsewhere. This concept, known as the "butterfly effect," suggests that financial markets are susceptible to initial conditions and that seemingly minor events can trigger significant market movements. This has important implications for risk management as it suggests that traditional models, which often assume linear relationships between variables, may underestimate the potential for extreme events.

Systems thinking, closely related to complexity theory, emphasizes the interconnectedness of financial markets and the importance of feedback loops in shaping market behavior. Feedback loops occur when the outcome of a process influences the process itself, either reinforcing or dampening the original effect. Positive feedback loops, in which an initial change leads to further changes in the same direction, can lead to market bubbles or crashes. Negative feedback loops, in which a change in one direction leads to a counteracting force, can stabilize markets.

Applying complexity theory and systems thinking to finance has led to the development of new models and tools for understanding market dynamics. Agent-based modeling, for example, simulates the interactions between individual agents in a market to study how their behavior leads to collective outcomes. These models can capture the nonlinearities and feedback loops characteristic of complex systems, providing a more realistic representation of how markets operate.

Network theory is another tool for studying the interconnectedness of financial markets. By mapping the relationships between financial institutions, assets, and markets, network theory can identify key nodes and connections that may pose systemic risks. For example, the collapse of Lehman Brothers in 2008 highlighted the importance of understanding the network of counterparty relationships in the financial system as the failure of a single institution had widespread implications for the entire market.

THE FUTURE OF MATHEMATICAL MODELING IN FINANCE

As financial markets continue to evolve, the role of mathematical modeling in finance will continue to grow. The development of new models and techniques will allow more accurate and sophisticated analysis of financial markets, helping to manage risk and optimize investment strategies.

One key trend shaping the future of mathematical finance is integrating ML and artificial intelligence (AI) into quantitative models. ML algorithms can analyze large datasets, identify patterns, and make predictions based on historical data. These algorithms can be used to develop models that are more accurate and adaptive than traditional models, particularly in the context of high-frequency trading and algorithmic trading.

Another significant trend is the increasing use of big data in financial modeling. The availability of vast amounts of data from various sources, including social media, market data, and economic indicators, has opened new possibilities for financial analysis. By integrating big data with quantitative models, financial institutions can gain deeper insights into market trends and develop more effective investment strategies.

However, as the use of quantitative models continues to expand, it is essential to recognize their limitations and the potential risks associated with their use. The GFC highlighted the dangers of overreliance on models that do not fully capture the complexities of financial markets. To mitigate these risks, it is essential to develop models that are robust, flexible, and capable of adapting to changing market conditions.

SUMMARY

In this chapter, we described the development and impact of mathematical models in finance. We began by discussing the historical origins of quantitative finance, tracing its roots back to early twentieth-century developments, such as Paul Samuelson's formalization of economic theories using mathematical notation. These early contributions laid the groundwork for developing sophisticated models, such as Harry Markowitz's portfolio theory, the Black-Scholes option pricing model, and the CAPM, revolutionizing portfolio management and asset pricing.

Modern portfolio theory, introduced by Harry Markowitz, and the development of CAPM by William Sharpe in the 1960s were highlighted as major financial breakthroughs. These models help quantify risk and optimize portfolios by assuming rational market behavior and normal distribution of asset returns. However, overreliance on these models, particularly before the GFC, revealed significant limitations, particularly in their assumptions about market efficiency and volatility, which failed to account for extreme market events.

We then shifted to discussing risk management models, including those incorporating VaR and CVaR measures. While the VaR has been widely used, the inability of models based on it to account for tail risks, or the potential for extreme losses, was exposed during the GFC. As a response, the CVaR was developed to focus on losses in worst-case scenarios, providing a more comprehensive view of risk. These developments have been crucial in shaping modern approaches to risk management, particularly in addressing fat-tailed distributions in financial markets.

Behavioral economics challenges traditional rational models. The chapter argues that cognitive biases, such as overconfidence and loss aversion, often lead to market inefficiencies that rational models such as the CAPM fail to account for. Behavioral insights have led to the development of alternative models that incorporate psychological factors, and these models have influenced the design of financial products aimed at addressing irrational investor behavior. While behavioral models are gaining traction, we acknowledge that rational models still hold a central place in finance owing to their simplicity and predictive power.

We then discussed the challenges of assuming normality in financial returns, highlighting that empirical studies since the 1960s have demonstrated the presence of fat tails and volatility clustering in asset returns. Models such as those based on EVT and GARCH were developed to capture better these tail risks, and stress-testing frameworks are used to simulate the impact of extreme market events. These advanced techniques are essential for improving risk assessment accuracy and portfolio management in volatile markets.

In this chapter, we advocated for integrating new economic thinking, such as behavioral economics and complexity theory, into mathematical models to better address modern financial markets' complexities. Combining rigorous mathematical models and insights from behavioral and complexity economics is essential for building more resilient financial systems. By continuously refining these models and incorporating interdisciplinary approaches, finance can better navigate the uncertainties and risks of today's interconnected markets.

6 Emerging Risks and the Future of Quantitative Finance

THE EVOLVING LANDSCAPE OF RISK IN FINANCE

The financial landscape constantly evolves, driven by technological advances, global economic shifts, environmental changes, and geopolitical tensions. These changes have introduced new risks, challenging traditional financial models and risk management practices. These emerging risks are often complex, less understood, and difficult to quantify, making them particularly challenging for financial institutions to manage. However, as discussed in Focardi and Fabozzi (2022), they also present opportunities for innovation in developing new models, strategies, and regulatory frameworks.

In this chapter, we explore some of the most significant emerging risks facing the financial industry today, including cyber risk, climate risk, geopolitical risk, and the risks associated with technological advances. We also discuss how these risks shape the future of quantitative finance and the steps financial institutions and regulators can take to address them.

CYBER RISK

The financial industry's digital transformation has brought significant benefits, such as increased efficiency, improved customer experiences, and the creation of new business models. However, it has also introduced new vulnerabilities, particularly cyber risk. Cyber risk is the potential for financial losses, operational disruptions, or reputational damage resulting from cyberattacks, data breaches, or other digital security threats to emerge.

The Nature of Cyber Risk

Given its reliance on digital infrastructure and the sensitive nature of the data it handles, the financial industry is particularly vulnerable to cyberattacks. These attacks can take various forms, such as distributed denial-of-service (DDoS) attacks, ransomware installation, phishing attempts, and data theft, each with the potential to cause significant harm.

The increasing sophistication of cyberattacks, coupled with the growing interconnectedness of financial systems, means that a successful cyberattack on one institution can have far-reaching consequences, potentially leading to systemic risk. For example, a cyberattack that disrupts the operations of a major financial institution could trigger a chain reaction, affecting counterparties, markets, and even the broader economy.

Quantifying Cyber Risk

One key challenge in managing cyber risk is the difficulty of quantifying it. Unlike traditional financial risks, such as credit or market risk, cyber risk is not easily captured by historical data or traditional risk metrics. This is because of the dynamic nature of cyber threats, the lack of standardized data on cyber incidents, and the difficulty of predicting the behavior of malicious actors.

To address this challenge, financial institutions are increasingly turning to advanced analytics and machine learning (ML) to assess and quantify cyber risk. These approaches involve analyzing large datasets, including threat intelligence assessments, network traffic, and historical incident reports to identify patterns and predict potential vulnerabilities. ML algorithms can be particularly effective in detecting anomalies in network traffic that may indicate a cyberattack in progress.

Scenario analysis and stress testing are also critical tools for quantifying cyber risk. By simulating different types of cyberattacks and assessing their potential impact on the institution's operations and financial position, financial institutions can better understand their exposure to cyber risk and develop strategies to mitigate it. For example, a scenario analysis might simulate a ransomware attack that encrypts critical data, allowing the institution to assess the potential financial losses and the effectiveness of its incident response plan.

Managing Cyber Risk

Managing cyber risk requires a comprehensive and multifaceted approach, including technical defenses, organizational strategies, and regulatory compliance. On the technical side, financial institutions must invest in robust cybersecurity measures, such as firewalls, encryption, multifactor authentication, and intrusion detection systems. These measures are essential for protecting against cyberattacks and ensuring the security of sensitive data.

In addition to technical defenses, financial institutions must also implement organizational strategies for managing cyber risk. These strategies include establishing a strong cybersecurity culture, providing regular employee training, and developing incident response plans. A well-prepared organization is better equipped to detect, respond to, and recover from cyber incidents, minimizing the potential impact on operations and reputation.

Regulatory compliance is another critical aspect of managing cyber risk. Financial regulators worldwide have introduced a range of cybersecurity requirements and guidelines that financial institutions must adhere to. These regulations often require institutions to implement specific cybersecurity measures, conduct regular risk assessments, and report any cyber incidents to the relevant authorities. Compliance with these regulations is essential for maintaining the trust of customers, investors, and regulators.

Case Study: The WannaCry Ransomware Attack

The WannaCry ransomware attack on May 12, 2017, serves as a stark reminder of the potential impact of cyber risk on financial institutions and other critical infrastructure. The attack, which affected over 200,000 computers in over 150 countries, exploited a vulnerability in Microsoft Windows to encrypt data on infected systems and demanded ransom payments in Bitcoin.

The financial impact of WannaCry was significant, with estimates of global losses reaching hundreds of millions of dollars. The attack disrupted operations at several major organizations, including the UK's National Health Service, which was forced to cancel appointments and divert emergency patients.

The WannaCry attack underscored the importance of maintaining up-to-date cybersecurity measures and implementing robust incident response plans for financial institutions. The attack also highlighted the potential for cyber risk to cause widespread disruption across multiple sectors, emphasizing the need for a coordinated and collaborative approach to cybersecurity.

CLIMATE RISK AND ESG INTEGRATION

Climate risk has emerged as one of the most pressing challenges facing the financial industry, with far-reaching implications for investment portfolios, risk management, and regulatory frameworks. Climate risk can be broadly categorized into two types: physical risk and transition risk. Physical risk refers to the direct impact of climate-related events, such as hurricanes, floods, and wildfires, on financial assets and infrastructure. Transition risk refers to the financial impact of the transition to a low-carbon economy, including changes in regulations, market preferences, and technology. Fabozzi, Focardi, Ponta, and others (2022) discuss these new types of risk and suggest that a new conceptual framework is needed to deal with these risks.

Physical Climate Risk

Physical climate risk is becoming increasingly apparent as the frequency and severity of climate-related events continue to rise. These events can cause significant damage to physical assets, disrupt supply chains, and lead to economic losses. For example, hurricanes and floods can damage infrastructure, reduce property values, and disrupt business operations, leading to financial losses for investors and insurers.

Quantifying physical climate risk is challenging as it requires modeling the potential impact of future climate events on specific assets and regions. Traditional risk models, which rely on historical data, may not fully capture climate-related events' increasing frequency and severity. To address this challenge, financial institutions are increasingly turning to climate models and scenario analysis to assess their exposure to physical climate risk.

Based on complex simulations of the Earth's climate system, climate models can provide insights into the potential impact of different climate scenarios on specific regions and assets. By integrating these models with financial data, institutions can assess the potential impact of physical climate risk on their portfolios and develop strategies to mitigate it. For example, an institution might use climate models to assess the risk of flooding in a specific region and adjust its real estate investments accordingly.

Transition Risk

Transition risk reflects the financial challenges created by the global shift toward a low-carbon economy. This transition is driven by regulatory changes, technological advances, and shifting market preferences. For example, governments worldwide are introducing regulations to reduce carbon emissions, such as carbon pricing and emissions trading schemes. At the same time, advances in renewable energy technology and changes in consumer preferences are driving a shift away from fossil fuels.

The transition to a low-carbon economy presents risks and opportunities for financial institutions. On the risk side, institutions with significant exposure to carbon-intensive industries, such as oil and gas, may face financial losses as these industries become less competitive. For example, introducing carbon pricing could increase business costs for these industries, leading to lower profitability and declining asset values.

On the opportunity side, the transition to a low-carbon economy also presents possibilities for investment in renewable energy, energy efficiency, and other sustainable technologies. The transition may benefit financial institutions that can identify and capitalize on these opportunities.

Financial institutions increasingly integrate environmental, social, and governance (ESG) factors into their investment strategies and risk management frameworks to manage transition risk. ESG integration involves assessing investments' environmental and societal impact and incorporating these considerations into investment decision-making. For example, an institution might divest from carbon-intensive industries and increase its investments in renewable energy and energy efficiency.

Perhaps the main transition risk is associated with erroneous industrial policies, that is, the risk of making wrong choices. In Europe, a striking example is the transition to electric cars. The European Union introduced a regulation stating that after 2035, all new cars and vans must be zero-emission vehicles. With current technology, this regulation implies that all cars and vans sold after 2035 must be electric.

This regulation has been severely criticized on many grounds. First, switching to electric cars will increase the demand for electric energy. Realistically, it will be challenging to meet the growing demand for energy with clean energy sources. Nuclear power is the only technology to increase energy production with zero emissions. Nuclear power is not without risk, as demonstrated by major atomic reactor incidents. In addition, the problem of storing waste is not resolved. And creating a network of rechargers that can satisfy the totality of new cars in all conditions is very challenging.

Second, European car manufacturers lament that switching to electric cars has dramatically worsened their competitive position against China. China has better technology for electric cars and much easier access to the rare materials needed to manufacture them. Of course, one might wonder how critical industrial policy decisions were made lightly without the serious participation of the car industry.

Without our entering this highly political debate, the risk of making a wrong decision is perhaps the main true transition risk. The task is daunting. Policymakers must consider a range of political, societal, and technological factors to arrive at a bona fide estimate of the consequences of a technological shift of unprecedented proportions.

Regulatory and Market Responses to Climate Risk

As awareness of climate risk has grown, regulators and market participants have taken steps to address its impact on the financial system. Central banks and financial regulators have begun incorporating climate risk into their supervisory frameworks, recognizing that climate-related risks could threaten financial stability.

For example, the Bank of England has conducted stress tests to assess the resilience of the UK financial system to climate-related risks. These tests entail modeling the impact of various climate scenarios on banks' balance sheets, including scenarios that assume a rapid transition to a low-carbon economy and a more gradual transition.

In addition to regulatory efforts, investors have been demanding greater transparency around the climate-related risks companies face. This has led to the development of disclosure frameworks, such as the Task Force on Climate-related Financial Disclosures (TCFD), which provides guidelines for companies to disclose their exposure to climate risk and the measures they are taking to manage it.

THE RISK RELATED TO THE EXHAUSTION OF NATURAL RESOURCES

In the 1970s the scientific community issued the first warning that the Earth cannot sustain an exponential increase in the use of natural resources. Two reports stand out in particular: *The Limits of Growth,* authored by Dennis Meadows and others (1972) and commissioned by the Club of Rome, and *The Entropy Law and the Economic Process,* by Nicholas Georgescu-Roegen (1971).

The MIT report, *The Limits of Growth,* was based on the model World3 created by a team of sixteen MIT researchers under the direction of Dennis Meadows using system dynamics, a method developed by Jay Forrester (1971). The report concluded that with the increase in population and consumption of natural resources, humankind will face a shortage of food and resources in a few decades.

At the same time, Georgescu-Roegen claimed that economic processes produce an irreversible degradation of resources. Even accepting that the inflow of solar energy permits a decrease in the Earth's entropy, Georgescu-Roegen claimed that there is a fourth law of thermodynamics according to which there is an irreversible degradation of materials. For example, the burning of coal is an irreversible process.

The political and business community ignored all these warnings. In 1987, the World Commission on Environment and Development, presided over by Gro Harlem Brundtland, released the report *Our Common Future.* This report introduced the idea of sustainable development. This term refers to the concept that it is possible to maintain growth with an intelligent and equitable use of resources. *Our Common Future* did not explain in detail how to avoid the exhaustion of natural resources. The term "green growth" later replaced "sustainable development." Green growth means that technology can aid continued growth without exhausting natural resources. Given the severity of the resource problem, many governments started promoting and marginally forcing the circular economy.

The circular economy is an economic system that minimizes waste and makes the most of resources. It contrasts with the traditional linear economy, which follows a "take, make, dispose" model. In a circular economy, products, materials, and resources are reused, repaired, refurbished, or recycled for as long as possible, creating a closed-loop system. This approach reduces environmental impact, conserves natural resources, and promotes sustainability by extending the life cycle of products and minimizing waste generation.

Green Growth, Degrowth, the Circular Economy, and Qualitative Growth

To sustain current growth, humans would need to be able to produce materials from abundant sources with acceptable energy consumption. We do not have the technology to synthesize basic materials from abundant sources on a large scale. Industrial chemical processes synthesize materials for industrial use. However, these processes are often very polluting, consume energy, and require nonabundant components. We do not have the technology for assembling molecules of basic materials.

Although the materials needed for industrial processes may be very abundant in theory, extracting them is becoming increasingly difficult. Extraction processes are often highly polluting and require an increasing amount of energy.

It seems clear that green growth is impossible with current technologies.[1] Therefore, several alternatives to the current growth trend have been proposed. The first and most obvious solution is degrowth. Many forms of degrowth have been proposed. All share the idea that the current trend of material growth is not sustainable. Therefore, material growth objectives must be abandoned and replaced by other objectives.

Some forms of degrowth require that a different concept of well-being replace growth. Proponents of this form of degrowth claim that the inordinate possession of objects is not a source of well-being. Therefore, economies must have the happiness of citizens, not their wealth, as an objective.

The peaceful implementation of full-fledged degrowth seems difficult in the present cultural and social climate. Implementing degrowth requires a highly egalitarian society in which the objective of well-being is widely accepted. Our societies, however, are highly competitive, unequal, and organized around a power structure. As Beckerman (1974) argued, attempting to organize a society without economic growth under current social and political conditions is likely to lead to significant economic and social challenges, including increased poverty and inequality. He was skeptical that a democratic society could successfully plan for zero or negative growth without major cultural and institutional changes, as such a strategy might result in increased hardship for the majority and a disproportionate benefit for elites. While he did not claim that democracy would collapse without growth, he warned of the potential risks and instability that could arise.

The circular economy is a concept often attributed to Kenneth Boulding (1966), who emphasized the need for self-sufficient economic systems to avoid resource waste, comparing the Earth to a spaceship that must rely only on its resources. A later report by Geneviève Reday-Mulvey and Walter Stahel (1977) suggested reducing energy-intensive automation by making better use of manpower and extending product life cycles. The Ellen MacArthur Foundation is actively promoting the circular economy.

The current conceptualization of a circular economy goes well beyond recycling waste. Recycling is not an easy process. Modern artifacts are highly engineered "things," even at the chemical level. Deconstructing products to reuse materials is a complicated and energy-consuming process. The circular economy must be engineered; we cannot dream of applying circularity as an add-on to present economies. Today, circularity entails designing products with a long operational life; that is, they are easily reparable and easy to disassemble at the end of their operational life.

The requirement of long operational life and reparability implies that the rate of innovation must slow. This is precisely the opposite of the current trend toward innovation and change. Transportation must be reduced to a minimum to reduce pollution and energy consumption—in other words, a major cultural and economic change. Not surprisingly, the level of circularity is currently very low. On a global basis, only 7–8% of materials are recovered; the remaining fraction is extracted.

It seems unlikely that the circular economy will be implemented on a large scale in the near future. Major changes are happening in some industrial sectors, such as agriculture, with a trend toward local production and distribution. However, current industrial policies do not truly commit to recycling and reducing material consumption.

The Brundtland Report's concept of "sustainable development" remains an extremely important but elusive objective. It emphasizes that development must meet present needs without compromising the ability of future generations to meet their own, recognizing the limits imposed by finite resources. Our societies must therefore adapt economic development to operate within the constraints of the Earth's physical resources.

The key point is that we need a social and economic system that permits us to set personal objectives and improve ourselves without harming others. Without growth, personal objectives inevitably imply the failure of others. In a growing society, we can all grow, though at different speeds. After satisfying primary needs such as food, shelter, and water, most people's personal objectives are social. People want to improve and to belong.

We need to unlink the concept of growth from using natural resources. We must dematerialize growth. One possibility is to make growth more qualitative and less quantitative. Qualitative growth is based on social consensus. Society must agree on what quality is. Quality can be associated with complexity. In general, products and services of better quality are more complex. But there are purely dematerialized sources of quality: culture, beauty, the relationship with nature, and rules of living. A more integrated treatment of circularity and qualitative growth has recently been proposed in the context of sustainability transitions.[2]

We have witnessed several periods in which society underwent major qualitative overhauls. Ancient Greece is an example of an enormous qualitative improvement. Humans developed a new way of thinking: logic, mathematics, philosophy, physics, and beauty started in Greece. The Renaissance marked another major qualitative leap forward. Simply put, we need a new Renaissance to allow qualitative growth.

Qualitative growth requires a significant overhaul of economic concepts. Economies must embrace fundamental notions from physics and accept that economic theories need abstract terms. The first economic theories were quantitative. The main variables were observables obtained through aggregation: the quantity of crops, food, and so on. Money was still based on gold, although advanced economies were based on transferable credit. Money and credit were the first genuinely abstract concepts introduced in the economy.

After World War II, abstract terms entered more frequently into economic theories. Utility functions, for example, are abstract terms. Still, economics remained biased toward quantity. Despite the increasing variety of rapidly evolving products and services, economic models continued to rely on functions such as the quantity of output and inflation. This was done by making solid assumptions that created idealized economies. Models made unrealistic assumptions, such as assuming that an economy produces one good. An innovative book such as that by Wynn Godley and Marc Lavoie (2007), *Monetary Economics,* assumed that the economy produces uniform "widgets."

Suppose we want to model a qualitative economy. In that case, we would need to adopt the principles of the physical sciences, where theories include abstract terms; respond globally to the empirical testing, consistent with the Duhem-Quine principle, which holds that scientific theories are tested as a whole rather than in isolation, and include observation processes that depend on the theory.

Fabozzi, Focardi, Ponta, and others (2022) and Focardi and Fabozzi (2023) thoroughly discuss the practical and conceptual issues related to the exhaustion of natural resources and possible solutions.

GEOPOLITICAL RISK IN A GLOBALIZED MARKET

Geopolitical risk refers to the potential impact of political events, such as wars, terrorism, trade disputes, and regulatory changes, on financial markets and investment portfolios. In an increasingly interconnected and globalized world, geopolitical risks have become more complex and unpredictable, with far-reaching implications for the financial industry.

The Impact of Geopolitical Risk on Financial Markets

Geopolitical tensions influence markets by triggering volatility, altering capital flows, and disrupting global supply chains. Events such as conflicts, trade disputes, and political instability can rapidly shift investor sentiment and challenge the resilience of financial systems. Understanding these dynamics is essential for developing strategies that mitigate risk and enhance portfolio stability. For example, the outbreak of conflict in a major oil-producing region can produce a spike in oil prices. As another example, trade disputes between major economies can disrupt global trade flows and affect the profitability of multinational corporations.

Quantifying geopolitical risk is challenging as it is inherently uncertain and its consequences are difficult to predict. Traditional risk models, which rely on historical data, may not fully capture the potential impact of geopolitical events on financial markets. To address this challenge, financial institutions are increasingly using scenario analysis and geopolitical risk indices to assess their exposure to geopolitical risk.

Scenario analysis involves simulating the potential impact of different geopolitical events on financial markets and investment portfolios. For example, an institution might simulate the effect of a trade war between the United States and China on global equity markets and assess the potential impact on its portfolio. Geopolitical risk indices, which track the level of geopolitical risk in different regions and sectors, can also provide insight into the potential impact of geopolitical events on financial markets.

Fabozzi (2025a, 2025b) proposes a resilience-based framework that complements traditional risk indices by identifying how institutions may be structurally vulnerable to geopolitical shocks, including disruptions to supply chains, critical infrastructure, and operational continuity.[3]

Managing Geopolitical Risk

Managing geopolitical risk requires strategic planning, scenario analysis, and diversification. Financial institutions must develop strategies to mitigate the potential impact of geopolitical events on their operations and investment portfolios. Such strategies can include diversifying investments across regions and sectors, hedging against specific risks, and developing contingency plans for different geopolitical scenarios.

Diversification is a crucial strategy for managing geopolitical risk as it reduces the potential impact of any single event on the overall portfolio. For example, an institution with significant exposure to a region with high geopolitical risk might diversify its investments into other regions or sectors to reduce its overall risk. Similarly, an institution with significant exposure to a specific commodity, such as oil, might hedge its risk by investing in alternative energy sources.

In addition to diversification, financial institutions can use scenario analysis to assess the potential impact of different geopolitical events on their operations and investment portfolios. By simulating various scenarios, institutions can identify potential vulnerabilities and develop strategies to mitigate them. For example, an institution might establish contingency plans for a sudden increase in oil prices due to a conflict in a major oil-producing region.

Case Study: The Impact of the U.S.-China Trade War

The U.S.-China trade war, which began in 2018, clearly shows how geopolitical risk can affect financial markets and global supply chains. The trade war was characterized by the imposition of tariffs on a wide range of goods traded between the two countries, leading to increased uncertainty and volatility in global markets.

The trade war had significant implications for companies exposed to the U.S. and Chinese markets, particularly those in technology, manufacturing, and agriculture. For example, U.S. technology companies that relied on Chinese components faced disruptions to their supply chains. At the same time, U.S. farmers experienced a decline in demand for their products as a result of retaliatory tariffs imposed by China.

For financial institutions, the trade war highlighted the importance of managing geopolitical risk through diversification and scenario analysis. Institutions heavily exposed to the U.S. and Chinese markets faced significant challenges, while those with more diversified portfolios were better positioned to weather the impact of the trade war.

TECHNOLOGICAL ADVANCES AND THE RISKS OF INNOVATION

Technological advances are transforming the financial industry, leading to new opportunities and challenges. The rise of big data, artificial intelligence (AI), and ML has enabled financial institutions to process vast amounts of information and identify previously undetectable patterns. However, these technological advances also introduce new risks, particularly cyber risk, operational risk, and market disruption.

The Promise and Perils of Big Data and Machine Learning

Big data refers to the vast amounts of data generated and collected daily from various sources, including social media, transaction records, market data, and sensors. The availability of big data has enabled financial institutions to gain deeper insights into market trends, customer behavior, and investment opportunities. ML, which involves using algorithms to analyze big data and identify patterns, has become an essential tool for quantitative finance.

ML algorithms can be used for various applications, including predicting asset prices, optimizing trading strategies, and managing risk. For example, they can be used to analyze historical price data to identify patterns and trends indicating future price movements. Similarly, they can be used to develop trading strategies that adapt to changing market conditions in real time.

While big data and ML offer significant opportunities for financial institutions, they also introduce new risks. One critical risk is the potential for overfitting, in which a model is too closely tailored to the specific data used in its development, leading to poor performance on new or out-of-sample data. Another risk is the potential for biases in the data, which can lead to biased or inaccurate model outputs.

To mitigate these risks, rigorous validation and testing methods, such as cross-validation and out-of-sample testing, must be used to assess the performance of ML models. Additionally, diverse and representative datasets that capture a wide range of market conditions must be used, and potential sources of bias in the data collection and interpretation process must be carefully assessed.

Overconfidence and Fear

The recent success of AI, especially generative AI, has created a climate of overconfidence and fear. Many think that AI has reached the stage of exhibiting superhuman cognitive abilities. Even in decision-making positions, many are fascinated by these capabilities and believe that AI can take on decision-making roles. However, others fear that giving decision-making power to machines will entail fundamental risks for humankind.

The notion of emerging properties is typical of complex systems. Though the idea that a complex system is more than the sum of its parts goes back to Aristotle, it is only with the development of a complex system that emerging properties have become a subject for scientific investigation.

Complex systems exhibit emerging properties in that they exhibit behavior that cannot be explained by the behavior and interaction of their parts. If and, eventually, why this happens is a subject for debate. One explanation is that the chain of deductions needed to explain global behavior is too long, possibly even infinite, to be implementable. Others claim that laws and general principles that describe complex systems are missing. However, there is the possibility that we lack sufficient knowledge.

The notion of emerging properties applies to biological systems. Although biological systems obey physical laws, there are no shared and validated explanations of how life formed and continues to grow. There is also no explanation of how the human brain works, and the relationship of self-consciousness to material structures such as the brain is not known.

AI is not the creation of a thinking machine but an engineering attempt to mimic human behavior. We do not really know how the brain works or how thoughts are related to human behavior. AI tries to mimic cognitive behavior using engineering principles.

It was generally believed that AI could do only what it was programmed to do. For example, an expert system is a collection of rules created by human experts. One expects an expert system to behave according to the rules. Neural networks are universal function approximators, a mathematical concept that is easy to understand.

The scientific community was surprised to discover that some systems, such as large language models (LLMs), were behaving in ways that surprised their creators. This fact raised the possibility that these new extensive AI systems exhibit emerging properties.

The verdict is still open. Many experts suggest suspending judgment. Melanie Mitchell at the Santa Fe Institute suggests we do not know enough about LLMs and human intelligence (Mitchell, 2021).

Despite the cautious opinion of top researchers, the recent development of AI has created an unprecedented level of both enthusiasm and fear. There are many risks associated with these new developments. On one side, overconfidence might lead to dangerous applications, while on the other side, fear might lead to an unjustified rejection of a technology that could be very useful.

Algorithmic and High-Frequency Trading

Algorithmic trading, which involves using computer algorithms to execute trades automatically, has become increasingly prevalent in financial markets. High-frequency trading, a subset of algorithmic trading, consists of executing trades at extremely high speeds, often in milliseconds or microseconds. These trading strategies have been credited with increasing market liquidity and reducing transaction costs, but they have also been associated with increased market volatility and the potential for flash crashes.

One of the critical risks associated with algorithmic and high-frequency trading is the potential for market disruption. For example, in 2010, a flash crash occurred in the U.S. stock market during which prices dropped sharply in seconds before quickly recovering. The crash was triggered by a large sell order in the futures market, which led to a cascade of selling across multiple asset classes. The event highlighted the potential for algorithmic trading to exacerbate market volatility and create systemic risks.

Financial institutions and regulators have implemented various measures, including circuit breakers, to halt trading when prices fall by a certain percentage, and stricter oversight of trading algorithms to manage the risks associated with algorithmic and high-frequency trading. Additionally, financial institutions must develop robust risk management frameworks that account for the potential impact of algorithmic trading on market stability.

Blockchain and Cryptocurrencies

Blockchain technology and cryptocurrencies have emerged as disruptive forces in the financial industry, potentially transforming traditional monetary systems. Blockchain, a decentralized and distributed ledger technology, provides a secure and transparent way to record transactions and verify the ownership of assets. Cryptocurrencies, such as Bitcoin and Ethereum, are digital currencies that operate on blockchain technology and offer an alternative to traditional fiat currencies.

While blockchain and cryptocurrencies offer significant opportunities for innovation, they also introduce new risks and challenges. One key risk is the potential for regulatory uncertainty as governments worldwide grapple with how to regulate these emerging technologies. For example, the regulatory status of cryptocurrencies varies widely from country to country, with some governments embracing them and others banning them outright.

Another risk is the potential for market manipulation and fraud. The relatively unregulated nature of the cryptocurrency market has led to concerns about market manipulation, such as pump-and-dump schemes, where the price of a cryptocurrency is artificially inflated before being sold off. Additionally, the security of cryptocurrency exchanges and wallets has been a significant concern, with several high-profile hacks resulting in the loss of millions of dollars' worth of digital assets.

To manage the risks associated with blockchain and cryptocurrencies, financial institutions must carefully assess their exposure to these emerging technologies and develop strategies to mitigate potential risks. This includes conducting thorough due diligence on cryptocurrency investments, implementing robust security measures to protect digital assets, and staying informed about regulatory developments.

Concerns with Capital Market Technologies

Throughout the history of technological advancements, split outcomes often emerge—each innovation brings about significant benefits but also introduces unintended challenges that complicate its implementation.

A major issue with new capital market technologies is the potential for increased systemic risk, which refers to the possibility of a widespread disruption in the financial system that could have severe economic consequences. Regulators worldwide are particularly concerned that new technologies, especially in trading platforms, may amplify systemic risk. This heightened risk can stem from several factors. First, the interconnectedness of trading platforms across global financial institutions and service providers means that a failure or significant disruption in one entity could trigger a cascade of problems throughout the financial system.

Second, technological advancements have enabled investment banks and fintech companies to introduce complex financial products to the market rapidly. These products are sometimes purchased by investors who do not fully understand their inherent risks, and a collapse in their value could have far-reaching consequences throughout the financial system. Algorithmic trading, including high-frequency trading, can also unintentionally create avenues for market manipulation. For instance, strategies like spoofing—where large buy or sell orders are placed and then quickly canceled—can mislead other market participants about true market conditions. Furthermore, the lack of transparency in algorithmic trading makes it difficult to track the origin of trades, complicating distinguishing legitimate transactions from manipulative ones.

Cyber risk is another significant concern as the increased adoption of digital technologies in financial markets has heightened the vulnerability of financial services firms to cyberattacks. The operational risks associated with new platforms, particularly during their early stages of adoption, can lead to disruptions in trading and substantial financial losses.

SUMMARY

This chapter has discussed the evolution of the financial industry in response to emerging risks, including cyber, climate, and geopolitical risks, and technological advances. These risks are complex and difficult to quantify and pose significant challenges to traditional financial models. However, they also provide opportunities for innovation, particularly in developing new strategies and regulatory frameworks to manage these risks. The chapter described these risks and their impact on the future of quantitative finance.

Cyber risk has become a prominent issue as financial institutions increasingly rely on digital infrastructure. Cyberattacks such as those involving ransomware and data breaches can cause severe financial and operational disruptions. Quantifying cyber risk remains challenging, for traditional financial metrics cannot easily capture the dynamic nature of cyber threats. Instead, financial institutions are turning to advanced analytics, ML, and scenario analysis to assess and manage cyber risk.

The climate risks of interest to financial managers are physical and transition risks, particularly in the integration of ESG factors into financial strategies. Physical risks arise from the increasing frequency of climate-related events, while transition risks stem from the shift to a low-carbon economy. Various regulatory and market responses to climate risks are occurring. It will be increasingly important to use climate models and scenario analysis to quantify these risks and adapt financial portfolios accordingly.

The chapter also explored geopolitical risk and technological advances, focusing on their potential to disrupt financial markets. Geopolitical events such as trade wars or conflicts can have significant financial impacts, leading to market volatility and supply chain disruptions. Technological advances such as ML, blockchain, and high-frequency trading come with both opportunities and risks, particularly in respect to market manipulation, the problem of overfitting, and regulatory uncertainty around these advances. Financial institutions must adapt to these emerging risks through robust risk management frameworks and diversification strategies.

7 Entangling Markets: The Role of Quantum Probability in Financial Systems

THE QUANTUM LEAP IN FINANCIAL PROBABILITY

In chapter 4, we discussed complexity science in financial modeling, which views markets as adaptive, nonlinear systems shaped by feedback loops and emerging behaviors. We now turn to a cutting-edge field that tackles uncertainty on an even deeper level: quantum finance. While complexity science offers valuable insights into the dynamic and interconnected nature of financial markets, rising volatility and unpredictability expose the shortcomings of traditional risk and uncertainty models. This brings us to quantum probability—a framework that goes beyond the limits of classical probability models, capturing the inherent uncertainty and reflexivity of modern financial markets.

Classical financial models often struggle to capture the uncertainty, reflexivity, and complexity of modern markets. This has prompted interest in approaches inspired by quantum theory, particularly quantum probability, which offers new tools for modeling decision-making under uncertainty. By shifting the focus from deterministic predictions to probabilistic frameworks, this chapter explores how quantum concepts can improve our understanding of pricing, risk, and market behavior.

Quantum finance allows us to move beyond traditional stochastic processes and explore new methodologies for pricing derivatives, managing portfolio risk, and understanding market anomalies. By incorporating the principles of superposition and entanglement, quantum finance provides a richer, more flexible framework for handling the uncertainty, feedback loops, and interdependencies that characterize financial markets today.

This chapter delves into the theoretical underpinnings of quantum finance as laid out in the foundational work on quantum probability of Focardi, Fabozzi, and Mazza (2020). We explore how this emerging field reshapes our understanding of risk, price dynamics, and market behavior, building on the complexity science foundation developed earlier while addressing the deeper, probabilistic challenges posed by financial modeling in an increasingly uncertain world. We introduce new ways of thinking about market behavior through quantum probability, offering a mathematically rigorous framework that is practically applicable to real-world financial problems.

SCOPE AND RELEVANCE OF QUANTUM FINANCE

In this chapter, we explore how the principles of quantum probability, initially developed for quantum mechanics, can provide a new framework for understanding and modeling financial markets. Chapter 4 introduced complexity science to model the intricate dynamics of financial systems, emphasizing feedback loops and emerging behavior. Quantum finance builds on this by addressing how uncertainty and self-reflexivity—core aspects of financial markets—can be modeled using a quantum probabilistic approach.

Quantum finance is not about quantum mechanics per se but rather about applying the probability theory derived from quantum mechanics to financial contexts. This approach offers several advantages over the classical probability theory that underpins traditional financial models. Classical probability assumes that uncertainties in the market are simply the result of incomplete information. Quantum probability, by contrast, recognizes that uncertainties are inherent in the market itself and that observing the market—whether through observing trades, evaluating prices, or assessing risks—can change the market.

This framework is beneficial for dealing with phenomena that classical models struggle to explain, such as significant, unexpected market shifts or self-reinforcing price movements. Quantum finance provides a more empirically faithful model for handling extreme events and uncertainty by considering observations and market actions as operators rather than random variables.

In the next section, we discuss the foundational concepts of quantum finance, including the role of self-reflexivity in markets and the need for a new probability theory to account for incompatible observations—a feature unique to quantum probability. This sets the stage for understanding how quantum finance can be applied to option pricing, risk management, and portfolio theory, offering new tools for academics and financial industry practitioners.

THE SCIENTIFIC FRAMEWORK OF QUANTUM FINANCE

The scientific basis for quantum finance stems from the inadequacies of traditional models to fully capture the complexity of financial markets, particularly in times of stress or extreme uncertainty. While classical models rely on assumptions of stationarity and ergodicity, quantum finance abandons these assumptions, replacing them with a dynamic and probabilistic framework.

Classical finance models, such as those built on Kolmogorov's probability theory, assume an objective financial reality (Kolmogorov, 1956). In this framework, financial systems are deterministic, with underlying "true" prices that can be revealed by accumulating market information. However, this assumption fails to account for the impact of human behavior, market self-reflexivity, and the real-world conditions that lead to market anomalies and crises.

Quantum finance entails a paradigm shift by focusing on observations rather than on "states of the world." It accepts that observing the market (such as trades and price movements) has an impact on the market itself, leading to quantization—the concept that financial variables, like prices, behave similarly to quantum particles in a probabilistic system.

One key element of this framework is the application of operators rather than random variables. Operators represent market observables, such as asset prices, under quantum finance. These operators allow the superposition of states—meaning that financial instruments can exist in multiple states of valuation simultaneously until an observation (such as a trade) "collapses" these states into a singular outcome. This reflects that ongoing participant actions constantly evolve and influence financial markets.

Furthermore, quantum probability introduces the notion of incompatible observations. In financial markets, two variables—price and volatility, say—cannot be precisely measured simultaneously without influencing each other. This concept aligns with Heisenberg's uncertainty principle in quantum mechanics, according to which measuring one variable affects the certainty of measurement of another. In finance, this translates to the idea that market participants cannot fully control or predict all outcomes as each decision or observation introduces new uncertainties into the system.

Consequently, quantum finance offers a revolutionary scientific framework that acknowledges modern financial systems' inherent uncertainties and complexities. By moving away from classical models and embracing the intrinsic probabilistic nature of markets, quantum finance provides more accurate tools for pricing, risk management, and understanding market dynamics under uncertainty. This framework aligns with the principles of complexity science and enhances our ability to model and navigate financial markets in a world of uncertainty and constant change.

Observations, Variables, and Operators

In traditional finance, we often think of financial variables—such as prices, interest rates, and returns—as values that can be observed and measured at any time. These values are treated as if they exist independently of the observer, much as physical quantities in classical physics are treated. However, when we apply the principles of quantum finance, we must rethink this approach. In quantum theory, observations are not passive but actively shape the observed system. This reflects a key insight of quantum probability: what we measure and how we measure it can fundamentally alter the outcomes we observe.

In this context, financial variables are no longer just independent, objective values but are better understood as observations. These observations are influenced by the actions of market participants, much as quantum particles behave differently when measured. For example, trading has an impact on market prices, introducing a kind of reflexivity. Market prices are not simply the result of independent forces but are influenced by traders' collective behavior, expectations, and actions.

Quantum finance introduces the idea of operators to represent these observations. Operators are mathematical entities that capture the relationships between different observations, much as in quantum mechanics. Instead of using variables that can take any value, quantum finance uses operators that define the possible outcomes and the probabilities of those outcomes.

Introducing operators provides a more sophisticated way to model financial systems, especially under uncertainty and market reflexivity.

In traditional finance, the concept of incompatible observations rarely appears. However, some quantum finance observations cannot be made simultaneously with complete precision. This is akin to Heisenberg's uncertainty principle, according to which specific pairs of variables, such as position and momentum in physics, cannot be observed together with complete certainty. In financial markets, we see a similar phenomenon when trying to predict future prices and volatility simultaneously; our ability to predict one might limit the accuracy of prediction of the other.

The transition from classical variables to quantum operators represents a fundamental shift in the approach to financial modeling. It allows better capture of the complexities and uncertainties inherent in financial markets by providing new tools for understanding such phenomena as extreme events, price discontinuities, and market volatility.

The Revolutions of Twentieth-Century Physics and Their Impact on Finance

The twentieth century witnessed revolutionary advances in physics that drastically altered our understanding of the universe. These breakthroughs did not just affect the scientific community; they reverberated across numerous disciplines, including economics and finance. Concepts from physics, especially quantum mechanics and relativity, have begun to shape how we understand and model financial systems. As finance grows more complex and interconnected, these once esoteric scientific theories are proving relevant in addressing the uncertainty and complexity that characterize global financial markets.

Relativity: Changing Our Perception of Space and Time In 1905, Albert Einstein published his groundbreaking theory of special relativity, which fundamentally changed how scientists viewed space and time. This theory postulates that time and space are not independent and absolute entities, as previously regarded under Newtonian physics, but rather are interconnected and relative, meaning they can stretch and contract depending on an observer's velocity and gravitational forces. A decade later, Einstein followed up with his general theory of relativity, which described how gravity is not merely a force but a curvature of spacetime that is a function of mass and energy.[1]

This revolutionary view of space and time provides a valuable metaphor for understanding financial systems. In the same way that massive objects warp spacetime, large economic actors—such as multinational corporations, central banks, or entire nations—distort the financial markets around them. These market "curvatures" affect how smaller participants interact, sometimes forcing them to adapt their strategies to the shifting environment.

Relativity also introduces the idea that observers—or, in financial terms, market participants—perceive events differently depending on their perspective. Just as time can appear to move more slowly near a massive object (owing to the warping of spacetime[2]), a financial crisis might look more severe or manageable depending on a market participant's position in the economic landscape. A retail investor might feel the pressure of market movements far more acutely than a large institutional investor whose diversified portfolio can better withstand volatility.

The key takeaway from relativity for finance is that context matters. Market dynamics are not static or uniform but vary according to the "mass" of the players and their position in the system. Just as no two observers in the universe experience space and time identically, no two market participants perceive financial risks and opportunities similarly. This has profound implications for how we model financial systems and evaluate risk.

Quantum Mechanics: Embracing Uncertainty and Superposition If relativity reshaped our understanding of the macroscopic world, quantum mechanics redefined how we view the microscopic world—the domain of atoms and subatomic particles. Quantum mechanics challenged the deterministic view of classical physics, introducing the concept that particles do not have definite positions and velocities until they are observed. This insight gave rise to the Heisenberg uncertainty principle, which states that the more precisely we measure one property (such as a particle's position), the less precisely we can know another property (such as its velocity).[3]

The implications of quantum mechanics are even more radical when we consider superposition, the idea that particles can exist in multiple states simultaneously until they are observed. Schrödinger's famous thought experiment, known as Schrödinger's cat, illustrates this paradox.[4] A cat inside a sealed box with a mechanism that can kill it can be both alive and dead at the same time until someone opens the box and observes its state.

In the context of finance, the principle of superposition can be applied to market uncertainty. Just as a particle exists in a superposition of states, financial assets, such as stocks or options, can be seen as existing in a superposition of potential values. Their true value is revealed only when key information—such as earnings reports or interest rate changes—becomes available, forcing the "observation" of the asset's value.

This insight underscores how markets are not always as deterministic as traditional models suggest. Classical financial theories, such as the efficient market hypothesis, assume that markets are rational and that prices reflect all available information. However, quantum finance, inspired by quantum mechanics, acknowledges that markets can be in a state of flux, with multiple potential outcomes coexisting until critical events collapse the uncertainty into a single reality.

Entanglement: The Interconnectedness of Financial Markets Another fundamental concept in quantum mechanics is entanglement. When two particles become entangled, their properties remain linked, regardless of distance. If the state of one particle is measured, the state of the other is immediately known, even if it is light-years away.[5] This "spooky action at a distance," in Einstein's words, has been demonstrated experimentally and challenges our classical understanding of how information and energy travel.

In financial markets, the concept of entanglement can be likened to the interconnectedness of global economies. In today's world, no market operates in isolation. A shock in one part of the financial system—such as a sudden policy change in the United States or a debt crisis in Europe—can have immediate and far-reaching effects on global markets. Just as entangled particles are linked in ways that defy classical physics, financial markets are linked in ways that defy classical economic models. The 2007–2008 Global Financial Crisis (GFC) is a perfect example of this entanglement: a collapse in the U.S. housing market triggered a worldwide recession.

This interconnectedness also applies to financial products. Derivatives, for example, are financial instruments whose value is derived from the performance of other assets. The performance of a derivative is entangled with the value of its underlying asset, just as the state of one quantum particle is linked to another. The collapse of one asset can pull down the value of derivatives tied to it, just as entanglement can cause instantaneous changes in entangled particles.

The Implications of Quantum Mechanics and Relativity for Financial Models The revolutionary ideas of relativity and quantum mechanics are not just abstract scientific concepts; they offer a new lens through which we can understand financial markets. In classical finance, uncertainty and risk are often treated as aberrations or errors to be minimized. However, the quantum view embraces uncertainty as an inherent and unavoidable system feature.

Traditional financial models struggle to capture the full scope of risks in a world increasingly characterized by volatility and complexity. Quantum finance provides an alternative by offering a more flexible framework that incorporates uncertainty, interconnectedness, and the dynamic nature of market forces. Just as quantum mechanics forces us to rethink the nature of reality, quantum finance encourages us to rethink how we model markets, assess risk, and make investment decisions.

REALISM AND DETERMINISM IN FINANCE THEORY

Traditional finance models often assume that market outcomes are influenced by a range of factors and that, with sufficient information, it is possible to make informed predictions about asset price movements. In these models, determinism refers to the idea that, given a set of inputs—such as interest rates, earnings, or economic growth—analysts can make probabilistic assessments of future asset price paths. However, while markets may respond to external conditions in ways that allow reasonable predictions to be made, the inherent uncertainty and risk mean perfect predictability is impossible.

This framework assumes that human actors (investors, traders, firms) behave in ways that maximize utility, following rational decision-making processes. These classical models, such as the capital asset pricing model (CAPM), assume that the distribution of future prices can be predicted deterministically based on current conditions. However, quantum finance moves beyond this framework by incorporating uncertainty and multiple potential outcomes.

Quantum finance allows for multiple possible outcomes, akin to the multiverse concept in physics, offering a more realistic view of financial risk and returns. This perspective acknowledges that financial markets do not always behave predictably and that outcomes can be influenced by many factors, not all of which are captured by traditional deterministic models.

The Limitations of Realism and Determinism

The deterministic view has limitations, especially in modern, complex financial markets. The assumption that financial markets behave in an entirely predictable manner has been challenged, especially after events like the GFC, during which markets exhibited behavior that deviated sharply from classical prediction models.

One of the key criticisms of realism and determinism in finance is that they tend to oversimplify human behavior. In reality, investors do not always act rationally. Behavioral biases, such as loss aversion, overconfidence, and herding, introduce an element of unpredictability that classical models struggle to account for. Additionally, financial markets are influenced by a web of interconnected factors—politics, technology, social trends, and global economics—which introduce layers of complexity that are difficult to model using deterministic approaches. As explained in chapter 4, complexity in finance refers to the interdependent and nonlinear behavior of financial markets, where multiple factors interact in ways that can lead to unpredictable outcomes.

Emerging Implications for Financial Markets

The movement away from determinism and realism in finance reflects a broader shift toward understanding markets as complex, adaptive systems. Rather than viewing markets as machines that respond predictably to external inputs, quantum finance encourages us to view markets as ecosystems that evolve and adapt based on the actions and decisions of participants.

This shift has profound implications for risk management and investment strategies. Traditional risk models, which rely on historical data and assume that the future will behave like the past, are increasingly being replaced by models that recognize the uncertainty inherent in financial systems. Quantum finance introduces new methods for dealing with this uncertainty, offering tools that better capture the unpredictability and interconnectedness of global markets.

In conclusion, as financial markets become more complex and interconnected, the deterministic models of the past are giving way to new approaches that embrace uncertainty. Quantum finance is one such approach, offering a more flexible and realistic framework for understanding the complexities of global markets. By moving beyond the rigid constraints of realism and determinism, quantum finance opens the door to new possibilities for modeling risk, understanding market dynamics, and making investment decisions in an uncertain world.

QUANTUM PROBABILITIES AND THEIR IMPORTANCE IN FINANCE

Quantum probability theory introduces a different way of thinking about uncertainty, measurement, and outcomes, contrasting with the more familiar classical probability models. While classical probability theory is based on fixed outcomes and a well-defined set of possible events, quantum probability shifts the focus to observations and interactions, significantly affecting how we model financial markets.

Oreste (2011) applies quantum principles and Einstein's theory of relativity to financial markets by interpreting the work of W. D. Gann through the lens of modern physics. Oreste proposes a novel technical analysis framework in which market price behavior, especially for intermediate and long-term trends, can be modeled and forecasted using ideas from quantum physics and relativity.[6]

Lee (2020) offers a comprehensive approach that bridges quantum mechanics, artificial intelligence, and financial forecasting. He introduces original models such as quantum price fields and quantum price-level (QPL) modeling, grounded in quantum field theory, to create new types of financial indicators analogous to traditional support/resistance levels. Lee also explores the application of AI (including chaos theory, fractals, and chaotic neural networks), and discusses the potential of quantum entanglement in forecasting major market events. His "quantum trader system" refers to a multi-agent AI framework that leverages quantum-inspired indicators to improve financial predictions. While similar AI-trading systems exist, these quantum finance tools are distinctive to Lee's research.

Classical versus Quantum Probability

In classical probability theory, the world is assumed to have an objective reality, where events occur with specific probabilities determined by an underlying probability space. This space contains all possible outcomes, and random variables assign probabilities. For example, we might model the likelihood of stock prices moving up or down in classical finance by using historical data or current market conditions.

Quantum probability, by contrast, does not assume a fixed reality of events. Instead, it is concerned with the likelihood of observations rather than predefined outcomes. In this framework, observation plays a crucial role in determining the state of a system. This reflects the underlying principles of quantum mechanics, where particles do not have definite positions or velocities until observed. Similarly, in quantum finance, financial quantities—such as prices—are not fixed but can exist in multiple potential states until they are "observed" through a trade or market event.

Why Quantum Probability Matters in Finance

The concept of quantum probability offers a new way of thinking about uncertainty, randomness, and decision-making in financial markets. Unlike classical probability, which assumes a well-defined structure of outcomes and measurable risks, quantum probability allows multiple potential outcomes to coexist until specific observations or events occur. Chakraborti et al. (2023) include several essays on decision-making in a quantum and complexity framework. This approach has profound implications for how we model financial markets and manage risks in an increasingly complex and interconnected world. Below are several key reasons why quantum probability is critical in modern finance.

Applications in Finance Quantum probability has begun to find applications in areas such as high-frequency trading, where the timing and volume of trades can influence market prices. By using operators and observables instead of random variables, quantum probability offers a more nuanced approach to understanding how trades and market conditions evolve in real time. It is also being explored in options pricing models and risk management, where traditional assumptions about market behavior are often insufficient.

Uncertainty and Nondeterminism One key reason quantum probability is important in finance is its ability to capture uncertainty and nondeterminism in markets better. Traditional financial models often assume that markets behave deterministically or at least probabilistically, but with an assumption of a fixed set of possible outcomes. However, financial markets are highly complex and influenced by numerous, often unpredictable factors. Quantum probability acknowledges that multiple potential outcomes can exist simultaneously, providing a more flexible and realistic way to model markets.

Incompatible Observables In quantum mechanics, some pairs of observables—such as position and momentum—cannot be known simultaneously with absolute precision. This principle, known as Heisenberg's uncertainty principle, has an analogy in finance. Quantum probability allows for this inherent uncertainty and noncommutativity of observables, which classical probability struggles to accommodate.

Market Dynamics and Self-Reflexivity Markets are inherently self-reflexive, meaning that observing or interacting with the market (such as placing trades) influences its behavior. Quantum probability accounts for this by recognizing that the observation can change the system's state. For instance, large trades or sudden influxes of market data can shift prices unpredictably, much as quantum systems change state when observed. Traditional finance models overlook this dynamic interaction between market participants and market outcomes.

Hilbert Spaces and Operators in Finance At the heart of quantum probability is the use of Hilbert spaces and operators to represent financial systems. In classical probability, random variables assign probabilities to outcomes. In quantum probability, observables—such as stock prices—are represented by operators in Hilbert space. The outcome of a financial observation, such as a price or a return, is determined by the eigenvalues of the corresponding operator. This shift from random variables to operators allows modeling quantized outcomes, where financial variables can take on a discrete set of values rather than a continuous range.

EVIDENCE IN FAVOR OF QUANTUM PROBABILITY

Quantum probability, a probabilistic framework derived from quantum mechanics that allows for the coexistence of multiple potential outcomes until a measurement or observation collapses these possibilities into a single result, has emerged as a useful tool for modeling complex systems, where classical probability falls short. Traditional financial models, which rely on classical probability, assume that markets behave predictably according to well-defined rules and that outcomes are either completely knowable or can be assigned fixed probabilities. However, real-world markets do not always conform to this simplicity. Quantum probability, derived from quantum mechanics, offers a framework for more flexible, adaptive models that better capture financial markets' uncertainty, interdependencies, and nonlinear behaviors. Orrell (2022) offers a broad perspective on quantum finance.

Capturing Human Behavior

One of the primary arguments favoring quantum probability in finance is its ability to model human behavior more effectively than classical methods. Cognitive biases, emotions, and incomplete information often influence decision-making in real-world markets. Quantum probability allows the coexistence of multiple potential outcomes, such as when an investor is uncertain about buying, holding, or selling a stock. These conflicting decisions can be modeled simultaneously, reflecting the actual decision-making process of a human under uncertainty. Cognitive biases, emotions, and incomplete information are crucial in decision-making. Quantum probability reflects these subjective influences by modeling uncertainty as overlapping decision states.

In classical finance, investors are assumed to make entirely rational decisions based on all available information. However, this assumption rarely holds in real-world markets, as various subjective factors influence people. Quantum probability incorporates the uncertainty inherent in human behavior by allowing overlapping states of decision-making, which are collapsed into a specific outcome only when an action is taken. In quantum mechanics, a particle exists in multiple states until it is observed. Similarly, in quantum finance, an investor's decisions, such as whether to buy or sell, exist in overlapping states until acted upon.

Addressing Market Volatility

Quantum probability also provides a better framework for dealing with market volatility and the unpredictability of financial crises. Classical models are based on the idea that events in the market follow a linear, predictable pattern. However, financial crises such as the GFC underscore that markets can behave in highly nonlinear and unpredictable ways. Quantum probability allows for superposition, or the simultaneous existence of multiple possible market states, and the eventual market movement becomes clear only after certain conditions are met (such as new economic data being released or unexpected geopolitical events occurring).

This ability to model overlapping potential market outcomes makes quantum probability especially valuable in high-volatility environments with frequent unexpected market shifts. Traditional models tend to underestimate the impact of rare, extreme events. In contrast, quantum probability can more effectively model the range of possible futures, providing a more resilient framework for risk management. Financial crises and market volatility often exhibit nonlinear behavior, which traditional models struggle to capture. Quantum probability allows more flexible modeling of these unpredictable events.

Handling Incompatible Observations

Another advantage of quantum probability is its capacity to deal with incompatible observations, a phenomenon well documented in quantum mechanics. In finance, incompatible observations might be understood as conflicting data or signals about the future of a market or asset. For example, a company's financial performance might indicate strong growth, but external economic indicators, such as a looming recession, might suggest caution. Classical models would struggle to reconcile these conflicting signals in a meaningful way. Quantum probability allows both signals to exist simultaneously until the market forces a decision (or collapse), leading to one outcome dominating.[7]

Predicting Complex Interactions

Markets are highly interconnected, and decisions made by one entity (such as a central bank) can have far-reaching effects across global economies. Classical models often fail to account for these interdependencies comprehensively. Quantum probability, through the concept of entanglement, allows a more accurate modeling of these complex relationships. In quantum mechanics, entangled particles remain linked regardless of distance, and in financial markets, economic events or policies can similarly have immediate global repercussions, no matter where they originate.

Quantum probability's ability to model these interconnected relationships makes it a valuable tool for understanding the ripple effects that one market event can have on the global financial system. For instance, a policy change by the Federal Reserve could immediately affect markets across Asia or Europe, reflecting the entanglement of global economies.

Why Quantum Probability Matters in Finance

The flexibility, adaptability, and holistic nature of quantum probability make it a more realistic model for financial markets, where uncertainty and unpredictability are the norm. By embracing the complexity and multilayered realities of financial systems, quantum probability equips analysts and risk managers with better tools for navigating crises, managing portfolios, and understanding market dynamics. It opens the door to more advanced risk management techniques better suited to deal with such market anomalies as crashes and bubbles and with the rapid spread of financial contagion.

QUANTIZATION AND BINOMIAL MODELS

As explored throughout this chapter, quantum probability offers a framework for addressing financial markets' inherent uncertainty and complexity. Traditional financial models often rely on assumptions that oversimplify the unpredictability of real-world markets, a situation that quantum approaches aim to address. The next step in this progression is to explore how quantization—a fundamental concept from quantum mechanics—can be applied to finance theory. This section examines how the tools of quantum mechanics can be used to reshape core financial models, providing more flexible and nuanced approaches to evaluating market behavior, especially with respect to options pricing.

Quantization of Finance Theory

In physics, quantization refers to transforming classical systems into quantum systems, where values that once were continuous now become discrete.[8] When applied to finance, this idea translates into breaking down complex financial systems into smaller, more manageable components that can be analyzed using quantum methods. This is particularly useful when attempting to model financial markets, which often involve variables that interact in ways too complex for classical models to capture accurately.

By applying quantization to finance theory, we can better explain how discrete events, such as economic reports, earnings announcements, or geopolitical developments, influence markets. These events do not occur continuously but at specific intervals, and their effects on markets can vary dramatically, depending on the timing and nature of the information released. Traditional models often assume that changes happen gradually, but quantization reflects the reality that markets move in response to distinct events as it can capture the steplike behavior of market reactions.

This approach allows market behaviors to be modeled more precisely, especially in environments where information is released in bursts, causing rapid shifts in market sentiment or asset prices. The concept of quantized finance acknowledges that financial systems are not smooth and continuous but are subject to abrupt, discrete changes in response to new data or events.

Binomial Model of Options Pricing One of the most direct applications of quantization in finance is the binomial options pricing model. This model breaks down asset price movement into two possible outcomes: the price goes up or it goes down. This binary outcome reflects the quantized states in quantum mechanics, where multiple possibilities exist until observed.

Chen (2004) introduced a quantum binomial options pricing model. This model is described as a discretized and simpler version of continuous quantum finance models. It is compared to how the Cox-Ross-Rubinstein classical binomial options pricing model relates to the Black-Scholes-Merton model. Chen's work showed that if stocks are assumed to behave according to Maxwell-Boltzmann statistics, the quantum binomial model collapses to the classical binomial model. The quantum binomial model uses concepts from quantum mechanics, such as density matrices and trace operations, to formulate options pricing. Additionally, Chen proposes a quantum model for the binomial market in finance. His paper demonstrates that, in this quantum model, the range of risk-neutral outcomes forms a disk-shaped region within three-dimensional space, and the size of this region depends on the risk-free interest rate.

This model is instrumental in options pricing because it simplifies the process by breaking down time into smaller steps. Potential price movements are calculated at each interval, and the sum of these movements gives a more accurate option valuation. Quantum finance's approach to the binomial model mirrors how quantum systems are broken into discrete states that evolve over time.

This model's strength lies in its simplicity and flexibility. It can be adapted to account for different market conditions, making it a versatile tool for valuing options in various contexts. This model ties directly to the concept of quantization as it mirrors how quantum systems are broken down into discrete states that evolve. In finance, this helps capture the realities of market fluctuations, which are often characterized by abrupt, steplike changes rather than smooth transitions.

Why This Matters in the Broader Context The quantization of finance theory and the binomial model of options pricing are critical extensions of the broader theme in this chapter: the classical models, while helpful, are insufficient to capture the full complexity of modern financial systems. Quantum finance, through quantization, offers tools that better mirror the discrete, nonlinear nature of financial markets. When applied to options pricing, these tools are invaluable because uncertainty and multiple possible outcomes must be modeled precisely.

Incorporating quantization into financial models represents a shift toward acknowledging the limitations of classical deterministic approaches, emphasizing the need for probabilistic and discrete methods that better capture real-world market behaviors.

QUANTUM STOCHASTIC PROCESSES AND THE QUANTUM BLACK-SCHOLES FORMULA

Stochastic processes describe how a system evolves under random influences, and these processes are foundational in classical finance. Quantum finance introduces *quantum stochastic processes,* which extend these ideas by integrating the uncertainty and probabilistic behaviors of quantum mechanics. This shift leads to more robust models, especially in pricing options and derivatives.

Baaquie (2004) elaborates on using path integrals and Hamiltonians in quantum stochastic processes, highlighting how these concepts improve the complexity of financial models, mainly when applied to interest rates and options pricing. The *quantum Black-Scholes formula* extends the classical Black-Scholes model by accounting for market behaviors too complex to be captured by traditional models, making it a valuable tool for managing financial risk.

Quantum Stochastic Processes

Classical stochastic processes assume that future prices evolve continuously and are influenced by random shocks based on known probabilities. In contrast, quantum stochastic processes integrate uncertainty and multiple potential outcomes fundamental to quantum mechanics. Unlike classical systems, where outcomes are predictable given enough information, quantum systems allow for several possible states until a measurement (or decision) is made. For example, financial markets can exhibit multiple potential price paths until an event—such as an earnings report—collapses the outcome into a single price.

The Quantum Black-Scholes Formula

The quantum Black-Scholes formula extends the classical model by using these quantum stochastic processes to account for market behaviors that are too complex or uncertain to capture by traditional models. The classical Black-Scholes formula assumes constant volatility and market conditions, but markets are influenced by various factors that can change unpredictably. Quantum finance introduces the idea that multiple potential volatilities and market states can coexist, which more accurately reflects real-world market fluctuations.

In summary, quantum stochastic processes and the quantum Black-Scholes formula offer a more flexible, sophisticated way of modeling asset prices and managing financial risk, especially in environments where traditional models fall short. By accounting for the inherent uncertainty in markets, these tools can provide deeper insights into options pricing and market dynamics.

QUANTUM OPTIONS PRICING AND QUANTUM ASSET PRICING THEORY

Quantum mechanics provides new avenues for improving how we model and predict financial markets. Traditional models, such the Black-Scholes formula, rely on classical probability theory and deterministic approaches. However, quantum finance introduces more advanced techniques that incorporate the principles of quantum mechanics, offering a more flexible and nuanced framework for pricing options and valuing assets.[9] This section describes two significant advances in quantum finance: options pricing through the Schrödinger equation and options pricing through quantum Itô processes.

Options Pricing Through the Schrödinger Equation

In quantum mechanics, the Schrödinger equation describes how the state of a quantum system evolves. When applied to finance, the same mathematical framework can be used to model the evolution of asset prices and the value of options. The Schrödinger equation takes into account a wave-like behavior of prices, meaning that multiple potential price paths can exist simultaneously until an event, such as a market decision or external factor, collapses the possibilities into a single outcome. As Focardi, Fabozzi, and Mazza (2020) explain, the Schrödinger equation plays a crucial role in modeling the dynamic behavior of financial derivatives, providing a more flexible approach than classical models.

By accounting for fluctuating market conditions, this approach offers a significant advantage over traditional models, such as the Black-Scholes model. While the Black-Scholes model assumes constant volatility, the quantum Schrödinger equation accommodates varying volatilities, which allows more accurate predictions, particularly in turbulent markets.

Options Pricing Through Quantum Itô Processes

Itô calculus is a fundamental tool in stochastic processes and is commonly used in classical finance to model the random movements of asset prices. In quantum finance, this concept is extended through *quantum Itô processes*, which incorporate the probabilistic nature of quantum mechanics into financial modeling. These processes describe how asset prices evolve in a quantum framework, accounting for stochastic noise and quantum systems' probabilistic, nondeterministic behaviors.

Hull (2017) explains that classical Itô processes are essential for modeling price movements in traditional finance, underpinning well-established models like Black-Scholes and the stochastic modeling of asset prices. By contrast, in the emerging field of quantum finance, researchers have explored how quantum Itô processes, which incorporate quantum noise and quantum probability, can model financial market uncertainties that classical models might overlook. These quantum approaches provide alternative perspectives for understanding asset price dynamics, especially in contexts with complex uncertainty or market microstructure effects. However, these quantum models are not discussed in Hull's work, but rather in recent quantum finance research.

Why Quantum Options Pricing Matters

Incorporating quantum mechanics into options pricing models is crucial because it allows a more flexible approach to understanding market dynamics. Traditional models, such as the Black-Scholes model, are limited by their assumptions of constant volatility and smooth price paths (Focardi, Fabozzi, & Mazza, 2020). Quantum models, however, embrace the uncertainty and multiple possible outcomes inherent in financial markets, providing a more accurate representation of how prices evolve over time.

By applying techniques like the Schrödinger equation and quantum Itô processes, quantum finance offers improved tools for managing risk, pricing derivatives, and making investment decisions under uncertainty (Baaquie, 2004). These models take into account the complexity of modern financial markets and offer a pathway to more advanced and adaptive financial strategies.

SUMMARY

This chapter has introduced quantum finance, a revolutionary approach that applies the principles of quantum mechanics to financial modeling. Traditional financial models, such as the efficient market hypothesis, rely on static and objective probabilities. However, as financial markets become increasingly complex, classical models struggle to capture market dynamics accurately. Quantum finance leverages quantum probability, a theory that recognizes the dynamic and subjective nature of probability. This new approach allows better modeling of market uncertainties, reflexivity, and the impact of observation, providing a more flexible and comprehensive framework for understanding financial markets.

The concept of quantum finance is built on the scientific framework of quantum mechanics. It abandons classical finance's deterministic assumptions, which are based on fixed and observable financial variables. Instead, quantum finance views these variables as probabilistic and influenced by observation, much as particles in quantum mechanics are influenced by observation. Quantum finance employs mathematical tools such as operators and density matrices to represent market observables, allowing for the superposition of states, where financial instruments exist in multiple states of valuation until observed. This paradigm shift helps capture modern financial markets' inherent uncertainty and reflexivity.

A key element of quantum finance is the concept of incompatible observations, which aligns with Heisenberg's uncertainty principle in quantum mechanics. In finance, this concept highlights the limitations of predicting multiple market variables, such as price and volatility, with absolute precision. The act of observing one variable can introduce uncertainty in the measurement of another, further emphasizing the complexity of financial systems. This recognition of interconnected uncertainties is a significant departure from traditional models, which assume markets behave predictably when enough information is available.

This chapter also explored how quantum finance can reshape options pricing and risk management strategies. Classical models such as the Black-Scholes formula assume constant volatility and fail to account for extreme market events. Quantum finance introduces quantum stochastic processes that incorporate quantum uncertainty into financial modeling. These processes allow more accurate modeling of asset price evolution, especially in volatile market environments, where traditional models fall short.

Quantum finance not only introduces new mathematical tools but also offers more profound insights into the behavioral dynamics of market participants. The chapter discussed how quantum finance can account for self-reflexivity in markets, where the actions and decisions of market participants influence the market itself. This aligns with the quantum concept of entanglement, in which the state of one particle is linked to another's state, no matter the distance. In financial markets, this interconnectedness is reflected in the global economy, where a shock in one region can have immediate and far-reaching impacts on other markets.

Quantum finance provides a forward-looking framework for understanding modern financial markets by combining insights from relativity and quantum mechanics. Differences in how market participants perceive events, akin to observers in relativity theory, and the concept of superposition, where assets can exist in multiple potential states until key information is revealed, offer a more realistic approach to modeling uncertainty. By embracing these principles, quantum finance moves beyond the limitations of classical models, enabling more accurate pricing, risk management, and portfolio optimization in an increasingly complex and interconnected global economy.

8 Rethinking Economics and Finance Through Complexity and Empirical Approaches

REDEFINING ECONOMIC THOUGHT FOR A COMPLEX WORLD

The global financial system has become more complex and interconnected, influenced by technological advances, evolving market structures, and the interaction of economic forces with human behavior. Traditional economic theories based on rational agents and equilibrium often fall short in capturing modern market realities. These models struggle with nonlinearity, feedback loops, and emergent dynamics that define today's markets. Consequently, there is growing recognition of the need for models grounded in empirical validation, behavioral insights, and a deeper understanding of complexity in financial systems.

In response to these challenges, there has been a growing recognition of the need for a new paradigm in economics and finance that better captures the dynamic, interconnected, and often unpredictable nature of global markets. This paradigm shift calls for a move away from overly simplistic models and toward approaches that embrace the complexity of economic systems, incorporate empirical validation, and take into account the behavioral nuances of market participants.

This chapter explores the evolution of economic and financial thought in light of these developments, offering a critique of traditional models while highlighting the potential of alternative approaches grounded in complexity science and empirical analysis. Through this lens, we seek to understand the limitations of mainstream economic theories, the challenges faced by traditional financial models such as the capital asset pricing model (CAPM), and the importance of developing more robust frameworks to better navigate modern markets' uncertainties.

THE CRITIQUE OF MAINSTREAM ECONOMICS

Mainstream economic theories have long been predicated on assumptions that simplify real-world markets' complexities into more manageable, mathematically tractable forms. These assumptions include rational behavior, utility maximization, and market equilibrium, which have provided the foundation for much of modern economic and financial theory. However, these assumptions often fail to capture the true nature of economic systems, leading to models that, while elegant in their simplicity, are often disconnected from empirical reality.

One of the central criticisms of mainstream economics is its reliance on the concept of the rational agent endowed with rational expectations. According to traditional economic theory, individuals are assumed to have rational expectations, a perfect probabilistic view of the future, and to make decisions by maximizing their utility, based on all available information and with a clear understanding of the risks and rewards involved. While useful for constructing models, this assumption does not align with the observed behavior of individuals in real-world markets. Cognitive biases, emotional responses, and social influences often lead to decisions that deviate significantly from the rational ideal, resulting in market outcomes that traditional models do not easily predict.

The disconnect between theory and reality becomes particularly apparent during periods of economic crisis. The GFC is a prime example: the prevailing economic theories could not adequately explain the widespread failure of financial institutions and markets. Traditional models, which assume that markets are self-correcting and that risk is well distributed, could not account for the systemic risks that had built up in the financial system. This failure highlighted the need for models that could better capture the interconnectedness of global markets and the potential for cascading failures.

Another critique of mainstream economics is its focus on equilibrium as a consequence of rationality and rational expectations. Many traditional models assume that markets naturally tend toward an equilibrium in which supply and demand are balanced and all available information is fully reflected in asset prices. However, this assumption overlooks the dynamic nature of markets and that prices can be influenced by various factors, including investor sentiment, technological change, and regulatory interventions. Markets are often in flux, with prices moving in response to new information, shifting expectations, and external shocks. Therefore, the focus on equilibrium limits traditional models' ability to capture the complexities and instabilities inherent in real-world markets.

GENERAL EQUILIBRIUM MODELS

Let's discuss general equilibrium models to understand better the changes that are needed. The French economist Leon Walras is credited with developing the first general equilibrium model (Walras, 1874). Many prominent economists espoused the idea of economic general equilibrium. The key idea is that supply equals demand at the current market prices in equilibrium. It is assumed that in a free market, market forces keep an economy in equilibrium, so that occasional deviations from equilibrium are immediately corrected. The Kakutani-Brouwer fixed point theorem proves that a general equilibrium exists.[1]

Many economists have criticized the idea of market equilibrium. General equilibrium is a mathematical theorem based on several strong assumptions about the agents that populate markets. In practice, these assumptions are not verified. John Maynard Keynes criticized the notion that market forces keep an economy in equilibrium (Keynes, 1936). Keynes states government intervention is needed to stabilize a free market economy.

Robert E. Lucas's (1976) critique was instrumental in shaping a new notion of dynamic general equilibrium. Lucas claimed that macroeconomics needs a microeconomic foundation. Several economists, including Lucas himself, Thomas Sargent, Finn E. Kydland, and Edward C. Prescott, worked on creating a dynamic general equilibrium model based on Lucas's idea of giving macroeconomics a micro foundation.

Based on John Muth's notion of rational expectations, developed in 1961, these authors progressively developed dynamic stochastic general equilibrium (DSGE) models (Muth, 1961). The idea of dynamic general equilibrium is conceptually simple. Given that agents are endowed with rational expectations, their decisions must be coherent with real economic evolution. DSGEs are stochastic control systems. Agents are generally aggregated into a single representative agent endowed with a utility function. The model maximizes the utility of the representative agent over lifetime consumption.

DSGEs are very far from reality. First, agents do not have rational expectations. Simply put, agents do not know the stochastic processes that describe economic variables in the infinite future. In addition, the Sonnenschein-Mantel-Debreu theorem gives strong arguments against aggregating utility functions of utility-maximizing rational agents. Eric Beinhocker (2007, p. 117) devotes paragraphs to describing a utility-maximizing, rational expectations agent who goes to the market to buy tomatoes and assigns a probability to any other thing he might in the infinite future buy with the same money versus the intuitive or "inductively rational" agent who makes the impulse purchase on the basis of a quick assessment: "Hmmm . . . tomatoes. They look nice and fresh. I kinda feel like salad tonight. Price looks OK." In addition, DSGE is based on a descriptive framework that does not allow representing the evolutionary nature of modern economies. The critical importance of financial systems to real economies is completely lost in the DSGE.

DSGEs are idealizations of economic rationality formulated in a sophisticated mathematical language. For several reasons, these models have become mainstream. They are elegant mathematical theories perfectly in line with the ideology of unconstrained, free markets. Though mathematically difficult to formulate, they are conceptually simple. After the GFC, many economists openly recognized the limitations of these models. However, the DSGE has rapidly regained the favor of academia.

In the 1950s, Herbert Simon proposed the framework of boundedly rational agents as an alternative to rational agents and proposed satisficing as a realistic alternative to economic rationality (Simon, 1957). Simon's agents make decisions based only on a finite set of data, and therefore they make errors. In addition, boundedly rational agents are happy with decisions that are not idealized optimization. Satisficing means making decisions based on heuristics.

It proved very difficult to write parsimonious sets of equations that describe the collective behavior of boundedly rational agents. However, agent-based-modeling (ABM), discussed in chapter 4, is an increasingly important and successful theoretical tool for studying economics. ABM agents are obviously boundedly rational agents, and their decision-making process is based on heuristics more than the formal maximization of a utility function. ABM models are very useful for creating simulations of the real economy. These simulations can be used either to study the statistical properties of economic variables or to create scenarios reflecting stress conditions.

ECONOMETRICS AND LEARNING

In a famous anecdote, Queen Elizabeth II paid a visit to the London School of Economics on November 5, 2008. During this visit, Queen Elizabeth asked the panel of distinguished professors who were hosting her visit why nobody had seen the crisis arrive and why it seemed nobody knew what to do. On July 22, 2009, Professors Tim Besley and Peter Hennessy addressed a letter to the queen responding to her question. The letter, available on the internet, offers several justifications that boil down to the consideration that economic theory is an idealized mathematical theory that fails to consider real-life systemic events of catastrophic proportions, such as the 2007–2008 GFC.

This formal answer recognizes that mainstream models have fundamental shortcomings that are not currently addressed. Therefore it is unsurprising that government agencies, central banks, and large organizations use methods other than mainstream theory to make forecasts. Statistical learning is increasingly used to make forecasts and understand economic relationships.

Supervised and unsupervised learning methods are both used. Supervised methods are based on approximating a sample. Every supervised method is a trade-off between the approximation accuracy and the number of parameters used. In general, by increasing the number of parameters, we can approximate the sample with arbitrary precision, but the model's generalization ability will be reduced. Unsupervised methods try to find a structure in a set of data. The simplest unsupervised algorithm separates a set of points into two classes, optimizing some target function.

Linear regressions tend to approximate a set of points with a linear function. Regression finds a straight line that best approximates a set of points in two dimensions. In two or more dimensions, we try to approximate a set of points with a plane or a hyperplane.

Perhaps the most widely used approach in economics and finance is vector autoregressive (VAR) models. Given a time series, a VAR model regresses data at time t on data at time $t-1$, $t-2$, and so on. The idea of VAR models is to choose a linear model and find an optimal approximation to the data. The number of lags gives the number of parameters. Therefore, we must find the best trade-off between the sample's approximation accuracy and the number of parameters.

Several criteria exist for determining the number of parameters, including the Bayesian information criterion and the Akaike information criterion.

Between 1960 and 1990, Vladimir Vapnik and Alexei Chervonenkis developed a general theory of statistical learning that provides a broader framework for model selection and learning. Vapnik (2000) details this theory.

Neural networks are currently one of the most powerful learning methods, especially deep learning, which uses multiple layers of artificial neurons. Deep learning is also one of the most powerful artificial intelligence (AI) techniques. It is the key technology behind modern image recognition and generative AI forms.

Without delving into the specifics of various methodologies, we would like to raise a key question: Is learning itself a scientific method? Can we trust learning in the same way we trust science? Furthermore, can we assert that models derived from learning are equivalent to scientific theories? The answer is not easy. Scientific theories are the product of human ingenuity and intelligence. There is no constructive method to make scientific discoveries. Scientific theories are hypotheses that result from many people's works. Physics was built progressively over 350 years. The development of modern physics went through several paradigm shifts, and most likely there will be new ones. Physical laws are verified through experiments and observations with very high accuracy. Many experiments have been performed and cross-validated.

In addition, behind physical theories is a strong belief that we are investigating a world that is not going to change. Though David Hume's questions on the possibility of generalization from a finite sample remain open, in practice, physicists believe they are investigating a real world whose fundamental laws are not going to change. If we investigate with learning methods a system that we know will not change, we can apply the general principles of scientific explanation.

However, when we investigate economic, financial, or social phenomena, we are never sure that the object of our investigation is not going to change. On the contrary, in the case of complex adaptive systems, the subject of chapter 4, we know or, better yet, we assume that we are investigating an evolving system. In this case, what we learn is a snapshot of a system that most likely will evolve and change.

The real issue with learning is that we do not know whether the system we are investigating will change. The intuition behind statistical learning is that our samples represent the system's true behavior. We cannot rule out the possibility that our sample is highly unlikely, but in practice, we exclude this possibility. However, when we learn an adaptive system, we know we are learning something that will change. In this case, learning is a local approximation; it is not a theory.

ECONOMICS AS AN EMPIRICAL SCIENCE

The critique of mainstream economics has led to a growing recognition of the importance of empirical validation in economic theories. Unlike the physical sciences, in which theories can be tested through controlled experiments, economics deals with complex, adaptive systems where controlled experiments are often impossible. As a result, economic theories must be tested against real-world data, with models continually refined and adjusted based on empirical observations.

One of the challenges of economics as an empirical science is the difficulty of making accurate predictions. Economic systems are influenced by a wide range of factors, including human behavior, technological change, and political decisions, all of which can introduce significant uncertainty into the system. Traditional economic models, which often rely on a limited set of variables, may struggle to capture the full range of influences on the economy, leading to predictions that are often inaccurate or incomplete.

The limitations of equilibrium-based models become particularly apparent in this context. While equilibrium models can provide useful insights into the behavior of markets under certain conditions, they often fail to capture the dynamic nature of economic systems. In reality, markets are rarely in a state of equilibrium, with prices constantly adjusting in response to new information and changing conditions. This dynamic nature of markets requires models that can account for the complex interactions between different economic variables and the potential for sudden shifts in market conditions.

The shift toward a more empirical approach in economics has led to the development of models that better capture the complexities of real-world markets. These models often incorporate a wider range of variables and rely on more sophisticated statistical techniques to analyze the relationships between different economic factors. By grounding economic theories in empirical observations, these models can provide more accurate predictions and offer a better understanding of the factors driving economic outcomes.

The Notion of Empirical Science

To discuss economics as an empirical science, we should first consider the scientific method. The concept of a method for understanding natural phenomena dates back to Aristotle, who distinguished between inductive and deductive reasoning in his work *Organon*. Inductive reasoning involves generalizing from many facts to a general law, while deduction involves drawing logical inferences from general laws.

For centuries, philosophers refined Aristotle's ideas without fundamentally challenging them. In fact, the scientific method as formulated by Aristotle was celebrated as a major human achievement throughout the Scientific Revolution of the sixteenth through eighteenth centuries. However, David Hume openly criticized Aristotle's inductive method and its many adherents. It is fair to say that Hume laid the foundation for empiricism as we understand it today. In essence, Hume argued that no finite collection of empirical observations can justify a conceptual leap to a generalization.

Hume's critique remains widely discussed and unresolved to this day (Hume, 1739). Empirical science is inherently hypothetical: empirical laws are hypotheses that align with observed phenomena. Several key points should be noted:

1. Any empirical theory is not the sole one that aligns with empirical observations; many potentially infinite theories can explain the same observations.
2. Observations are not purely objective data but are influenced by the theory itself. In modern science, observations are often obtained through measurement devices that depend on the underlying theory.
3. Theories often include abstract terms that are connected to observations through the theory.
4. The Duhem-Quine thesis posits that empirical testing applies to entire theories rather than to individual statements because individual statements can always be made true within the context of the broader theory.
5. As new empirical evidence accumulates, theories must evolve. According to Thomas S. Kuhn, these changes occur not gradually but in significant leaps or paradigm shifts, which alter both theoretical laws and the descriptive framework (Kuhn, 1970). As a result, old and new theories are incommensurable as they are based on fundamentally different observations.

6. The Copenhagen interpretation of quantum mechanics suggests that physics does not describe an objective reality but is merely a set of mathematical rules for describing observations.

Following Hempel and Oppenheim (1948), scientific explanation involves creating parsimonious general theories that represent physical facts through sequences of logical-mathematical deductions. The scientific explanation of empirical facts means that these facts can be deduced from a theory. For example, to understand how the body of a car behaves on the road, we solve the equations of elasticity with the appropriate initial and boundary conditions that describe the vehicle.

Therefore, empirical science is based on both observations and theories. We often encounter statements that refer to "empirical laws," which are collections of observations not explained by a comprehensive theory. In general, empirical laws are later included in the general theory, perhaps in some modified form. If a theory cannot explain many important empirical facts, then it is likely that it needs a paradigm shift.

Reductionism, which claims that all physical phenomena can be explained through deductions from basic laws, has been challenged by the science of complexity. Philip Anderson criticized reductionism and argued that science is inherently hierarchical and stratified (Anderson, 1972).

The above points represent a widely shared view of the scientific method, though not one universally agreed on. Some scientists and philosophers challenge the idea that science only describes observations, arguing that science implies ontological commitments. Some sciences cannot be formulated in axiomatic terms, leaving open the question of scientific explanation. The concept of observation itself is complex, mainly when the observer is human, as observation becomes a conscious act—a process we do not yet fully understand.

Moreover, many argue that scientific explanation is not synonymous with knowledge. They contend that some knowledge is not scientific and cannot be acquired through observation and theoretical formulation. These topics, however, are beyond the scope of this book.

To discuss economics as an empirical science, we must mention econophysics. In 1995, at a conference in Kolkata, India, the physicist Harry Eugene Stanley coined the term *econophysics* to describe efforts by physicists and economists to use methods from physics, mainly statistical physics, to address problems in finance theory. Econophysics has fostered an interdisciplinary approach, applying methods from physics and complexity theory to economics and finance. One of the significant achievements of econophysics has been the explanation of the inverse power law distributions observed in financial quantities.[2]

Finally, it is essential to consider whether econometrics and, more broadly, learning can be regarded as a form of scientific explanation. Econometrics makes assumptions about models and learns the model's parameters. More generally, learning can involve the estimation of parameters and the discovery of the models themselves.

When we learn an econometric or another model, can we claim that we have uncovered a law of nature? The answer is not straightforward because we typically estimate models of evolving economies. We often apply learning methods to only approximately valid models for a limited period. This is not simply the metaphysical issue of generalizing from a finite number of past events but rather the challenge of applying static models to dynamic and ever-changing datasets. If we accept econometrics and learning as legitimate forms of scientific explanation, we must broaden our understanding of what constitutes an explanation.

What Is Needed for Economics to be an Empirical Science

Current economic theory is not inherently empirical. General equilibrium models represent idealized economies that embody the notion of economic rationality, but they do not function as empirical theories. In contrast, econometrics is empirical by nature, based on a process of learning from data. However, the role of econometrics as a form of scientific explanation is open to debate. A critical aspect of econometrics is that it deals with evolving models where the models are hypotheses like those in any scientific discovery process. Yet the parameters of these models are learned from past data, with no guarantee that they will apply to future data as economies are constantly evolving systems.

For economics to become an empirical science in the classical sense, it must adhere to the principles of a global empirical scientific framework. First, it is impossible to separate data from laws. While it might be tempting to think that the future of economics lies in modeling ever-larger datasets of financial and economic information using a mix of learning, causal modeling, and theoretical hypotheses, this view is overly simplistic. Surprisingly, there are very few pure data points in economics. While monetary data can be observed, real data are difficult to capture because modern economies are evolving, complex systems in which products and services are constantly changing. As a result, it is impossible to aggregate basic physical data such as production quantities.

Consequently, many fundamental variables, such as inflation, output, and productivity, are not directly observable. For example, inflation cannot be directly observed in complex, evolving economies. To create a descriptive framework for modern economies, we must use abstract terms and link them to empirical data through observation procedures. As discussed earlier, we must consider observations, variables, and equations simultaneously.

The next point concerns money and its circulation. In modern economies, money plays a crucial role often underappreciated by economic theories. The banking system, a specialized industry, creates money. As Moore (1988) describes, the banking system generates money through a process of transferable credit, essentially a set of numbers stored in bank computers. Rules govern the transfer of money from one bank's client to another's. Money has become completely dematerialized; writing a number on a computer has no physical constraint, as the constraints are built into the banking system. Money is initially created when someone incurs a debt with a bank. Central banks can also create money by purchasing assets representing credit.

The third point concerns the symbolism associated with products and services. Purchasing goods and services is akin to using a language. When we make a purchase, we communicate greatly about our ideas, social status, culture, and willingness to integrate and conform. Both money and symbolism are powerful forces that shape economic dynamics.

Finally, the fourth point addresses the treatment of human behavior and decision-making in the context of an empirical theory, which is discussed in the next subsection.

Self-Referentiality

Individuals are information processors who, among other things, make decisions. Forecasting human decisions is very challenging, possibly even impossible. Aggregating the decision-making processes of groups is not simply a matter of averaging individual decisions; groups have internal dynamics, and their collective decisions are often unpredictable.

Moreover, markets and economies are self-referential, meaning that knowledge about them feeds back into them, influencing their behavior. In 1976, Robert Lucas argued in a famous article that economic agents anticipate the effects of policy changes, rendering these policies ineffective—a concept known as the Lucas critique (Lucas, 1976). He advocated basing macroeconomics on microeconomic foundations.

John Muth (1961) claimed that agents have rational expectations. When rational expectations are combined with Lucas's critique, it suggests that economic processes must be in equilibrium. We arrive at stochastic general equilibrium models by adding agent optimization and making strong assumptions about the aggregation of utility functions.

However, agents do not always have rational expectations; they have cognitive biases and often use heuristics instead of formal optimization. As a result, the economic system may experience crises, and the system does not automatically recover after a crisis. Modeling these complexities is far more challenging than modeling general equilibrium. Various models have been proposed, including one by Steve Keen (2013) based on Richard Goodwin's (1982) model, which effectively exhibits economic crises.

In conclusion, economics has the potential to become an empirical science. However, developing an empirical economic theory that can become a mainstream model will be a significant challenge. An empirical model would require a clear statement of its objectives, which would be difficult to achieve, particularly at the political level.

COMPLEX SYSTEMS IN ECONOMICS AND FINANCIAL MARKETS

As the limitations of traditional economic models have become increasingly apparent, there has been a growing interest in understanding economies as complex adaptive systems. The exploration of complex systems in economics and financial markets represents a significant shift in understanding how these systems operate. Traditional economic models, often based on equilibrium and rational behavior assumptions, have proved inadequate in capturing real-world markets' intricate and dynamic nature. These models typically rely on linear relationships and simplified representations of market behavior, which fail to take into account the complexities observed in actual economic and financial environments.

As explained in chapter 4, complex systems are characterized by a high degree of interconnectedness, nonlinearity, and emerging behavior. These systems consist of numerous interacting components, each of which can influence the behavior of the system as a whole. In economics and finance, this interconnectedness can lead to unpredictable outcomes that traditional models do not easily explain. For instance, a sudden increase in market volatility can trigger a cascade of sell-offs, leading to a sharp decline in asset prices and potentially causing a broader financial crisis. Understanding these dynamics requires a departure from linear models and adopting approaches that embrace the richness and unpredictability inherent in complex systems.

One of the most promising tools for exploring the dynamics of complex financial systems is ABM. Unlike traditional models, which often rely on the assumption of a representative agent, ABMs simulate the interactions between a large number of heterogeneous agents, each with its own unique characteristics, preferences, and decision-making processes. This approach allows the modeling of diverse behaviors and the capture of emerging phenomena such as bubbles, crashes, and contagion. ABM provides a more realistic representation of market dynamics by facilitating the exploration of various market structures and institutional arrangements as well as the modeling of bounded rationality, where agents use heuristics and rules of thumb rather than optimizing based on complete information.

In addition to ABM, network analysis has emerged as a critical tool for studying complex financial systems. Financial markets can be conceptualized as networks of interconnected agents where the relationships between these agents—such as financial institutions, investors, and borrowers—are represented as links in the network. Network analysis examines the structure and dynamics of these relationships, providing insights into systemic risk and the potential for cascading failures. For example, during the GFC, the interconnectedness of global financial markets meant that the failure of one institution could trigger a chain reaction of failures across the system. Network analysis helps identify key nodes within the financial network that are critical for maintaining stability and can be used to develop strategies to enhance the financial system's resilience.

The rise of big data, machine learning, and AI has further expanded the toolkit available for analyzing complex systems in economics and finance. These technologies enable the processing and analysis of vast amounts of data, contributing to the identification of patterns, trends, and anomalies that were previously undetectable. Machine learning (ML) models can adapt to changing market conditions, offering new approaches to risk management, asset pricing, and portfolio optimization. However, using these advanced technologies also presents challenges, such as the risk of overfitting, whereby models are too closely tailored to the specific data used in their development, leading to poor performance on new or out-of-sample data.

COMPLEX SYSTEMS

Behavioral finance has also played a pivotal role in advancing the understanding of complexity in financial markets. By incorporating insights from psychology into economic and financial models, behavioral finance has helped explain many of the anomalies and deviations from rational behavior observed in real-world markets. Concepts such as bounded rationality, where individuals use heuristics to make decisions under uncertainty, challenge the traditional assumption of the rational agent and provide a more accurate representation of decision-making in financial markets. The role of emotions in financial decision-making, as highlighted by behavioral finance, further underscores the importance of understanding the psychological factors that drive market dynamics.

Basically, the study of complex systems in economics and financial markets offers a more nuanced and realistic understanding of market behavior. By moving beyond the limitations of traditional models, which often fail to capture the intricacies of real-world markets, approaches such as ABM, network analysis, ML, and behavioral finance provide valuable tools for analyzing the dynamics of financial systems. These methods enable the exploration of emerging phenomena, the identification of systemic risks, and the development of more robust strategies for managing financial markets. As the financial landscape continues to evolve, the need for models that embrace the complexity of economic systems will become increasingly important, offering new opportunities for research, policy development, and risk management.

Measures of Complexity

Intuition suggests that measuring the level of complexity in a system is essential. However, as discussed in previous sections, any measure of complexity not grounded in a theory of complexity has limited utility. Since there is no general theory of complexity, there is no universally accepted measure.

It's important to note that information is not a reliable measure of complexity. This might seem counterintuitive, as one might naturally assume that a highly complex system would contain a large amount of information. However, Shannon's theory of information is fundamentally a communication theory, not complexity. It shows that the average information produced by a source equals the average length of optimally encoded messages. Consequently, purely random messages carry the highest level of information because they cannot be compressed or encoded in a shorter form.

Similarly, the Kolmogorov-Chaitin theory of algorithmic complexity does not provide a direct measure of complexity. The Kolmogorov-Chaitin measure refers to the shortest program length describing a data stream. A completely random message, for instance, cannot be defined by a program shorter than the message itself, highlighting that algorithmic compressibility is more about the ability to compress data streams than about measuring complexity.

Various measures of complexity have been proposed, particularly in computer science. Ladyman and Wiesner (2020) discuss different approaches to measuring complexity. In economics, a beneficial measure is the Economic Complexity Index, developed by César Hidalgo and Ricardo Hausmann (2009).

THE ROLE OF UNCERTAINTY AND RISKS IN ECONOMICS AND FINANCIAL SYSTEMS

Traditional economic models often assume that individuals make decisions based on a clear understanding of all available information and a rational assessment of the risks and rewards involved. However, individuals usually face significant uncertainty and are limited in processing information and making rational decisions. This concept, known as bounded rationality, challenges the traditional assumption of the rational agent and has important implications for economic theory.

Bounded rationality suggests that individuals use heuristics, or rules of thumb, to make uncertain decisions. These heuristics can lead to systematic biases in decision-making, such as overconfidence, loss aversion, and anchoring, which can significantly affect market outcomes. For example, during periods of market euphoria, overconfidence can lead investors to take on excessive risk, driving up asset prices with the potential formation of bubbles. Conversely, during periods of market panic, loss aversion can lead to a rush to sell assets, exacerbating market declines.

Incorporating uncertainty into economic models is critical for capturing the true nature of decision-making in financial markets. Traditional models often assume that individuals can accurately assess probabilities and make decisions based on expected utility. However, individuals frequently face ambiguity and uncertainty, making it difficult to assess probabilities accurately. This can lead to decision-making that deviates from the predictions of traditional models.

One approach to incorporating uncertainty into economic models is the use of *probability weighting functions,* which capture the tendency of individuals to overweight low-probability events and underweight high-probability events. This approach can help to explain observed behaviors such as the preference for lottery-like investments, where individuals are willing to take on high levels of risk in the hope of achieving a large payoff, despite the low probability of success.

Another approach is the use of robust decision-making frameworks, which focus on developing strategies that perform well across a range of possible scenarios, rather than optimizing for a single expected outcome. This approach acknowledges the inherent uncertainty in economic systems and seeks to develop strategies that are resilient to unexpected events and changes in market conditions.

Uncertainty and Financial Markets

Uncertainty has always been a central theme in finance, influencing decision-making, risk management, and the development of financial models. Traditional financial theories, such as the CAPM and the efficient market hypothesis, have often assumed that markets are fundamentally predictable and that risks can be quantified and managed through diversification and other risk management techniques. However, the real world is far more complex, with uncertainty manifesting in various forms, from market volatility to economic shocks and unforeseen events.

Here we discuss the multifaceted nature of uncertainty in financial markets, the limitations of traditional models in addressing uncertainty, and emerging approaches that seek to better capture and manage financial systems' inherent unpredictability. We delve into the concepts of Knightian uncertainty, risk management frameworks, the role of behavioral finance in understanding uncertainty, and the implications of uncertainty for financial stability and policymaking.

Knightian Uncertainty The distinction between risk and uncertainty, first introduced by economist Frank Knight in his 1921 book, *Risk, Uncertainty, and Profit*, remains a foundational concept in studying financial markets. Knightian risk refers to situations where the probability distribution of outcomes is known, allowing risk to be quantified and managed through techniques such as diversification, insurance, and hedging. In contrast, Knightian uncertainty refers to situations where the probability distribution of outcomes is unknown or unknowable, making it impossible to quantify or predict outcomes accurately.

Knightian uncertainty poses significant challenges to financial decision-making and risk management. Traditional economic models, which often assume risks can be quantified and managed, are ill-equipped to deal with situations of true uncertainty. For example, during the GFC, many risks associated with complex financial instruments, such as mortgage-backed securities and collateralized debt obligations, were not fully understood, leading to widespread uncertainty and market turmoil.

The limitations of traditional models in addressing Knightian uncertainty have led to the development of alternative approaches that seek to better capture the complexities of uncertainty in financial markets. These approaches often involve the use of robust decision-making frameworks that focus on developing strategies that perform well across a range of possible scenarios rather than optimizing for a single expected outcome. By acknowledging the inherent uncertainty in financial markets, these frameworks aim to create more resilient strategies to withstand unexpected shocks and changes in market conditions.

One of the critical insights from Knightian uncertainty is the importance of flexibility and adaptability in financial decision-making. In a world of uncertainty, rigid strategies that rely on precise predictions and assumptions are more likely to fail when faced with unforeseen events. Instead, methods that are flexible, adaptive, and capable of evolving in response to new information and changing conditions are better equipped to navigate the uncertainties of financial markets.

Risk Management in the Face of Uncertainty

Risk management has traditionally been centered on identifying, quantifying, and mitigating risks through various techniques or financial instruments, including diversification, hedging, and financial derivatives. However, the limitations of these traditional approaches have become increasingly apparent in the face of uncertainty, particularly during periods of market stress and economic crises.

The limitations of traditional risk models stem from their reliance on assumptions such as normality, linearity, and stable market conditions. These approaches often struggle to reflect the dynamic and interdependent nature of financial systems, especially under stress. They may fail to account for changing correlations, feedback loops, and path-dependent risks that emerge during market dislocations. As financial systems grow more complex, risk management must shift toward frameworks that recognize nonlinear dynamics, behavioral responses, and the potential for rare but highly disruptive events.

In response to these challenges, there has been a growing emphasis on developing more robust and comprehensive risk management frameworks that can better account for uncertainty. One approach uses stress testing and scenario analysis, which involve simulating a range of potential scenarios, including extreme events, to assess the resilience of financial institutions and portfolios. These techniques recognize that historical data may not always be a reliable guide to future risks and that markets can be subject to sudden and unexpected shocks.

Another critical development in risk management is the increasing use of tail risk management strategies. Tail risks refer to the risks of extreme events that lie in the tails of the probability distribution of outcomes, such as market crashes, natural disasters, or geopolitical crises. These events are often characterized by their low probability but high impact, making them difficult to predict and manage using traditional risk management techniques. Tail risk management strategies seek to protect portfolios from these extreme events using options, derivatives, and other financial instruments that can provide downside protection.

The role of behavioral finance in risk management has also gained attention in recent years. Behavioral finance challenges the traditional assumption that investors are fully rational and that markets are efficient. Instead, it highlights the cognitive biases, emotions, and psychological factors that can influence decision-making and lead to suboptimal outcomes. By incorporating insights from behavioral finance into risk management frameworks, financial institutions can develop strategies that account for the human factors that can drive market behavior and contribute to market volatility.

The Role of Behavioral Finance in Understanding Uncertainty

As explained in chapter 2, behavioral finance has significantly contributed to our understanding of how individuals and markets respond to uncertainty. Traditional financial theories often assume that individuals make decisions based on a rational assessment of risks and rewards, using all available information to maximize utility. However, behavioral finance reveals that cognitive biases, emotions, and social influences often lead to decisions that deviate from the predictions of traditional models.

One of the key insights from behavioral finance is the concept of loss aversion, which refers to the tendency for individuals to be more sensitive to losses than gains. This bias can have a significant impact on decision-making in the face of uncertainty as individuals may be more likely to avoid taking risks, even when the potential rewards outweigh the risks. Loss aversion can also lead to behaviors such as the disposition effect, whereby investors hold on to losing stocks too long in the hope that prices will recover, leading to suboptimal portfolio performance.

Another important concept from behavioral finance is the availability heuristic, which refers to the tendency for individuals to base their judgments on readily available information rather than on a comprehensive analysis of all relevant data. In the context of financial markets, this can lead to an overemphasis on recent events or trends, resulting in an underestimation of the likelihood of rare or extreme events. For example, during periods of market stability, investors may become complacent and underestimate the risks of a market downturn, leading to inadequate preparation for a potential crisis.

Behavioral finance also highlights the role of overconfidence in decision-making. Overconfident investors may overestimate their ability to predict market movements or identify profitable opportunities, leading to excessive trading and risk-taking. This can contribute to market bubbles and crashes as overconfident investors drive prices higher during market exuberance, only to see those prices collapse when reality sets in. Understanding the role of overconfidence in financial markets is critical for developing strategies to mitigate the risks associated with this bias.

The insights from behavioral finance have important implications for risk management and investment strategies in the face of uncertainty. By recognizing the cognitive biases that influence decision-making, financial institutions can develop strategies that help mitigate these biases' impact and improve decision-making in uncertain environments. For example, precommitment strategies that enforce discipline in portfolio management can help investors avoid the emotional pitfalls of loss aversion and overconfidence.

Financial Stability and Policymaking in the Face of Uncertainty

The inherent uncertainty in financial markets has important implications for financial stability and policymaking. Traditional approaches to financial regulation and monetary policy often assume that markets are fundamentally stable and that risks can be managed through appropriate regulatory oversight and intervention. However, financial markets are subject to a wide range of shocks and disruptions, many of which are difficult to predict or control.

The GFC exposed the limitations of traditional regulatory frameworks in maintaining financial stability. The crisis was characterized by major financial institution failures, collapses in international credit markets, and severe economic recessions. In the aftermath of the crisis, there has been a growing recognition of the need for more proactive and adaptive regulatory approaches to better address modern financial systems' uncertainties and complexities.

One of the key challenges in maintaining financial stability is the potential for systemic risk, whereby the failure of one financial institution or market triggers a cascade of failures across the system. Systemic risk is often exacerbated by the interconnectedness of global financial markets because shocks in one part of the system can quickly spread to other parts. Policymakers must therefore develop strategies to monitor and mitigate systemic risk, including identifying systemically important financial institutions (SIFIs) and implementing measures to enhance the financial system's resilience.

Stress testing and scenario analysis have become increasingly important tools for assessing financial institutions' resilience to systemic risk. These techniques involve simulating a range of potential scenarios, including extreme events, to assess the financial system's impact and identify potential vulnerabilities. Stress testing is now a key component of regulatory oversight in many countries, with central banks and regulatory agencies conducting regular stress tests of major financial institutions.

Another important development in financial regulation is the increasing emphasis on macroprudential policy, which focuses on maintaining the financial system's stability, rather than just the stability of individual institutions. Macroprudential policies are designed to address systemic risks and prevent the buildup of vulnerabilities in the financial system. Examples of macroprudential policies include countercyclical capital buffers, which require banks to hold additional capital during periods of credit growth, and limits on loan-to-value ratios for mortgage lending.

Monetary policy also plays a critical role in maintaining financial stability in the face of uncertainty. Central banks have traditionally used interest rates as their primary tool for managing economic growth and inflation. However, in recent years, they have increasingly turned to unconventional monetary policy tools, such as quantitative easing and forward guidance, to address the challenges of low inflation and weak economic growth. These tools involve the central bank purchasing financial assets and communicating future monetary policy intentions to influence market expectations.

The use of unconventional monetary policy tools has raised important questions about these policies' effectiveness and potential risks. For example, a policy of quantitative easing has supported economic recovery and boosted asset prices, but it has also raised concerns about the potential for asset bubbles and increased financial instability. Policymakers must carefully consider the trade-offs involved in using these tools and the potential risks they may pose to financial stability.

Navigating Uncertainty in Financial Markets

The development of alternative approaches to risk management, such as robust decision-making frameworks, stress testing, and tail risk management, represents an important step forward in addressing the challenges of uncertainty. These approaches recognize that financial markets are dynamic and unpredictable, and they emphasize the importance of flexibility, adaptability, and resilience in navigating uncertainty.

CHALLENGES TO TRADITIONAL FINANCIAL MODELS

The limitations of traditional economic models are particularly evident in finance, where models such as the CAPM have long been used to guide investment decisions and assess risk. While these models have provided valuable insights into the behavior of financial markets, they are also based on assumptions that often do not hold in the real world.

The CAPM, for example, assumes that investors are rational, markets are efficient, and asset prices fully reflect all available information. It also assumes that investors can borrow and lend at a risk-free rate and that there are no taxes or transaction costs. While these assumptions simplify the modeling process, they also limit the model's ability to capture the complexities of real-world markets.

One of the key criticisms of the CAPM is its reliance on the concept of beta, which measures the sensitivity of an asset's returns to the returns of the market as a whole. According to the CAPM, an asset's expected return is determined solely by its beta, with higher-beta assets expected to deliver higher returns in compensation for their higher risk. However, empirical evidence has shown that beta alone does not fully explain the variation in asset returns and that other factors, such as size, value, and momentum, also play significant roles.

The limitations of the CAPM have led to the development of multifactor models, such as the Fama-French three-factor model (Fama & French, 1993), five-factor model (Fama & French, 2015), and the model with momentum as formulated by Carhart (1997), the so-called four-factor model, which incorporates additional factors beyond beta to explain asset returns. These models have been more successful in capturing the observed behavior of asset prices, but they also raise questions about the validity of the assumptions underlying traditional financial models.

Another challenge to traditional financial models is their focus on equilibrium. As with traditional economic models, financial models often assume that markets are in a state of equilibrium, with supply and demand balanced and prices fully reflecting all available information. However, markets often are in a state of disequilibrium, with prices moving in response to new information, changing expectations, and external shocks. This dynamic nature of markets requires models that take into account the potential for sudden shifts in market conditions and the emergence of market anomalies.

The need for models predicting tail events and market anomalies has become increasingly apparent after the GFC. Traditional models, which often rely on normal distributions and the assumption of efficient markets, could not predict the extreme events that characterized the crisis, such as the collapse of major financial institutions and the sudden freeze in global credit markets. These events highlighted the need for models to better capture the tail risks and nonlinear dynamics inherent in financial markets.

ALTERNATIVE APPROACHES TO ECONOMIC AND FINANCIAL MODELING

The challenges facing traditional economic and financial models have led to the exploration of alternative approaches that can better capture the complexities and uncertainties of real-world markets. These approaches often draw on insights from complexity science, behavioral finance, and empirical analysis, emphasizing the importance of flexibility and adaptability in modeling economic and financial systems.

One promising approach uses multiagent systems and artificial economies that simulate the interactions between many heterogeneous agents, each with unique characteristics and decision-making processes. These models can capture the emerging behavior that arises from the interactions between agents, such as the formation of bubbles, crashes, and contagion. By allowing for a wide range of behaviors and interactions, multiagent systems provide a more realistic representation of the complexities of economic and financial systems.

Behavioral finance has also played a key role in developing alternative models. By incorporating insights from psychology into economic and financial models, behavioral finance has helped explain many anomalies and deviations from rational behavior observed in real-world markets. For example, models incorporating loss aversion, overconfidence, and other cognitive biases can better explain asset price and investor behavior patterns.

Another significant development has been the increasing emphasis on empirical validation in economic and financial modeling. Rather than relying solely on theoretical assumptions, many researchers and practitioners now focus on testing models against real-world data and refining them based on empirical observations. This approach has led to the development of more robust models that can better capture the complexities of economic and financial systems.

The move toward more empirically grounded and adaptive models represents a significant shift in economic and financial thought. These models recognize that markets are complex, dynamic systems that cannot be fully understood through simplified, equilibrium-based frameworks. Instead, they emphasize the importance of incorporating flexibility, adaptability, and empirical validation to better navigate the uncertainties and complexities of modern markets.

CASE STUDIES AND APPLICATIONS

To illustrate the practical applications of the concepts discussed in this chapter, we next offer several relevant examples.

Uncertainty in Financial Markets

The European Sovereign Debt Crisis: The European sovereign debt crisis, which began in 2009, provides a clear example of the role of uncertainty in financial markets. Concerns about the sustainability of government debt levels in several eurozone countries, including Greece, Ireland, Portugal, and Spain, triggered the crisis. As these concerns grew, investors began to demand higher yields on government bonds, leading to a sharp increase in borrowing costs for these countries.

The Impact of Brexit on Financial Markets: The uncertainty surrounding Brexit was compounded by the lengthy and complex negotiations between the UK and the European Union over the terms of the UK's departure. This uncertainty had a significant impact on business investment, consumer confidence, and financial markets as companies and investors were unsure about the future trading relationship between the UK and the European Union and the potential impact on the UK economy. The Brexit process highlights the challenges of managing risk and uncertainty in a rapidly changing political and economic environment. The uncertainty surrounding Brexit had a marked influence on financial markets, leading to increased volatility and changes in investor behavior. Policymakers and financial institutions had to adapt to this uncertainty and develop strategies to mitigate the risks associated with Brexit.

The COVID-19 Pandemic and Financial Markets: The initial market reaction to the pandemic was panic as investors rushed to sell risky assets and sought safety in government bonds and cash. Central banks and governments around the world responded with a range of policy measures, including interest rate cuts, quantitative easing, and fiscal stimulus, to stabilize financial markets and to support the economy. These measures helped restore confidence and reduce uncertainty, but the pandemic highlighted the challenges of managing risk in the face of an unprecedented global crisis.

The 2007–2008 Global Financial Crisis: This crisis is a stark reminder of the limitations of traditional economic and financial models. The crisis was characterized by the widespread failure of financial institutions and markets, leading to a severe global recession. Conventional models, which rely on assumptions of rational behavior and efficient markets, could not predict or mitigate the crisis. One of the critical factors that contributed to the crisis was the widespread use of complex financial instruments, such as mortgage-backed securities (MBS) and collateralized debt obligations (CDOs), which were priced using traditional models that failed to capture the full extent of the risks. These models often rely on historical data and assumptions of normality, and so could not take into account the extreme tail risks associated with the housing market's collapse. The crisis highlighted the need for models to capture better the interconnectedness of global markets and the potential for systemic risk. In response to the crisis, there has been a growing emphasis on developing models that incorporate the complexities of real-world markets, such as multiagent systems and models that take into account tail risks and nonlinear dynamics.

The Rise of Complexity-Based Models in Risk Management: In the years following the GFC, there has been a growing interest in using complexity-based models in risk management. These models recognize that financial markets are complex adaptive systems in which small changes in one part of the system can lead to large and often unpredictable effects elsewhere. One of the key advantages of complexity-based models is their ability to capture the emerging behavior that arises from interactions between different market participants. For example, these models can simulate the spread of financial contagion, whereby the failure of one institution triggers a cascade of failures across the financial system. By capturing these dynamics, complexity-based models can provide a more realistic assessment of financial institutions' risks. Complexity-based models have led to the development of new risk management strategies to better navigate the uncertainties of modern markets. For example, stress testing and scenario analysis have become increasingly important tools for assessing the resilience of financial institutions to extreme events. These approaches recognize that markets are not always in equilibrium and that sudden shifts in market conditions can have significant and far-reaching consequences.

Applications of Alternative Models in Portfolio Management: The limitations of traditional financial models have also led to the exploration of alternative approaches in portfolio management. One example is using behavioral finance principles to develop more robust investment strategies. By recognizing the impact of cognitive biases on investor behavior, these strategies can be applied to better navigate the complexities of financial markets and deliver more consistent returns. Another example is multifactor models, which incorporate a more comprehensive range of variables beyond traditional measures such as beta. These models recognize that various factors influence asset prices, including size, value, momentum, and volatility. By incorporating these factors into portfolio construction, investment managers can develop more diversified portfolios that can better withstand market shocks. The move toward more adaptive and empirically grounded models has also led to the development of new approaches to portfolio optimization. For example, robust optimization techniques, which account for uncertainty and model risk, have become increasingly popular in constructing investment portfolios. These techniques recognize that traditional optimization models, which rely on precise estimates of expected returns and covariances, may be overly sensitive to estimation errors and can lead to suboptimal portfolios.

SUMMARY

This chapter began by critiquing traditional economic models, particularly those that rely on rational behavior and equilibrium assumptions. While mathematically tractable, these models often fail to capture the complexities of real-world markets, as was evident during the GFC. We argued for a paradigm shift toward models that better account for modern economies' dynamic and interconnected nature, emphasizing the importance of empirical validation and the incorporation of complexity science into economic theory.

We also discussed the need to reconceptualize economics as an empirical science, highlighting the challenges of applying the scientific method to economic systems. Unlike physical sciences, where controlled experiments are possible, economics must rely on real-world data to test theories, making accurate predictions difficult. Traditional equilibrium-based models are inadequate for capturing the true nature of economic systems, which are rarely in equilibrium and are influenced by various variables, including human behavior and technological change.

Furthermore, we explored the concept of complexity in economics and finance, noting that traditional models often overlook complex systems' nonlinear and emerging behavior. The discussion introduced alternative approaches, such as ABM and network analysis, which offer more realistic representations of market dynamics by simulating the interactions of heterogeneous agents and examining the interconnectedness of financial systems. These methods provide valuable tools for understanding systemic risks and developing more resilient financial strategies.

In addition to complexity, we addressed the role of uncertainty in economics and finance, critiquing the limitations of traditional models such as the CAPM that assume market predictability. We explained Knightian uncertainty, which differentiates between risks that can be quantified and those that cannot, and emphasized the need for robust decision-making frameworks that can adapt to various scenarios. We highlighted the contributions of behavioral finance to understanding how cognitive biases and emotional responses influence decision-making under uncertainty.

Finally, we emphasized the importance of developing alternative economic and financial models grounded in empirical evidence capable of capturing real-world markets' complexities. We advocate shifting from overly simplistic models to approaches that embrace global markets' dynamic, interconnected, and often unpredictable nature. This new direction in economic thought holds the potential to provide more accurate predictions and better tools for navigating the uncertainties of modern financial systems.

9 Navigating Financial Innovation: From Data-Driven Decisions to Technological Disruption

INNOVATION AS A CATALYST FOR FINANCIAL EVOLUTION

Financial innovation has always been at the heart of economic progress, driving efficiency, creating new markets, and providing tools for managing risk. In recent decades, the pace of financial innovation has accelerated, fueled by technological advances and the increasing interconnectedness of global markets. This rapid evolution has reshaped the financial landscape, introducing new opportunities and challenges.

The importance of innovation in finance cannot be overstated. Historically, innovations such as financial derivatives, for example, have fundamentally altered how economies function. Today, we are witnessing a new wave of innovation driven by advances in digital technology, artificial intelligence (AI), and interdisciplinary approaches that borrow from fields as diverse as physics, biology, and sociology. However, financial innovation has also played a role in financial instability. For instance, the 2007–2008 Global Financial Crisis (GFC) was partly precipitated by the proliferation of complex financial products, obscuring underlying risks and leading to widespread defaults. This underscores the dual nature of innovation in finance: while it drives progress, it also necessitates careful regulation and risk management.

Central to our discussion is the role of data and technology. Machine learning (ML), AI, and big data analytics are now integral to financial engineering, enabling more precise risk modeling and portfolio management. However, these technologies are surrounded by questions about transparency, ethical use, and the potential for unintended biases.

One of the most pivotal financial innovations in recent history was the development of derivatives in the 1970s. Instruments such as options, futures, and swaps allow investors to hedge against various types of risk, speculate on future price movements, and gain synthetic exposure to different asset classes. These innovations fundamentally transformed financial markets, increasing their efficiency and liquidity while providing new tools for risk management.

To deepen understanding of the role of interdisciplinary approaches in financial innovation, it is essential to consider how concepts from other scientific disciplines have been integrated into financial modeling and analysis. For instance, the field of econophysics, which applies methods from statistical physics to financial markets, has provided valuable insights into market dynamics, particularly in understanding the distribution of asset returns and the clustering of volatility. Similarly, integrating psychological insights into financial models has led to the development of behavioral finance, which better accounts for cognitive biases and emotional influences on investor behavior.

Additionally, the role of mathematical modeling in finance has evolved significantly. As explained in chapter 5, there is a growing recognition of traditional mathematical models' limitations in capturing the full spectrum of market behavior. This has led to incorporating more adaptive and flexible modeling techniques that can better account for financial markets' dynamic and often unpredictable nature.

Moreover, as highlighted by Fabozzi, Focardi, and Jonas (2014) and in chapter 2, integrating behavioral insights into financial models significantly advances our understanding of market behavior. Traditional models that rely solely on rational assumptions have been increasingly supplemented by models that account for cognitive biases and psychological factors, providing a more accurate reflection of how markets operate in practice.

The introduction of interdisciplinary approaches and the ongoing innovation in financial markets underscore the need to reevaluate existing models and theories continuously. Integrating insights from diverse fields will be crucial in developing more robust and resilient financial systems as the financial landscape evolves.

In sum, while financial innovation holds immense potential, it must be guided by strong regulatory frameworks, ethical considerations, and a commitment to social responsibility. The future of finance lies in striking the right balance between embracing new technologies and mitigating the risks they introduce.

THE ROLE OF DATA AND TECHNOLOGY IN FINANCIAL ENGINEERING

Financial engineering has transformed modern finance by creating innovative financial products that have reshaped markets and investment strategies. At the heart of this transformation is the increasing role of data and technology, which has enabled the development of more sophisticated financial instruments, improved risk management practices, and optimized portfolio management.

The evolution of data's role in finance has been transformative, moving from reliance on traditional data sources, such as historical prices and economic indicators, to integrating big data and alternative data. Big data refers to the vast volumes of structured and unstructured data generated from various sources, including social media, satellite imagery, and transactional data. The availability of big data has enabled financial institutions to gain deeper insights into market trends, consumer behavior, and economic conditions, allowing more informed decision-making.

Alternative data, such as social media sentiment, web traffic, and geospatial data, have become increasingly important in modern finance. These nontraditional data sources provide unique perspectives on market dynamics not captured by conventional financial metrics. For example, hedge funds and asset managers use alternative data to identify emerging trends, assess market sentiment, and develop new investment strategies that offer a competitive edge.

The Evolution of Financial Products

The origins of financial engineering can be traced back to the development of derivatives markets in the 1970s. Derivatives such as options, futures, and swaps have transformed financial markets. These instruments allow market participants to hedge against various risks, such as price volatility, interest rate changes, and currency fluctuations. For instance, options give investors the right, but not the obligation, to buy or sell an asset at a predetermined price, providing flexibility in managing potential future risks. On the other hand, futures contracts oblige the parties to transact an asset at a predetermined future date and price, offering a straightforward mechanism for hedging and speculation.

The widespread adoption of these instruments has significantly enhanced market liquidity and efficiency. By enabling the transfer and management of risk, derivatives have become indispensable tools for investors, allowing more precise control over financial exposures and contributing to the overall stability of financial markets.

As technology has advanced, so also have the complexity and variety of financial products. Structured products, hybrid financial instruments combining different asset classes, derivatives, and other financial components, have emerged as a key innovation. Structured products are customized financial instruments that combine various derivatives and other financial assets to create tailored investment solutions. These products are often designed to meet specific investor needs, such as providing principal protection, enhancing yield, or gaining exposure to a particular market or asset class. One common type of structured product is the equity-linked note, which combines a fixed income instrument with an equity option. This structure allows investors to benefit from potential equity market gains while limiting downside risk. However, the complexity of structured products, including the use of leverage and the multiple underlying assets, can make them difficult to value and understand, posing significant risks to less sophisticated investors.

The customization of structured products offers significant benefits in terms of aligning investment strategies with individual risk profiles. However, it also requires rigorous risk management practices and transparent communication to ensure investors fully understand these products' potential risks and rewards.

These products can be tailored to meet specific investment goals, such as providing principal protection, enhancing yield, or gaining exposure to particular markets. However, their complexity has also posed transparency and risk management challenges, particularly during times of market volatility.

Near Money and the Shadow Banking System As we look at the transformative impact of financial innovation on traditional banking and financial markets, it is critical to examine how new systems, such as shadow banking, have emerged to play pivotal roles in liquidity provision and risk management. Shadow banking represents a significant financial innovation, operating outside the regulated framework of traditional banks while performing many similar functions. This evolution has given rise to new forms of "near money"—highly liquid assets that function similarly to traditional money—further expanding the scope of modern financial systems. Here we delve into the role of shadow banking in the creation of near money and its implications for financial stability, offering a deeper understanding of how financial innovation extends beyond conventional banking channels.

The term "shadow banking," introduced by Paul McCulley in 2007, refers to a financial system in which nonbank entities, which are not subject to the same regulations as traditional banks, play a similar role in providing liquidity to the market. This system involves a complex network of participants (McCulley, 2007). According to Pozsar, Ashcraft, and Boesky (2013), shadow banking involves the processes of credit, maturity, and liquidity transformation occurring without direct access to public liquidity or government backstops. These activities are conducted by specialized financial intermediaries known as shadow banks, which operate within a broader network called the shadow banking system.

In a related analysis, Pozsar (2014) identifies four key institutions in the modern financial system responsible for issuing different types of money claims: central banks, commercial banks, dealer banks, and money market funds. Each institution issues a distinct form of money: central banks provide reserves, commercial banks issue deposits, dealers engage in repos (repurchase agreements), and money market funds issue constant net asset value (NAV) shares. A repo is a short-term contract in which a dealer sells a security and agrees to repurchase it later for a higher price, with the difference reflected in the repo rate. Money market funds, composed of safe and highly liquid assets, maintain a stable value and can be sold at face value on demand. Both repos and money market funds, along with other highly liquid assets, are often categorized as near money owing to their liquidity and cashlike characteristics.

The shadow banking system has gained significant importance since the early 2000s. Although it experienced a temporary decline during the GFC, its growth resumed in the following years. Pozsar views the shadow banking system as a critical part of the overall financial structure. However, opinions on its role differ. For instance, Laura Kodres, former division chief for the Global Financial Stability Division at the International Monetary Fund, argues that shadow banking represents one of the key failures of the financial system that contributed to the GFC, as noted in the IMF's Back to Basics series.[1]

Securitization and Structured Products Securitization is a financial process that involves pooling various types of debt—such as mortgages, auto loans, and credit card receivables—and repackaging them into securities that can be sold to investors. These tradable securities allow financial institutions to convert illiquid assets into liquid assets, enhancing liquidity in the financial system.

The key advantage of securitization is that it enables banks and other financial institutions to transfer the risks associated with these debts to investors, freeing up capital for further lending. By selling these securities, banks reduce their exposure to the underlying assets, which can improve their balance sheet and lower their risk profiles.

However, the complexity of securitized products often makes it difficult to fully assess the risks associated with the underlying assets. This was particularly evident during the GFC, when many investors were unaware of the high risk embedded in subprime MBS. Misaligned incentives between originators, who earned fees from issuing loans, and investors, who assumed the risk, led to an excessive buildup of poor-quality loans.

The securitization market has evolved in response to these challenges. Financial innovations, such as blockchain technology, promise greater transparency in securitized products by allowing real-time tracking of underlying assets. This shift could help reduce the opacity that characterized the precrisis era, offering investors a clearer view of the risks they are assuming.

The Transformative Impact of Data and Technology in Financial Engineering

The rapid expansion of data and advances in computational technology have fundamentally reshaped financial engineering. Rather than relying solely on historical prices or limited financial metrics, modern financial institutions now harness large, diverse, and often real-time data to inform decision-making. These resources, ranging from transaction records to alternative sources such as satellite imagery and social media sentiment, enable analysts to identify emerging patterns, design innovative products, and manage risk with greater precision. The transformative impact lies not only in the volume of data but also in the ability to convert raw information into actionable insights, supporting more adaptive and resilient financial strategies.

The Evolution of Data in Finance Historically, financial decision-making relied on relatively limited datasets, primarily from financial statements, economic indicators, and market prices. While these traditional data sources remain essential, the landscape has evolved dramatically with the advent of big data. The volume, velocity, and variety of data available to financial institutions have increased exponentially, providing new opportunities for analysis and insight.

Big data encompasses a wide range of information, from transaction records and customer behavior data to social media activity and sensor data from the internet of things (IoT). The ability to analyze these diverse datasets in real time has transformed financial services, enabling more accurate risk assessment, personalized customer experiences, and more effective fraud detection.

One critical development in using data in finance is the rise of alternative data. Alternative data refers to data from nontraditional sources that provide insights into financial markets and economic activity. Examples include satellite imagery, data from web scraping and credit card transactions, and sentiment analysis of news articles and social media. By integrating alternative and traditional financial data, financial institutions can better understand market trends, consumer behavior, and economic conditions.

The rise of big data has been accompanied by significant advances in data analytics, particularly in ML and AI. These technologies enable the processing and analysis of vast amounts of data, allowing financial institutions to identify patterns, make predictions, and optimize decision-making processes.

Applications of ML in Finance Machine learning, a subset of AI, involves algorithms that learn from data and improve performance over time. In finance, ML is used for various applications, from credit scoring and fraud detection to algorithmic trading and portfolio management. One of the critical strengths of ML is its ability to handle unstructured data, such as text, images, and audio, which accounts for a significant portion of the data generated today. For example, natural language processing, a branch of ML, analyzes text data from news articles, earnings reports, and social media posts, providing insights into market sentiment and company performance. Similarly, image recognition algorithms can analyze satellite imagery, social media photos, and other visual data to detect economic trends and consumer behavior.

ML is transforming modern finance by enabling institutions to process massive data efficiently and adaptively. A key application is fraud detection, where algorithms continuously monitor transaction patterns to identify unusual behavior that may signal fraudulent activity. These systems learn and improve over time, making them increasingly effective at detecting new and evolving forms of fraud. ML also powers algorithmic trading, where models analyze historical price data, news sentiment, and market signals to identify trading opportunities and execute strategies at high speeds, allowing firms to capture short-term market movements that would be difficult to exploit manually. In addition, credit scoring models leverage alternative and nontraditional data to improve predictive accuracy, expanding access to credit while enhancing risk management. Collectively, these applications illustrate how ML and AI can enhance efficiency, accuracy, and profitability across multiple areas of finance.

Blockchain technology, another revolutionary advance, has introduced new possibilities for creating secure and transparent records of financial transactions. In securitization, blockchain can track the ownership and performance of asset-backed securities in real time, reducing the risk of fraud and enhancing investor confidence. Furthermore, the advent of smart contracts—self-executing contracts with the terms of the agreement directly written into code—can automate and streamline complex financial transactions, reducing the need for intermediaries and lowering transaction costs.

Challenges in ML and AI Despite their promise in finance, ML and AI also present several challenges. One of the main challenges is the risk of overfitting, where a model is too closely tailored to the specific data used in its development, leading to poor performance on new or out-of-sample data.

Another challenge is the interpretability of ML models. Many ML algorithms, particularly deep learning models, operate as "black boxes," where the internal workings of the model are not easily understood. This lack of transparency can make it challenging to explain the model's predictions and ensure they are based on sound reasoning.

The increasing reliance on data in finance has brought significant challenges related to data management, privacy, and security. As financial institutions collect and analyze vast amounts of data, they must ensure that these data are stored, processed, and used to protect the privacy and security of individuals and organizations. Data management is a critical aspect of modern finance as accessing and analyzing data in real time is essential for decision-making, risk management, and regulatory compliance.

Data governance is also essential as financial institutions must ensure their data are accurate, consistent, and compliant with regulatory requirements. Doing so entails establishing data governance frameworks that define the roles, responsibilities, and processes for managing data throughout their life cycle.

Data privacy is a growing concern in the financial industry, particularly with the implementation of regulations such as the General Data Protection Regulation in the European Union and the California Consumer Privacy Act in the United States.

Cybersecurity is another challenge in the context of data management in finance. The increasing digitization of financial services has made financial institutions a prime target for cyberattacks, which can result in significant financial losses, reputational damage, and regulatory penalties.

The Future of Data-Driven Finance

As the financial industry evolves, data and advanced analytics will become more central to its operations. Harnessing the power of big data, alternative data, and ML will be key to staying competitive in an increasingly complex and dynamic market environment. One of the key trends shaping the future of data-driven finance is the increasing integration of AI and ML into all aspects of financial operations.

Another significant trend is the growing importance of data collaboration and sharing in the financial industry. As financial institutions recognize the value of data, they are increasingly seeking ways to collaborate and share data with other organizations, including competitors, regulators, and third-party service providers.

Another trend reshaping the financial landscape is the rise of open banking. Open banking refers to sharing financial data, such as transaction histories and account information, with third-party providers through secure application programming interfaces.

The future of data-driven finance will also be shaped by the increasing role of regulation in governing the use of data and technology in financial services. As data become more central to financial operations, regulators are expected to take a more active role in overseeing data practices.

The Central Role of Data in Shaping the Future of Finance

Data have become the lifeblood of modern finance, driving industry decision-making, risk management, and innovation. The exponential growth of data, combined with advances in analytics, ML, and AI, has transformed how financial institutions operate, enabling more accurate insights, personalized services, and efficient operations.

THE RISE OF DIGITAL CURRENCIES AND BLOCKCHAIN TECHNOLOGY

The advent of digital currencies and blockchain technology represents one of the most transformative developments in the financial sector in recent years. Digital currencies, such as Bitcoin, Ethereum, and stablecoins, offer a decentralized alternative to traditional fiat currencies, while blockchain technology provides a secure, transparent, and immutable ledger for recording transactions. Digital currencies, particularly cryptocurrencies such as Bitcoin and Ethereum, have introduced a decentralized approach to money, removing the need for traditional intermediaries such as banks and central governments. This decentralization offers greater security and privacy for users as transactions are verified by a network of nodes using cryptographic techniques rather than by a central authority.[2]

Moreover, digital currencies can disrupt global finance by enabling faster, cheaper, and more transparent cross-border transactions. This is particularly valuable in regions with underdeveloped financial infrastructures and limited access to traditional banking services. By offering an alternative to conventional fiat currencies, digital currencies challenge central banks' monopoly and have sparked discussions on the future of monetary policy in a digitized economy. These innovations can revolutionize the financial system by enabling faster, cheaper, and more efficient transactions, reducing reliance on traditional financial intermediaries, and increasing access to financial services for underserved populations.

The Evolution of Digital Currencies

Digital currencies have rapidly evolved since the launch of Bitcoin in 2009. Initially viewed with skepticism by many in the traditional financial sector, digital currencies have gained widespread adoption and recognition as a legitimate asset class. This shift has been driven by several factors, including the increasing digitization of the global economy, the growing mistrust of traditional financial institutions following the GFC, and the desire for more efficient and inclusive financial systems.

To further explore the evolution of digital currencies, it is essential to consider how advances in technology have shaped their development. As Fabozzi, Focardi, and Jonas (2010) note, the rise of digital currencies was closely linked to advances in cryptography, distributed computing, and the internet. These technologies have created secure, decentralized networks that make possible peer-to-peer transactions without intermediaries. Moreover, adopting blockchain technology has provided a robust foundation for digital currencies, ensuring the integrity and security of transactions while enabling transparency and reducing the risk of fraud.

Blockchain Technology: The Backbone of Digital Currencies

Blockchain technology is the underlying infrastructure that supports most digital currencies. At the heart of blockchain technology is the concept of a distributed ledger, where all transactions are recorded across multiple nodes in a network. Each transaction is grouped into a block and linked to the previous block, forming an immutable chain of records. This structure ensures that once a transaction is added to the blockchain, it cannot be altered or deleted, providing high security and trust.

The decentralized nature of blockchain means that no single entity controls the entire network, reducing the risk of centralized failures or malicious attacks. This is particularly important in digital currencies, where the security and integrity of transactions are paramount. Additionally, blockchain's transparency allows real-time verification of transactions, further enhancing trust among users.

The implications of blockchain technology extend well beyond the realm of digital currencies. Blockchain can disrupt various industries, from finance to supply chain management, by enabling decentralized, transparent, and secure systems. For example, as highlighted in Focardi, Fabozzi, and Mazza (2020), blockchain technology is being explored for its potential to revolutionize the trading of financial instruments, including options and derivatives. By automating the execution of contracts through smart contracts, blockchain can reduce the need for intermediaries, lower transaction costs, and increase market efficiency. Additionally, blockchain's ability to create immutable records of transactions provides a powerful tool for combating fraud and ensuring compliance with regulatory requirements.

The Impact of Digital Currencies on Global Finance

Digital currencies have the potential to significantly affect global finance by challenging the traditional roles of central banks, financial institutions, and payment systems. As more individuals and businesses adopt digital currencies, the demand for traditional fiat currencies could decrease, potentially undermining central banks' ability to control the money supply and influence economic conditions through interest rate adjustments.

Moreover, the rise of digital currencies has sparked interest in central bank digital currencies (CBDCs), or digital currencies central banks create to retain control over monetary policy in a digital economy. CBDCs could provide digital currencies' efficiency and financial inclusion benefits while maintaining traditional fiat currencies' stability and regulatory oversight. This development could lead to a hybrid financial system in which decentralized cryptocurrencies and state-controlled digital currencies coexist, each serving different purposes in the global economy.

However, the rise of digital currencies also challenges the existing financial system. These developments raise concerns about monetary policy effectiveness and overall financial stability.

It is worth noting that unlike traditional currencies, digital currencies challenge the foundations of how money is created and trusted. Digital currencies differ fundamentally from traditional, credit-based money, which is created without direct profit to the issuer. By contrast, most digital currencies are issued for the benefit of their creators, even if governed by technological protocols. Because money ultimately relies on trust, this profit-driven model may hinder the broad adoption of digital currencies.

To address these challenges, some central banks are exploring the possibility of issuing their own digital currencies, CBDCs. As discussed in

Focardi and Fabozzi (2010), CBDCs could provide the benefits of digital currencies—such as increased efficiency and financial inclusion—while maintaining the stability and control offered by traditional central banking systems. The introduction of CBDCs could also help central banks retain their monetary policy tools in a digital economy, ensuring they could effectively manage inflation, unemployment, and economic growth.

Regulatory Challenges and the Path Forward

The rise of digital currencies has exposed significant regulatory challenges, as their decentralized nature complicates the enforcement of traditional financial regulations. Different jurisdictions have taken varying approaches, from outright bans to the development of comprehensive regulatory frameworks to foster innovation while protecting consumers.

A key challenge is the potential for regulatory arbitrage, where activities migrate to jurisdictions with less stringent regulations, increasing the risk of financial instability. This lack of global coordination highlights the growing need for international cooperation to harmonize regulatory standards across borders.

Moreover, the decentralized nature of digital currencies complicates enforcing regulations and monitoring financial crimes such as money laundering and terrorist financing. Regulatory bodies must balance the need to protect consumers and maintain financial stability with the desire to foster innovation. Doing so may require creating new regulatory frameworks that address the unique characteristics of digital currencies while ensuring that they do not stifle the growth and adoption of these technologies.

The future of digital currencies will likely depend on the ability of regulators, policymakers, and industry participants to collaborate on developing standards and best practices that ensure the stability, security, and inclusivity of digital currency systems. As these standards take hold, the continuing evolution of digital currencies and blockchain technology will shape the financial landscape, presenting both opportunities and challenges for market participants worldwide.

ETHICS IN THE AGE OF FINANCIAL INNOVATION

As financial innovation continues to evolve with the adoption of digital currencies and blockchain technologies, it is crucial to consider the ethical challenges these advances bring. The increasing reliance on AI, ML, and decentralized finance (DeFi) has revolutionized the industry and raised significant concerns about fairness, transparency, and accountability. To navigate these challenges, we must examine the ethical implications of these innovations and their broader social impacts.

This section discusses the ethical and social implications of technological advances in finance. We examine the potential risks and benefits of AI and ML, the ethical challenges associated with algorithmic decision-making, the social impact of digital currencies and DeFi, and the role of financial institutions in promoting ethical behavior and corporate social responsibility. We also discuss the importance of developing ethical guidelines and frameworks to ensure that technological innovations in finance align with societal values and contribute to the common good.[3]

The Ethical Challenges of AI and ML in Finance

AI and ML are at the forefront of technological innovation in finance, driving significant improvements in risk management, fraud detection, and customer service. However, using AI and ML also presents several ethical challenges that must be carefully considered.

One of the primary ethical concerns associated with AI and ML is the potential for bias in algorithmic decision-making. Because AI algorithms are trained on large datasets, and if these datasets contain biases—whether related to race, gender, socioeconomic status, or other factors—the algorithms may learn and perpetuate these biases. This could lead to unfair outcomes, such as discriminatory lending practices or biased credit scoring models that disadvantage certain groups. For example, suppose an ML model is trained on historical lending data that reflect past discriminatory practices. In that case, the model may continue to recommend higher interest rates or deny loans to individuals from marginalized communities, even if they are creditworthy. This raises important questions about fairness and the responsibility of financial institutions to ensure that their AI systems are designed and implemented in ways that do not perpetuate existing inequalities.

Another ethical challenge is the lack of transparency and interpretability in many AI and ML models and the intense learning techniques. These models often operate as black boxes, meaning their internal decision-making processes are not easily understood or explained. This lack of transparency can make it difficult for financial institutions to justify their decisions to regulators, customers, and other stakeholders, undermining trust in the financial system.

To address these challenges, there is a growing movement toward "explainable AI," which seeks to develop AI models that are both accurate and interpretable. Explainable AI aims to provide clear and understandable explanations for how AI models arrive at decisions, thereby promoting greater transparency and accountability. This is particularly important in finance, where decisions can have significant financial and social consequences.

Additionally, using AI and ML in finance raises concerns about the potential for job displacement and the broader impact on employment. As financial institutions increasingly automate tasks previously performed by humans, there is a risk that specific jobs may become obsolete, leading to unemployment and economic inequality. While AI and automation can create new opportunities and improve efficiency, it is essential to consider the social implications and develop strategies for supporting workers affected by these changes.

Social Impact of Digital Currencies and Decentralized Finance

Digital currencies and DeFi are among the most disruptive innovations in the financial industry. As just noted, they offer new possibilities for financial inclusion, cross-border transactions, and the democratization of financial services. However, these technologies also raise important ethical and social questions, particularly regarding access, equity, and the potential for financial exclusion.

One of the key promises of digital currencies is their potential to expand access to financial services, particularly in regions where traditional banking infrastructure is limited or nonexistent. Digital currencies can enable individuals in developing countries to participate in the global economy, access savings and credit, and make secure and low-cost payments. These abilities could reduce poverty and promote economic development, particularly for the unbanked and underbanked populations.

However, adopting digital currencies also presents challenges related to financial exclusion. While digital currencies offer new opportunities for financial inclusion, they may also exacerbate existing inequalities, mainly if access to the necessary technology, such as smartphones and the internet, is limited. Additionally, the volatility of certain digital currencies, such as Bitcoin, can pose risks to individuals, who may not fully understand the implications of using these assets for everyday transactions or savings.

DeFi platforms, which operate without traditional intermediaries such as banks or payment processors, offer new ways for individuals to borrow, lend, trade, and invest in digital assets. While DeFi has the potential to democratize access to financial services, it also raises concerns about the lack of regulatory oversight, the potential for fraud and market manipulation, and the risks associated with smart contract vulnerabilities.

The social impact of DeFi is further complicated by the concentration of wealth and power within specific digital currency ecosystems. While DeFi platforms are often touted as decentralized and open to all, a small number of early adopters and large holders of digital assets, known as "whales," can exert significant influence over these platforms. This concentration of power can undermine the democratic principles that DeFi platforms are intended to promote and may lead to unequal outcomes for users.

Ethical guidelines and regulatory frameworks must be developed to address these challenges and ensure digital currencies and DeFi platforms are accessible, transparent, and secure. The ethical guidelines should aim at promoting digital literacy and financial education to help individuals understand the risks and opportunities associated with these technologies, and the regulatory framework should include measures to protect consumers from fraud, market manipulation, and other risks.

With the rise of DeFi, there are growing concerns about the potential social and environmental impacts of these new financial systems. As financial institutions continue to innovate, they must integrate principles of corporate social responsibility to ensure that technological advancements, such as DeFi, contribute to societal well-being and financial inclusion.

Ethics, Social Responsibility, and Innovation in Finance

Corporate social responsibility (CSR) has become a critical component in modern finance, ensuring that technological innovations contribute to societal well-being and promote ethical practices. As financial institutions develop new tools and technologies, such as AI, ML, and DeFi, there is increasing pressure to align these advances with the principles of fairness, transparency, and accountability. CSR provides the framework that enables financial institutions to operate in ways that meet regulatory requirements and promote positive social and environmental outcomes.

One of the key ethical challenges in financial innovation is how best to apply AI and ML technologies. While these tools can improve efficiency and decision-making, they also introduce bias, fairness, and transparency concerns. Financial institutions must address issues such as algorithmic bias, whereby automated systems may unfairly disadvantage certain groups, and AI models' lack of explainability, which can obscure accountability. By embedding ethical considerations into the development and deployment of AI systems, institutions can help mitigate these risks and promote trust in their operations.

DeFi represents another area where financial innovation intersects with ethical concerns. While it promises to democratize access to financial services, it also introduces risks related to security, regulatory oversight, and financial exclusion. As DeFi platforms grow in popularity, financial institutions must consider how to ensure equitable access while managing the risks associated with a largely unregulated and rapidly evolving sector. Ethical leadership will be essential in shaping the future of DeFi to ensure that it benefits all participants rather than exacerbating inequality.

In addition to ethical concerns, financial institutions are increasingly focused on sustainability. Participating in sustainable finance through the issuance of green bonds, impact investing, and the provision of sustainability-linked loans allows institutions to align profitability with environmental and social goals. By engaging in sustainable finance, institutions can contribute to global efforts to combat climate change, reduce carbon emissions, and promote broader social responsibility.

Financial inclusion is another critical aspect of CSR in financial innovation. Technological advances can bring banking and financial services to underserved populations, particularly in developing economies. Mobile banking, digital currencies, and blockchain technology provide new avenues for increasing access to financial services, helping to reduce inequality and foster economic development. Institutions prioritizing financial inclusion in their innovation strategies can be crucial in driving positive social change.

By integrating CSR and ethics into their innovation strategies, financial institutions can ensure that they contribute to a fairer, more inclusive, and sustainable financial system. Addressing these challenges will help institutions meet regulatory expectations, build stakeholder trust, and create long-term societal value.

EVOLVING FINANCIAL MODELS: INTEGRATING PHYSICS, PSYCHOLOGY, AND NETWORK THEORY

The complexity and interconnectedness of modern financial markets have prompted a shift toward interdisciplinary approaches in financial modeling. Traditional economic models, which often rely on assumptions of rational behavior and market efficiency, have proven inadequate in fully capturing the dynamics of financial markets, particularly in times of crisis. As a result, researchers and practitioners have increasingly turned to insights from such disciplines as physics, psychology, network theory, and biology to develop more robust and realistic models that better reflect the behavior of market participants and the systemic risks inherent in financial systems.

Econophysics and Financial Market Dynamics

One of the most significant interdisciplinary contributions to financial modeling comes from the field of econophysics. As explained in the previous chapter, *econophysics* is a term coined by the physicist Eugene Stanley. This field emerged in the 1990s as physicists began to recognize the parallels between financial markets and physical systems, particularly regarding the statistical properties of market data. For example, just as particles in a gas exhibit random motion, asset prices in financial markets can be modeled as random walks, leading to models that describe the distribution of price changes and the clustering of volatility.[4]

Econophysics has introduced significant concepts to financial modeling, such as fat tails and power law distributions, which describe the probability of extreme events in financial markets. Unlike the traditional Gaussian models, which assume normal distributions, econophysics models recognize that financial markets exhibit heavy tails, meaning that extreme events such as market crashes are more likely than conventional models suggest.

These insights have profound implications for risk management and asset pricing. By incorporating fat tails into financial models, analysts can better estimate the likelihood of large price movements and the potential risks associated with market turbulence. This approach challenges the assumptions of market equilibrium and rational behavior, turning instead to more sophisticated models that capture the complexities of real-world financial markets. These concepts challenge the traditional Gaussian assumptions of many financial models, which underestimate the likelihood of large price movements and the risk of market crashes. By incorporating these insights, econophysics provides a more accurate framework for understanding the risks associated with financial markets. It has led to the development of models that better capture the complex behavior of market participants.

To further expand on the contributions of econophysics, it is crucial to consider how these models have been applied in practice. As detailed in Focardi and Fabozzi (2010), models incorporating the principles of econophysics have been used to analyze market liquidity, price formation, and the emergence of market bubbles and crashes. These applications highlight the limitations of traditional economic theories that assume markets are always in equilibrium, showing instead that financial markets often operate far from equilibrium, with small perturbations potentially leading to significant and unpredictable outcomes.

Network Theory in Financial Systems

Another interdisciplinary approach that has gained traction in financial modeling is network theory, which originated in sociology and graph theory. Network theory provides a framework for analyzing the interconnections between and among market participants, financial institutions, and markets, allowing researchers to study the structure and dynamics of financial networks. This approach is valuable in understanding systemic risk as it highlights how the failure of one financial institution or market can propagate through the network and trigger broader financial instability.

Network theory provides a framework for analyzing the interconnectedness of financial institutions and markets. It highlights how the effects of one entity failing can cascade through the system and trigger broader financial instability. By mapping out these connections, network theory identifies critical nodes or hubs within the financial system—such as major banks or central clearinghouses—that are particularly vulnerable to failure.

Understanding these interconnections is crucial for preventing systemic crises. For example, during the GFC, the collapse of Lehman Brothers illustrated how the failure of a single institution could propagate through the financial network, leading to a worldwide financial meltdown. Network theory has since been used to design more resilient financial systems by focusing on reducing the concentration of risk in critical nodes and improving the robustness of the overall network.

Network theory has been used to model the relationships among banks, insurers, and other financial entities, revealing how the concentration of risk in certain network parts can lead to systemic vulnerabilities.

As explored in Fabozzi, Focardi, and Jonas (2010), network theory has been instrumental in understanding how financial shocks can spread across global markets, leading to systemic crises. By identifying the most interconnected institutions and markets, policymakers and regulators can better anticipate and mitigate the spread of financial contagion, enhancing the overall stability of the financial system.

A key feature of many types of networks is the existence of connection probability thresholds. Each network type has its unique threshold. Below this threshold, the size distribution of the network's connected components typically follows a Gaussian or exponential pattern. However, as the probability of connections nears the threshold, the distribution shifts to an inverse power law. At the threshold itself, the entire network becomes fully connected. In other words, below the threshold, the network consists of numerous small, disconnected components, but as the threshold is approached, more significant connected components begin to form.

Like a phase transition, this abrupt transition has garnered interest from economic theorists because it provides a geometric framework for understanding crises. Drawing on percolation theory, Focardi and Fabozzi (2004a) proposed a market connectivity parameter as a risk factor for credit risk. Focardi and Fabozzi (2005) introduced the autoregressive conditional duration model to explain the ARCH-like behavior observed in aggregate credit risk.

Behavioral Finance and Psychological Insights

Behavioral finance is another interdisciplinary approach that has significantly contributed to financial modeling by incorporating insights from psychology and cognitive science. Traditional financial models often assume that investors are rational and markets are efficient. However, behavioral finance challenges these assumptions by demonstrating that investors are subject to cognitive biases and emotional influences that can lead to irrational decision-making and market inefficiencies.

Behavioral finance can explain various market anomalies, such as overconfidence, herding behavior, and loss aversion. By incorporating psychological insights into financial models, behavioral finance challenges the traditional assumption of rational investors. For example, overconfidence can lead investors to underestimate risks and overestimate their ability to predict market movements, often resulting in excessive trading and suboptimal returns. Herding behavior, or investors following the actions of others rather than relying on their own analysis, can amplify market trends and contribute to bubbles or crashes.

Another critical concept is loss aversion, which suggests investors are more sensitive to losses than to gains. This has been used to explain phenomena such as the equity premium puzzle, that is, historical returns on stocks that are significantly higher than can be justified by traditional risk models. By integrating these insights, behavioral finance provides a more accurate reflection of market dynamics, allowing the development of investment strategies that take into account human biases. These insights have led to the development of models that better capture the psychological drivers of market behavior and have inspired new investment strategies that seek to capitalize on these biases.

To expand on the role of behavioral finance, it's essential to consider how these insights have been integrated into financial products and services. As discussed in Fabozzi, Focardi, and Jonas (2014), financial institutions have increasingly used behavioral insights to design products that align with the psychological tendencies of investors. For example, automatic enrollment in retirement savings plans takes advantage of inertia—a common behavioral bias—to encourage higher rates of saving. Similarly, financial advisers use framing techniques to present investment choices in a way that mitigates the impact of loss aversion, helping clients make more rational decisions.

Evolutionary Finance: A Biological Perspective

Evolutionary finance is an emerging interdisciplinary field that draws on concepts from evolutionary biology to model financial markets as dynamic systems in which different strategies and behaviors compete for survival. In this framework, market participants are species that adapt and evolve in response to changing market conditions. This perspective challenges the traditional equilibrium-based economics models, suggesting instead that markets continuously evolve in response to changing conditions rather than tending toward a stable state. An evolutionary finance perspective suggests that markets are more accurately described as ecosystems in which periods of stability are punctuated by sudden shifts in market dynamics, much as natural ecosystems experience phases of equilibrium and disruption.

This approach has practical applications in portfolio management, where recognizing that specific strategies may become less effective over time can help investors adapt their portfolios proactively. For example, investment strategies must evolve to retain effectiveness as market participants adjust to new information or changing economic conditions. Evolutionary finance thus provides a framework for understanding market dynamics as a process of constant adaptation and competition.

This perspective provides a more dynamic view of markets, where strategies that succeed in one environment may fail in another and the continuous process of adaptation and competition drives market dynamics.

Expanding on evolutionary finance, it is critical to highlight the practical applications of this approach in portfolio management and investment strategy. As noted in Focardi and Fabozzi (2023), evolutionary finance provides a framework for understanding how investment strategies evolve as market participants adapt to changing economic conditions. This perspective can help investors develop more resilient strategies better suited to navigating the uncertainties of financial markets. For instance, by recognizing that specific strategies may become less effective as market conditions change, investors can adjust their portfolios proactively to maintain optimal performance.

Challenges in Model Validation and Interpretation

While interdisciplinary approaches have enriched financial modeling, they have also introduced challenges, particularly in model validation and interpretation. Models drawn from physics, network theory, and biology often rely on complex mathematical frameworks that can be difficult to validate using real-world data. Additionally, the assumptions underlying these models may not always hold in financial markets, where human behavior and institutional factors play a significant role.

Moreover, the use of interdisciplinary models raises questions about their interpretability and applicability. For instance, while network theory can provide insights into systemic risk, it may not fully capture the strategic interactions between financial institutions or the role of regulatory interventions. Similarly, behavioral finance models may struggle to account for the factors influencing investor behavior, particularly in rapidly changing market environments.

Efforts are ongoing to improve the robustness and applicability of interdisciplinary models in finance. As discussed in Fabozzi, Focardi, and Ma (2005), one approach is to use out-of-sample validation and stress testing, both of which entail testing models against data not used in their development to assess their robustness in different market conditions. Additionally, integrating qualitative insights into quantitative models, as advocated by Focardi and Fabozzi (2023), can help improve the interpretability of models by incorporating a broader range of factors that influence market behavior.

CHALLENGES, OPPORTUNITIES, AND THE PATH FORWARD IN FINANCIAL INNOVATION

As the financial landscape evolves at an unprecedented pace, innovation brings both promise and peril. This section examines the critical challenges that arise in developing, adopting, and regulating new financial products and technologies, setting the stage for a deeper exploration of the key obstacles that must be addressed to ensure sustainable progress in financial innovation.

Key Challenges in Financial Innovation

The rapid pace of financial innovation presents complex challenges that market participants, regulators, and policymakers must navigate. One of the most pressing regulatory challenges posed by financial innovation is the need to develop frameworks that can keep pace with rapid technological advancements. Traditional regulatory approaches, often reactive and jurisdiction-specific, struggle to address the global and decentralized nature of many financial innovations, such as cryptocurrencies and DeFi platforms.

The lack of international coordination on financial regulation exacerbates the problem, leading to what is known as *regulatory arbitrage*, or firms moving operations to jurisdictions with more lenient rules. Regulatory arbitrage can undermine the effectiveness of regulation, increase the risk of financial instability, and create uneven playing fields across markets. To mitigate these risks, there is a growing call for greater international cooperation and harmonizing regulatory standards, which would help ensure that financial innovations are safe and sustainable.

One of the foremost challenges is the need for effective regulation in an era in which financial products and services evolve faster than the regulatory frameworks designed to oversee them. The global nature of modern finance, characterized by cross-border transactions and decentralized platforms, exacerbates this issue, making it difficult for regulators to monitor activities and enforce compliance.

DeFi products, such as cryptocurrencies and blockchain-based platforms, operate outside traditional financial systems, posing a significant hurdle to regulation and oversight. The anonymity and global reach of these platforms complicate efforts to prevent financial crimes, such as money laundering and terrorist financing. The rapid adoption of such technologies often outpaces the development of appropriate regulatory frameworks, leading to potential gaps in oversight and an increased risk of financial instability.

Another significant challenge is the potential for financial innovation to create new forms of systemic risk. Complex financial instruments, such as derivatives, particularly customized derivatives, have demonstrated the ability to amplify risk rather than mitigate it, as seen during the GFC. The interconnectedness of financial markets means that the failure of one institution or product can have far-reaching implications, threatening the entire system's stability.

Opportunities in Financial Innovation

Despite these challenges, financial innovation also presents substantial opportunities. Financial innovation offers significant opportunities to enhance financial inclusion, particularly in underserved regions with limited access to traditional banking services. For instance, mobile banking and digital wallets have transformed financial access in many developing countries by enabling millions of people to participate in the formal financial system for the first time. These innovations provide essential financial services, such as savings and payments, and facilitate microloans and insurance, helping to improve economic resilience and reduce poverty.

In addition to financial inclusion, there is growing momentum around sustainable finance, where financial innovations are aligned with ESG goals. Green bonds, sustainability-linked loans, and impact investing are examples of how finance can be directed toward projects that promote environmental stewardship and social good. These innovations allow investors to generate financial returns while contributing to the broader sustainable development goal.

Integrating advanced technologies, such as blockchain, AI, and ML, also offers the potential to revolutionize financial markets. These technologies can increase efficiency, reduce costs, and enhance transparency across various financial activities, from trading to risk management. However, realizing these benefits requires careful management of the associated risks, particularly those related to data privacy, cybersecurity, and the ethical use of AI.

The Path Forward

Looking ahead, the future of financial innovation will be shaped by how effectively these challenges are addressed. The path forward in financial innovation will require a careful balance of fostering innovation and managing the associated risks. This will entail developing robust regulatory frameworks and encouraging responsible innovation on the part of financial institutions. Stress testing, scenario analysis, and the development of explainable AI models can help ensure that financial innovations do not introduce undue risks into the system.

Greater collaboration is needed between regulators, industry participants, and academia to develop best practices and standards that can guide the development of new financial products and services. By aligning innovation with broader societal goals—such as financial inclusion, sustainability, and economic resilience—we can create a financial system that is both dynamic and stable, capable of supporting long-term economic growth and development.

Regulatory frameworks must evolve to keep pace with technological advances while ensuring that innovation does not threaten financial stability. This will require greater international cooperation and harmonizing regulatory standards across jurisdictions.

The development of regulatory sandboxes—controlled environments where new financial products and services can be tested under the supervision of regulators—offers a promising approach to balancing innovation with oversight. These sandboxes allow innovators to explore the potential of new technologies while ensuring adequate safeguards are in place to protect consumers and maintain market stability.

In addition to regulatory advancements, the financial industry must embrace a more holistic approach to risk management through developing robust models, applying more rigorous stress-testing techniques, and acquiring a deeper understanding of financial innovation's broader economic and social implications. By considering how financial products interact with the wider economy and contribute to systemic risk, financial institutions can create strategies that enhance resilience and promote long-term stability.

Finally, the path forward must include a commitment to ensuring that financial innovation benefits all segments of society. Steps toward this goal include assuring digital inclusion, expanding access to financial services, and designing products that meet the needs of diverse populations. By aligning innovation with broader societal goals, the financial industry can contribute to a more inclusive, resilient, and sustainable global economy.

Balancing Innovation with Risk Management

Financial innovation, while offering new tools for managing risk, also has the potential to introduce new forms of systemic risk. For example, the GFC was exacerbated by the proliferation of complex financial instruments, which obscured underlying risks and led to widespread defaults. The crisis highlighted the dangers of relying too heavily on financial models that do not adequately account for extreme events or the interconnectedness of financial markets.[5]

To prevent similar crises in the future, it is essential to incorporate rigorous stress testing and scenario analysis into the development of new financial products. These tools can help identify potential vulnerabilities in financial systems and ensure that innovative products are resilient under various market conditions. Additionally, ongoing regulatory oversight is crucial to monitor financial innovations' evolution and intervene when necessary to maintain financial stability.

For example, the development of complex financial derivatives has allowed market participants to hedge against various types of risk. Still, it has also contributed to the buildup of systemic risk, as seen during the GFC. The challenge lies in ensuring that innovative financial products are designed and used to enhance market stability rather than undermine it.

One key opportunity in financial innovation is the potential to improve risk management practices through advanced analytics, AI, and ML. These technologies can help market participants better understand and manage risk by providing more accurate and timely insights into market dynamics. However, using these technologies also raises concerns about the transparency and interpretability of risk models and the potential for new forms of systemic risk.

Addressing Inequality and Financial Exclusion

Another significant challenge in financial innovation is its potential to exacerbate inequality and financial exclusion. As explained earlier, while digital currencies, DeFi platforms, and other innovations can expand access to financial services, their use also raises concerns about deepening the digital divide and creating new forms of financial exclusion. For example, individuals lacking internet access, digital devices, or financial literacy may be left behind as financial services become increasingly digitized.

The potential for financial innovation to increase inequality is particularly pronounced in developing economies, where access to digital infrastructure is often limited. To ensure that the benefits of financial innovation are widely shared, targeted efforts are needed to promote digital inclusion, financial literacy, and equitable access to financial services. Here, public-private partnerships, regulatory initiatives, and investments in digital infrastructure can help bridge the gap between those with access to digital financial services and those without access.

Efforts to address financial exclusion through innovation can be further explored by considering the role of mobile banking and fintech in promoting financial inclusion. Mobile banking has revolutionized access to financial services in many parts of the world, particularly in regions with limited traditional banking infrastructure. By leveraging mobile technology, financial institutions can reach underserved populations, providing access to savings accounts, credit, and payment services. Expanding financial services can reduce inequality and promote economic development in marginalized communities.

Furthermore, developing financial products tailored to the needs of low-income individuals and small businesses can play a critical role in promoting financial inclusion. Microfinance, for instance, has provided entrepreneurs who would otherwise be excluded from traditional banking services access to credit. Microfinance institutions have developed innovative financial products that are specifically designed to meet the needs of low-income borrowers, helping to lift millions of people out of poverty and into the formal economy.

Opportunities for Sustainable Finance

Despite the challenges, financial innovation also presents significant opportunities, particularly in sustainable finance. As the global economy faces increasing pressure to transition to a more sustainable and low-carbon future, financial markets have a critical role to play in mobilizing capital for sustainable investments. Innovations such as green bonds, impact investing, and sustainability-linked loans are examples of how financial products can be designed to align with ESG goals.

The rise of digital technologies also offers opportunities for enhancing transparency and accountability in sustainable finance. For example, blockchain technology can track and verify the impact of sustainable investments, providing investors with greater confidence that their capital is being used to achieve positive environmental and societal outcomes. Additionally, AI and big data analytics can help identify and manage ESG risks, enabling investors to make more informed decisions.

Exploring the role of green financial products and services in promoting environmental sustainability can further expand the growth of sustainable finance. As Focardi and Fabozzi (2010) discuss, green bonds have proved to be a powerful tool for financing environmentally friendly projects, such as renewable energy and energy efficiency initiatives. By offering investors a way to align their portfolios with their values, green bonds have attracted significant interest from institutional investors seeking to have a positive impact on the environment while achieving competitive returns.

The integration of ESG factors into investment decision-making processes has become increasingly important in the context of sustainable finance. ESG integration involves incorporating ESG considerations into traditional financial analysis to assess investments' long-term risks and opportunities better. This approach helps investors manage risks related to climate change, social unrest, and regulatory changes and contributes to the broader goal of creating a more sustainable and responsible financial system.

While managing innovation-related risks is essential, addressing financial innovation's broader societal and environmental impacts is equally important. Innovation in finance has the potential to promote inclusivity and sustainability, offering solutions to some of society's most pressing global challenges. Below, we explore how financial innovation can support greater financial inclusion, sustainable finance, and the future of these transformative changes. Financial innovation fosters inclusivity and sustainability and drives advances in risk management practices. However, these advances come with challenges.

Using big data and ML in financial risk management represents a significant advance but poses challenges regarding model transparency and accountability. The complexity of ML algorithms can make it difficult for users to understand how decisions are being made, leading to concerns about the black box nature of these models. To mitigate these risks, there is a growing emphasis on the need for explainable AI in finance, which aims to make ML models more transparent and interpretable. This can help ensure that the models effectively manage risk and are understandable and trustworthy for market participants and regulators.

Additionally, the potential for financial innovation to create new forms of systemic risk cannot be overlooked. The interconnectedness of modern financial markets means that the failure of one financial institution or product can have far-reaching implications for the entire system. The development of stress testing and scenario analysis techniques has become increasingly important in assessing the resilience of financial institutions and products under different market conditions. By incorporating these techniques into the design and regulation of new financial innovations, the industry can better manage the risks associated with these developments.

The Future of Financial Innovation

The future of financial innovation will likely be shaped by how effectively the challenges outlined above are addressed. While the potential benefits of financial innovation are significant, their realization will depend on developing robust regulatory frameworks, the effective management of risk, and a commitment to ensuring that innovation benefits all segments of society. By embracing these challenges and opportunities, the financial industry can play a pivotal role in shaping a more inclusive, resilient, and sustainable global economy.

SUMMARY

This chapter has explored the role of innovation in reshaping the financial sector. Beginning with a historical perspective, we traced the evolution of financial innovation, particularly in developing financial products such as derivatives, options, and futures. These instruments have proved to be critical tools for managing risk and enhancing liquidity and have become integral to modern financial systems. However, innovation is a double-edged sword, often bringing significant benefits and systemic risks.

A central issue is the increasing integration of technology and data into finance. The rise of data-driven decision-making has transformed how financial institutions operate, with ML, AI, and big data analytics driving new risk management methods, portfolio optimization, and fraud detection. These technologies have redefined efficiency in financial operations, yet they also present challenges around transparency, accountability, and the potential for biased decision-making.

Blockchain technology and digital currencies are other focal points of the chapter. Blockchain, the underlying technology for cryptocurrencies such as Bitcoin, is a revolutionary tool that could potentially disrupt traditional banking systems. The decentralized and immutable nature of blockchain allows secure, transparent transactions to be conducted without intermediaries. More broadly, digital currencies both create opportunities for innovation and carry risks associated with lack of regulation and volatility.

The technological advances discussed in the chapter also have ethical and social implications. The use of AI and ML—both powerful tools for financial analysis—raises concerns about data privacy, security, and ethical use. We call for the development of robust ethical frameworks to ensure that technological innovations contribute to the common good rather than exacerbate social inequalities or creating new risks.

The chapter also highlighted interdisciplinary approaches to financial innovation, drawing from physics, psychology, and biology. For example, econophysics applies concepts from statistical physics to better understand market dynamics, whicle behavioral finance integrates psychological insights to account for cognitive biases and irrational behavior in financial decision-making. These approaches offer a more nuanced understanding of market behavior, particularly during times of crisis.

Another key theme is the regulation of financial innovation. The GFC serves as a stark reminder of the potential dangers of unchecked innovation, particularly when financial products obscure the risks they carry. We argue for more robust regulatory frameworks to keep pace with rapid technological advancements, ensuring innovation is balanced with effective risk management practices.

We also considered the social impact of financial innovation, with a focus on financial inclusion. New financial technologies have the potential to bring banking services to underbanked populations and create more inclusive financial systems. However, without careful management, these technologies could deepen existing inequalities by excluding those without access to digital infrastructure.

The chapter highlighted the importance of sustainability in addressing the future of financial innovation. ESG considerations are becoming increasingly relevant as financial institutions seek to align innovation with long-term societal goals. We suggest that sustainable finance, supported by innovative financial products, can be crucial in addressing global challenges such as climate change.

While financial innovation can drive significant positive change, it must be managed within a framework that prioritizes ethical considerations, robust regulation, and social responsibility. By embracing these principles, the financial industry can harness the full potential of innovation to build a more inclusive, resilient, and sustainable global economy.

Financial innovation is transforming the financial landscape through AI, ML, and DeFi. However, alongside these advancements comes the need for robust risk management strategies to mitigate the systemic risks they introduce. Furthermore, integrating ethical considerations and CSR principles is critical to ensuring these innovations contribute positively to society. Financial institutions can drive profitability and foster trust and long-term value creation by focusing on fairness, transparency, and sustainability.

As financial institutions continue to innovate, the future of finance will depend on the delicate balance between leveraging new technologies and adhering to ethical standards. By fostering a culture of moral leadership, prioritizing sustainability, and embracing CSR, the financial industry can navigate the challenges ahead while promoting a more inclusive, transparent, and resilient financial system. Moving forward, financial innovation's success will be measured both by profitability and by the societal impacts it has.

Notes

CHAPTER 2

1. Later work by Statman (1999) further contributed to understanding mental accounting, showing how investors compartmentalize their money and investments in ways that do not follow strict rationality. He also explores how framing affects investor decisions, with investors reacting differently to gains and losses depending on how information is presented.

2. Thaler (1993) compiles research that forms the basis of behavioral finance, explaining how psychological biases influence financial markets. Many key concepts have become central to behavioral finance.

3. The traditional life-cycle hypothesis, developed by Franco Modigliani and Richard Brumberg (1954), is an economic theory that explains how individuals plan their consumption and saving behavior throughout their lifetime. According to this theory, individuals aim to smooth consumption across different stages of life, saving during their working years and dissaving during retirement. The idea is that people want to maintain a stable standard of living despite fluctuations in income due to changes in employment, aging, or retirement. According to this theory, individuals are assumed to act rationally, making financial decisions based on their expected lifetime income and planning accordingly to optimize their consumption and savings.

CHAPTER 3

1. Frisch won the Nobel Prize in Economics in 1969 (shared with Jan Tinbergen), Haavelmo won in 1989, and Heckman and McFadden were corecipients in 2000.

2. Differential equations are a mathematical tool based on functional relationships between variables and their rates of change. They help us understand the relationship between changing quantities, which can be anything from the speed of a car

to the spread of a disease. Differential equations are unique because they don't just give a direct answer; instead, they show how one quantity changes in response to another.

3. A wave function is a concept used in quantum mechanics to describe the behavior of any physical system that doesn't always act like solid objects but more like waves. Instead of telling us exactly where a particle is, the wave function gives us a picture of the particle's probability of being in different places or having certain properties, like energy or momentum.

4. See Angrist and Krueger (1991), Imbens and Angrist (1994), and Card and Krueger (1994).

5. P-hacking refers to manipulating data analysis to achieve statistically significant results, even if those results are misleading or not meaningful. Common examples of p-hacking are running many tests on a dataset and only reporting the ones that yield significant results, reporting data or experiments that confirm a hypothesis while ignoring those that do not, changing variables, excluding specific data points, or rerunning models until desired results are obtained. Here is how p-hacking relates to causal modeling. The goal of causal modeling is to understand the true relationships between variables, not just to find statistically significant correlations. P-hacking, by contrast, focuses on achieving statistical significance, often without regard to whether the findings reflect true causal relationships, leading to unreliable or unstable models.

6. Overfitting occurs when a statistical or machine learning model is trained too closely to the specific patterns and noise in the training data rather than capturing the underlying, general relationships. As a result, the model performs well on the data it was trained on but poorly on new, unseen data. An overfitted model has learned the random fluctuations, quirks, or noise in the training dataset instead of the broader trends that would generalize to other datasets. Ways to avoid overfitting in causal models include testing the model on different subsets of data to ensure it generalizes well via cross-validation, keeping the model as simple as possible by limiting the number of variables and focusing on those with clear causal relevance, building models based on established theories or causal reasoning, not just statistical correlations, which helps ensure the relationships are meaningful and not just the result of noise.

CHAPTER 4

1. Mandelbrot's fractal theory offers a nonlinear perspective on market behaviors, aligning with our discussion of complex and emerging phenomena in finance. See Mandelbrot and Hudson (2004).

2. Farmer and Foley (2009) underscore the need for ABMs in understanding complex economic systems, reinforcing the benefits of this modeling approach.

3. Buchanan (2009) focuses on the potential of ABMs to model financial crises, adding depth to our discussion of their practical applications in understanding systemic events. Bookstaber (2012) surveys ABMs and their application to financial markets and institutions to understand potential vulnerabilities and risk paths. He argues that ABMs can help fill gaps in standard risk tools like VaR and stress testing, particularly in dealing with crisis dynamics. He suggests ABMs can be used as a tool for crisis management and to gauge the effects of policy actions.

4. For comprehensive coverage of network models and their applications to asset management, see Konstantinov and Fabozzi (2025).

5. Systemic risk arises when the failure of a single entity or a small group of entities triggers a chain reaction that leads to the collapse of other entities and, ultimately, the broader financial system. Haldane and May (2011) explore systemic risk using network theory, directly supporting our points about contagion and the role of interconnectedness in financial crises.

6. Gai and Kapadia (2010) offer empirical support for our claims about how network topology influences financial stability and risk.

CHAPTER 5

1. These models are used to model the time intervals between events, typically in high-frequency financial data. They account for clustering event times by modeling durations as a function of past durations, like how GARCH models handle volatility.

2. Percolation theory is a mathematical framework used to study the movement and connectivity of elements within a network. It often models phenomena like fluid flow through porous media or the spread of information. It helps determine the critical threshold at which a system transitions from disconnected to connected, revealing insights into phase transitions and network robustness.

3. See chapter 2 for further discussion.

4. For a further discussion of EVT for risk management, see Embrechts, Resnick, and Samorodnitsky (1999) and McNeil (1999).

5. Engle (1982) developed the autoregressive conditional heteroscedasticity (ARCH) model, which introduced time-varying volatility to account for volatility clustering in financial data. Bollerslev (1986) created the GARCH model, improving upon the ARCH model by incorporating past variances, making it more efficient and widely applicable. Engle, Focardi, and Fabozzi (2012) describe their use in asset management to improve risk management strategies and enhance decision-making related to asset allocation and hedging. Engle, Focardi, and Fabozzi (2017) explain the use of factor GARCH models to capture time-varying volatility in financial markets, highlighting the challenge of applying these models to large datasets owing to the

curse of dimensionality and propose solutions such as dimensionality reduction and dynamic conditional correlation models.

CHAPTER 6

1. According to Focardi and Fabozzi, green growth is not feasible with today's technology, leading to proposals such as degrowth (Focardi & Fabozzi, 2023).

2. See Focardi and Fabozzi (2025), who outline a conceptual and operational link between circular economy principles and the reorientation of economic development toward qualitative rather than quantitative expansion. They argue that circularity, when framed within broader systemic goals, can support well-being and ecological balance without relying on material throughput growth.

3. The framework proposed, ARMOR-CAP (Allocation for Resilient Markets and Operational Readiness-Capital Allocation Protection) introduces diagnostic tools to assess how firms and portfolios withstand sustained geopolitical disruption, offering a more forward-looking complement to existing geopolitical risk indices.

CHAPTER 7

1. The theory of general relativity is a theory of gravity proposed by Albert Einstein that describes gravity as the warping of spacetime by mass and energy, rather than a force acting at a distance, as described by Newtonian physics.

2. Spacetime is a four-dimensional continuum where time and the three spatial dimensions are woven together, as described in Einstein's theory of relativity. Massive objects, such as stars and planets, warp the fabric of spacetime, which is what we perceive as gravity.

3. The Heisenberg uncertainty principle is a fundamental concept in quantum mechanics. It states that it is impossible to know the exact position and momentum of a particle simultaneously.

4. Schrödinger's cat is a thought experiment devised by physicist Erwin Schrödinger to illustrate the concept of superposition in quantum mechanics, where a cat in a box can be considered both alive and dead until observed.

5. Quantum entanglement is a phenomenon in quantum mechanics where two or more particles become linked, and the state of one particle instantaneously affects the state of the other, no matter how far apart they are.

6. Oreste (2011) explains that both Einstein's theory of relativity and quantum mechanics are required to fully understand price behavior and to accurately forecast intermediate and long-term tops and bottoms in financial markets.

7. Quantum mechanics deals with incompatible observations, where two measurements cannot be known simultaneously with precision. In finance, quantum probability models conflicting market signals or data.

8. Quantization in physics is a process by which classical systems are transformed into quantum systems, where previously continuous values become discrete. This translates to modeling financial markets as systems influenced by distinct, discrete events in finance.

9. See Baaquie (2004).

CHAPTER 8

1. The Kakutani-Brouwer fixed point theorem refers to two foundational results in fixed-point theory, the Brouwer fixed point theorem and the Kakutani fixed point theorem. The former is a result in topology that states that for any continuous function mapping a compact convex set to itself in a finite-dimensional Euclidean space, there exists at least one point such that the function maps the point to itself (i.e., a fixed point). The Kakutani fixed point theorem is a generalization of Brouwer's theorem. It applies to set-valued functions (multifunctions) instead of single-valued functions and is commonly used in the study of equilibria in economics and game theory, particularly for proving the existence of Nash equilibria.

2. Stanley and Mantegna (2000) discuss how financial markets exhibit properties similar to physical systems, such as self-organization and criticality, and how these can be studied using techniques from physics.

CHAPTER 9

1. https://www.imf.org/en/Publications/fandd/issues/Series/Back-to-Basics/Shadow-Banks

2. Blockchain technology has introduced new ways to ensure transparency, and it has reduced reliance on intermediaries in financial transactions. As noted by Fabozzi, Focardi, and Jonas (2010), innovations such as smart contracts are enhancing the efficiency of markets and reducing transaction costs.

3. The importance of due diligence and transparency in investment practices became evident after scandals such as those involving Bernie Madoff and Galleon. As Fabozzi, Focardi, and Jonas (2010) note, ethical considerations and governance are increasingly critical in protecting investors from unethical practices.

4. Mantegna and Stanley (1999) is the foundational text in the field of econophysics. The authors propose using methods from physics to analyze economic systems, particularly emphasizing the investigation of correlations, scaling laws, and the

complexity inherent in financial markets. This approach applies physical concepts and quantitative tools to better understand and model the intricate behaviors and interconnectedness observed in financial data, aiming to reveal patterns and structures that traditional economic methods might overlook.

5. As Fabozzi, Focardi, and Jonas (2010) discuss, the GFC demonstrated the critical role of asset allocation in determining returns, and a more dynamic approach to asset allocation has gained prominence due to heightened market volatility.

References

Anderson, P. W. (1972). More is different: Broken symmetry and the nature of the hierarchical structure of science. *Science, 177*(4047), 393–396.

Angrist, J. D., & Krueger, A. B. (1991). Does compulsory school attendance affect schooling and earnings? *Quarterly Journal of Economics, 106*(4), 979–1014.

Artzner, P., Delbaen, F., Eber, J. M., & Heath, D. (1999). Coherent measures of risk. *Mathematical Finance, 9*(3), 203–228.

Baaquie, B. (2004). *Quantum finance: Path integrals and Hamiltonians for options and interest rates.* Cambridge University Press.

Beckerman, W. (1974). *In defense of economic growth.* Jonathan Cape.

Beinhocker, E. D. (2007). *The origin of wealth: Evolution, complexity, and the radical remaking of economics.* Harvard Business Review Press.

Black, F., & Scholes, M. (1973). The pricing of options and corporate liabilities. *Journal of Political Economy, 81*(3), 637–654.

Bollerslev, T. (1986). Generalized autoregressive conditional heteroskedasticity. *Journal of Econometrics, 31*(3), 307–327.

Bookstaber, R. (2012). *Using agent-based models for analyzing threats to financial stability.* Office of Financial Research Working Paper 0003. U.S. Department of the Treasury.

Boulding, K. E. (1966). The economics of the coming spaceship Earth. In H. Jarrett (Ed.), *Environmental quality in a growing economy* (pp. 3–14). Johns Hopkins University Press.

Brundtland, G. H. (1987). *Our common future, from one earth to one world.* UN Document A/42/427. World Commission on Environment and Development.

Buchanan, M. (2009). Meltdown modeling: Could agent-based computer models prevent another financial crisis? *Nature, 460,* 680–682.

Card, D. (1991). Do minimum wages reduce employment? A case study of California, 1987–89. *Industrial and Labor Relations Review, 44*(1), 38–54.

Card, D., & Krueger, A. B. (1994). Minimum wages and employment: A case study of the fast-food industry in New Jersey and Pennsylvania. *American Economic Review, 84*(4), 772–793.

Carhart, M. M. (1997). On persistence in mutual fund performance. *Journal of Finance, 52*(1), 57–82.

Chakraborti, A., Haven, E., Patra, S., & Singh, N. (2023). *Quantum decision theory and complexity modelling in economics and public policy*. Springer.

Chen, Z. (2004). Quantum theory for the binomial model in finance theory. *Journal of Systems Science and Complexity, 17*(4), 567–573.

Cont, R. (2001). Empirical properties of asset returns: Stylized facts and statistical issues. *Quantitative Finance, 1*(2), 223–236.

Cootner, P. H. (1964). *The random character of stock market prices*. MIT Press.

Cox, J. C., Ross, S. A., & Rubinstein, M. (1979). Option pricing: A simplified approach. *Journal of Financial Economics, 7*(3), 229–263.

Duffie, D., & Singleton, K. J. (2003). *Credit risk: Pricing, measurement, and management*. Princeton University Press.

Duhem, P. (1954). *The aim and structure of physical theory*. Princeton University Press.

Embrechts, P., Resnick, S. I., & Samorodnitsky, G. (1999). Extreme value theory as a risk management tool. *North American Actuarial Journal, 3*, 30–41.

Engle, R. F. (1982). Autoregressive conditional heteroscedasticity with estimates of the variance of United Kingdom inflation. *Econometrica, 50*(4), 987–1007.

Engle, R., Focardi, S., & Fabozzi, F. J. (2012). ARCH/GARCH models in applied financial econometrics. In F. J. Fabozzi (Ed.), *Encyclopedia of financial models: Vol. 2* (pp. 359–374). John Wiley & Sons.

Engle, R., Focardi, S., & Fabozzi, F. J. (2017). Issues in applying financial econometrics to factor-based modeling in investment management. *Journal of Portfolio Management, 42*(5), 94–106.

Fabozzi, F. J. (2025a). ARMOR-CAP investing: Building resilient portfolios for a geopolitical era. *Journal of Portfolio Management, 52*(6).

Fabozzi, F. J. (2025b). ESG isn't enough: Why portfolio resilience needs its own framework. *Journal of Investing, 34*(6).

Fabozzi, F. J., Focardi, S., & Jonas, C. (2010). *Investment management after the global financial crisis*. CFA Institute Research Foundation.

Fabozzi, F. J., Focardi, S., & Jonas, C. (2014). *Investment management: A science to teach or an art to learn?* CFA Institute Research Foundation.

Fabozzi, F. J., Focardi, S., & Jonas, C. (2017). *Equity valuation: Science, art, or craft?* CFA Institute Research Foundation.

Fabozzi, F. J., Focardi, S., & Ma, C. K. (2005). Implementable quantitative research and investment strategies. *Journal of Alternative Investments, 8*(2), 71–79.

Fabozzi, F. J., Focardi, S., Ponta, L., Rivoire, M., & Mazza, D. (2022). The economic theory of qualitative green growth. *Structural Change and Economic Dynamics, 61,* 242–254.

Fabozzi, F. J., Focardi, S., and Simonian, J. (2024). Paradigm shift: Embracing holism in causal modeling for investment applications. *Journal of Portfolio Management, 51*(1), 159–177.

Fabozzi, F. J., Focardi, S., Ponta, L., Rivoire, M., & Mazza, D. (2022). The economic theory of qualitative green growth. *Structural Change and Economic Dynamics, 61,* 242–254.

Fama, E. F. (1965). The behavior of stock market prices. *Journal of Business, 38*(1), 34–105.

Fama, E. F., & French, K. R. (1993). Common risk factors in the returns on stocks and bonds. *Journal of Financial Economics, 33*(1), 3–56.

Fama, E. F., & French, K. R. (2015). A five-factor asset pricing model. *Journal of Financial Economics, 116*(1), 1–22.

Farmer, J. D., & Foley, D. (2009). The economy needs agent-based modeling. *Nature, 460*(7256), 685–686.

Focardi, S., & Fabozzi, F. J. (2003). Fat tails, scaling, and stable laws: A critical look at modeling extremal events in financial phenomena. *Journal of Risk Finance, 5*(1), 5–26.

Focardi, S., & Fabozzi, F. J. (2004a). Clustering economic and financial time series: Exploring the existence of stable correlation conditions. *Finance Letters, 2*(3), 1–9.

Focardi, S., & Fabozzi, F. J. (2004b). A percolation approach to modeling credit loss distribution under contagion. *Journal of Risk, 7*(1), 75–94.

Focardi, S., & Fabozzi, F. J. (2005). An autoregressive conditional duration model of credit-risk contagion. *Journal of Risk Finance, 6*(3), 208–225.

Focardi, S., & Fabozzi, F. J. (2009). Black swans and white eagles: On mathematics and finance. *Mathematical Methods of Operations Research, 69*(3), 379–394.

Focardi, S., & Fabozzi, F. J. (2010). The reasonable effectiveness of mathematics in economics. *American Economist, 49,* 3–15.

Focardi, S., & Fabozzi, F. J. (2012). What's wrong with today's economics? *Journal of Portfolio Management, 38*(3), 104–119.

Focardi, S., & Fabozzi, F. J. (2014). Can we predict stock market crashes? *Journal of Portfolio Management, 40*(5), 183–195.

Focardi, S., & Fabozzi, F. J. (2016). Mathematics and economics: Saving a marriage on the brink of divorce? *Journal of Portfolio Management, 42*(4), 1–3.

Focardi, S., & Fabozzi, F. J. (2022). Why should asset management be interested in new economic thinking? *Journal of Portfolio Management, 48*(10), 276–295.

Focardi, S., & Fabozzi, F. J. (2023). *The theory of economic qualitative growth: A new framework for economic growth theory*. Nova Science Publishers.

Focardi, S., & Fabozzi, F. J. (2025). Reconciling circularity and growth: The model of qualitative economic growth. *Journal of Economic Analysis, 4*(2), 105.

Focardi, S., Fabozzi, F. J., & Mazza, D. (2020). Quantum option pricing and quantum finance. *Journal of Derivatives, 28*(1), 143–159.

Forrester, J. W. (1971). *World dynamics*. Wright-Allen Press.

Frisch, R. (1934). Statistical confluence analysis by means of complete regression systems. University Institute of Economics, Oslo.

Galilei, G. (1623). Il Saggiatore [The assayer]. Lyncean Academy.

Gai, P., & Kapadia, S. (2010). Contagion in financial networks. *Proceedings of the Royal Society Series A, 466*(2120), 2401–2423.

Georgescu-Roegen, N. (1971). *The entropy law and the economic process*. Harvard University Press.

Godley, W., & Lavoie, M. (2007). *Monetary economics: An integrated approach to credit, money, income, production and wealth*. Palgrave McMillan.

Goodwin, R. (1982). A growth cycle. In *Essays in economics dynamics*. Palgrave Macmillan.

Grinblatt, M., & Keloharju, M. (2001). What makes investors trade? *Journal of Finance, 56*(2), 589–616.

Haavelmo, T. (1944). The probability approach in econometrics. *Econometrica, 12,* 1–115.

Haldane, A. G., & May, R. M. (2011). Systemic risk in banking ecosystems. *Nature, 469,* 351–355.

Heckman, J. J. (1979). Sample selection bias as a specification error. *Econometrica, 47*(1), 153–161.

Hempel, C. G., & Oppenheim, P. (1948). Studies in the logic of explanation. *Philosophy of Science, 15*(2), 135–175.

Hidalgo, C. A., & Hausmann, R. (2009). The building blocks of economic complexity. *Proceedings of the National Academy of Sciences, 106*(26), 10570–10575.

Hull, J. C. (2017). *Options, futures, and other derivatives* (10th ed.). Pearson.

Hume, D. (1739). *A treatise of human nature.* John Noon.

Imbens, G. W., & Angrist, J. D. (1994). Identification and estimation of local average treatment effects. *Econometrica, 62*(2), 467–475.

Jorion, P. (2007). *Value at risk: The new benchmark for managing financial risk* (3rd ed.). McGraw-Hill.

Kahneman, D., & Tversky, A. (1979). Prospect theory: An analysis of decision under risk. *Econometrica, 47*(2), 263–292.

Kahneman, D., Knetsch, J. L., & Thaler, R. H. (1991). Anomalies: The endowment effect, loss aversion, and status quo bias. *Journal of Economic Perspectives, 5*(1), 193–206.

Keen, S. (2013). A monetary Minsky model of the Great Moderation and the Great Recession. *Economic Behavior and Organization, 86*(2), 221–235.

Keynes, J. M. (1921). *A treatise on probability*. Macmillan.

Keynes, J. M. (1936). *The general theory of employment, interest, and money*. Macmillan.

Knight, F. H. (1921). *Risk, uncertainty, and profit.* Houghton Mifflin.

Kolmogorov, A. N. (1956). *Foundations of the theory of probability.* (2nd ed., N. Morrison, Trans., 1950). Chelsea Publishing Company (Original work published in 1933).

Konstantinov, G., & Fabozzi, F. J. (2025). *Network models in finance.* John Wiley & Sons.

Kuhn, T. S. (1970). *The structure of scientific revolutions* (2nd ed.). University of Chicago Press.

Ladyman, J., & Wiesner, K. (2020). *What is a complex system?* Yale University Press

Laudy, O., Denev, A., & Ginsberg, A. (2022). Building probabilistic causal models using collective intelligence. *Journal of Financial Data Science, 4*(2), 83–109.

Lee, R. S. T. (2020). *Quantum finance: Intelligent forecast and trading systems.* Springer.

López de Prado, M. (2023). *Causal factor investing: Can factor investing become scientific?* Cambridge University Press.

López de Prado, M., Lipton, A., & Zoonekynd, V. (2024). The case for causal factor investing. *Journal of Portfolio Management, 51*(1), 146–158.

Lucas, R. E. Jr. (1976). Econometric policy evaluation: A critique. In K. Brunner & A. H. Meltzer (Eds.), *Carnegie-Rochester Conference Series on Public Policy* (Vol. 1, pp. 19–46). North-Holland.

Mach, E. (1883). *The science of mechanics: A critical and historical account of its development* (T. J. McCormack, Trans.). Open Court Publishing.

Mandelbrot, B. (1963). The variation of certain speculative prices. *Journal of Business, 36*(4), 394–419.

Mandelbrot, B. B., & Hudson, R. L. (2004). *The (mis)behavior of markets: A fractal view of risk, ruin, and reward.* Basic Books.

Mantegna, R. N., & Stanley, E. H. (1999). *Introduction to econophysics: Correlations and complexity in finance.* Cambridge University Press.

Markowitz, H. (1952). Portfolio selection. *Journal of Finance, 7*(1), 77–91.

McCulley, P. (2007). Teton reflections. *PIMCO Global Central Bank Focus.*

McFadden, D. (1974). Conditional logit analysis of qualitative choice behavior. In P. Zarembka (Ed.), *Frontiers in econometrics* (pp. 105–142). Academic Press.

McNeil, A. J. (1999). Extreme value theory for risk managers. https://www.sfu.ca/~rjones/econ811/readings/McNeil%201999.pdf

Meadows, D. H., Meadows, D. L., Randers, J., and Behrens, W. W. III. (1972). *The limits to growth: A report for the Club of Rome's Project on the Predicament of Mankind.* Potomac Associates.

Merton, R. C. (1973). Theory of rational option pricing. *The Bell Journal of Economics and Management Science, 4*(1), 141–183.

Mitchell, M. (2021). Why AI is harder than we think. arXiv:2104v2. https://arxiv.org/pdf/2104.12871

Modigliani, F., & Brumberg, R. (1954). Utility analysis and the consumption function: An interpretation of cross-section data. In K. K. Kurihara (Ed.), *Post-Keynesian economics* (pp. 388–436). Rutgers University Press.

Moore, B. (1988). *Horizontalists and verticalists: The macroeconomics of credit money.* Cambridge University Press.

Muth, J. F. (1961). Rational expectations and the theory of price movements. *Econometrica, 29*(3), 315–335.

Newton, I. (1687). *Philosophiæ naturalis principia mathematica* [Mathematical principles of natural philosophy]. Royal Society Press.

Odean, T. (1998). Are investors reluctant to realize their losses? *Journal of Finance, 53*(5), 1775–1798.

Oreste, F. (2011). *Quantum trading: Using principles of modern physics to forecast the financial markets*. John Wiley.

Orrell, D. (2022). *Quantum economics and finance: an applied mathematics introduction*. Panda Ohana Publishing.

Parthasarathy, K. (1992). *An introduction to quantum stochastic calculus*. Birkhauser.

Pearl, J. (2000). *Causality: Models, reasoning, and inference*. Cambridge University Press.

Phoa, W., Focardi, S., & Fabozzi, F. J. (2007). How do conflicting theories about financial markets coexist? *Journal of Post Keynesian Economics, 29*(3), 365–392.

Pozsar, Z. (2014). *Shadow banking: The money view*. Office of Financial Research Working Paper 14-04. U.S. Department of the Treasury.

Pozsar, Z., Adrian, T., Ashcraft, A., & Boesky, H. (2013). Shadow banking. *Economic Policy Review* (Federal Reserve Bank of New York).

Quine, W. V. O. (1951). Two dogmas of empiricism. *The Philosophical Review, 60*(1), 20–43.

Reday-Mulvey, G., & Stahel, W. R. (1977). *The potential for substituting manpower for energy: Final report 30 July 1977 for the Commission of the European Communities*. Battelle Institute, Geneva.

Reichenbach, H. (1956). *The direction of time*. University of California Press.

Ross, S. A. (1976). The arbitrage theory of capital asset pricing. *Journal of Economic Theory, 13*(3), 341–360.

Russell, B. (1913). On the notion of cause. *Proceedings of the Aristotelian Society, 13*, 1–26.

Samuelson, P. A. (1947). *Foundations of economic analysis*. Harvard University Press.

Shapira, Z., & Venezia, I. (2001). Patterns of behavior of professionally managed and independent investors. *Journal of Banking & Finance, 25*(8), 1573–1587.

Sharpe, W. F. (1964). Capital asset prices: A theory of market equilibrium under conditions of risk. *Journal of Finance, 19*(3), 425–442.

Shefrin, H. M., & Statman, M. (1985). The disposition to sell winners too early and ride losers too long: Theory and evidence. *Journal of Finance, 40*(3), 777–790.

Shefrin, H. M., & Thaler, R. H. (1988). The behavioral life-cycle hypothesis. *Economic Inquiry*, 26(4), 609–643.

Shrimali, G. (2022). Scope 3 emissions: Measurement and management. *Journal of Impact and ESG Investing, 3*(1), 31–54.

Simon, H. A. (1953). Causal order and identifiability. In W. C. Hood and T. C. Koopmans (Eds.), *Studies in econometric methods*. John Wiley & Sons.

Simon, H. A. (1957). *Models of man: social and rational: Mathematical essays on rational human behavior in a social setting*. Wiley.

Simonian, J. (2021). Causal uncertainty in capital markets: A robust noisy-or framework for portfolio management. *Journal of Financial Data Science, 3*(1), 43–55.

Simonian, J. (2022). Investment decisions under almost complete causal ignorance. *Journal of Portfolio Management, 49*(1), 33–38.

Simonian, J. (2023). A causal analysis of market contagion: A double machine learning approach. *Journal of Financial Data Science, 5*(2), 9–22.

Stanley, H. E., & Mantegna, R. N. (2000). *An introduction to econophysics: Correlations and complexity in finance*. Cambridge University Press.

Statman, M. (1999). Behavioral finance: Past battles and future engagements. *Financial Analysts Journal, 55*(6), 18–27.

Statman, M., & Shefrin, H. (2000). Behavioral portfolio theory. *Journal of Financial and Quantitative Analysis, 35*(2), 127–151.

Thaler, R. H. (1985). Mental accounting and consumer choice. *Marketing Science, 4*(3), 199–214.

Thaler, R. H. (Ed.). (1993). *Advances in behavioral finance*. Russell Sage Foundation.

Thaler, R. H., & Sunstein, C. R. (2008). *Nudge: Improving decisions about health, wealth, and happiness*. Yale University Press.

Vapnik, V. (2000). *The nature of statistical learning theory*. Springer-Verlag.

Von Neumann, J., & Morgenstern, O. (1944). *Theory of games and economic behavior*. Princeton University Press.

Walras, L. (1874). Éléments d'économie politique pure. *Revue de Théologie et de Philosophie et Compte-rendu des Principales Publications Scientifiques, 7*, 628–632.

Weaver, W. (1948). Science and complexity. *American Scientist, 36*, 536–544.

Wigner, E. P. (1960). The unreasonable effectiveness of mathematics in the natural sciences. *Communications on Pure and Applied Mathematics, 13*(1), 1–14.

Publisher contact:
The MIT Press
Massachusetts Institute of Technology
77 Massachusetts Avenue, Cambridge, MA 02139
mitpress.mit.edu

EU Authorised Representative:
Easy Access System Europe, Mustamäe tee 50,
10621 Tallinn, Estonia
gpsr.requests@easproject.com

Printed by Integrated Books International,
United States of America